MW00779684

Waiting on the Moon

Waiting on the Moon

Artists, Poets, Drifters, Grifters, and Goddesses

Peter Wolf

Little, Brown and Company

New York Boston London

Little, Brown and Company
Hachette Book Group
1290 Avenue of the Americas, New York, NY 10104
littlebrown.com

First Edition: March 2025

Little, Brown and Company is a division of Hachette Book Group, Inc. The Little, Brown name and logo are trademarks of Hachette Book Group, Inc.

The publisher is not responsible for websites (or their content) that are not owned by the publisher.

The Hachette Speakers Bureau provides a wide range of authors for speaking events. To find out more, go to hachettespeakersbureau.com or email hachettespeakers@hbgusa.com.

Little, Brown and Company books may be purchased in bulk for business, educational, or promotional use. For information, please contact your local bookseller or the Hachette Book Group Special Markets Department at special.markets@hbgusa.com.

Book interior design by Marie Mundaca

ISBN 9780316571708 (hardcover) / 9780316588386 (signed edition)
LCCN 2024942643

Printing 1, 2024

LSC-C

Printed in the United States of America

*For Grace
and
Nora*

I'm not such a fool as to not take the moon very seriously.

— Orson Welles

Contents

CONTENTS

Prologue

THERE IS A certain conceit involved in writing a memoir, taking on the assumption that one's life is a story worth telling. Over the years I have found myself regaling others, either at intimate dinner parties, in backstage dressing rooms, or during concert performances, with stories of the fascinating range of people, both known and unknown, I have encountered throughout my life. "You should write a book" was often the response.

I made numerous starts. I tried writing longhand, dictating into a recorder, and even using my one-finger typing, but nothing seemed to provide me with any fulfillment. I just couldn't seem to find my voice on the page. I didn't want an "as told to" or "written with" book. But after I reread numerous autobiographies, novels, collections of short stories, and my favorite noir mysteries, curiously, they seemed to kick-start my one-finger typing. Finally, one chapter led to another...and another and another.

In *Goodbye to Berlin*, Christopher Isherwood wrote, "I am a camera with its shutter open." With that goal in mind, I have remained as true to the events and encounters as my memory allows. In recounting the dialogue, I have tried to convey both the tone and essence of the conversations with as much accuracy as I can recall. While writing these chapters, I experienced both joy and sadness — the exaltation of rediscovery combined with the realization of the profound loss of the many people who played such important roles in my life.

In the past, I've read the acknowledgments pages of many books in which the authors thank their editors for helping shape the direction of their works. I thought it would be wise for me to pursue an editor of my own who could guide me, help me focus, and keep me from losing faith in completing this endeavor. After many referrals, there were several interesting leads, but surprisingly, I found what I was searching for not with a formal editor but with a friend, the painter Grace O'Connor, whose talents, vast interests, and enthusiasm for knowledge I greatly admire. During our friendship, we have enjoyed many lengthy conversations not only about painting but also about all the arts — and of course the many works of literature, each for our own reasons, we thought were worthwhile reading. It's to her and her sister Nora I dedicate this book.

Growin' Pains

"SOME THINGS YOU JUST CAN'T EXPLAIN"

1

I SLEPT WITH MARILYN MONROE
Miller and Monroe

I WAS TEN YEARS old when I stood alone on the sidewalk, squinting my eyes and waving up to a fifteenth-floor window of the Rockefeller University Hospital, in Manhattan. My older sister, Nancy, was undergoing treatment for rheumatic fever, and I was too young to be allowed in. Her isolation lasted for more than a year, during which my mother and father made daily visits from the Bronx.

After a lengthy discussion with the doctor, my parents left the hospital, concerned that things were not progressing in a positive direction, and were told to return later that day. In an effort to ease their anxiety, my mother suggested we go to the cinema as a distraction. Although I was worried about my sister, the prospect of a trip to the movies was exciting. My parents chose a foreign film, *He Who Must Die*, a French interpretation of the Passion of Christ directed by Jules Dassin. The midtown cinema was one of those small art-house theaters once scattered throughout New York City. We found our way to a middle row as the lights slowly dimmed and a large red velvet curtain opened to the beauty of the flickering screen. French-language credits began rolling and subtitles appeared, but for me, an energetic dyslexic boy, there was no movie magic in sight.

A woman in a mink coat and a tall man in glasses rushed into our row. When their view was obstructed by another couple who sat directly in front of them, they moved closer to us, until the woman was sitting next to me.

I was bored and restless, watching a lot of people jabbering in French. As I munched away on M&Ms, I became aware of a pleasant and intoxicating aroma coming from the woman beside me. Her exotic scent was utterly captivating, though I had no experience of perfume and how enticing it could be. I accidentally dropped my box of candy, and as I bent down to pick it up, I noticed she was wearing house slippers with a fuzzy lining and under her mink coat, an ivory silk nightgown bordered in white lace. As I was looking for my candy under the seat, she moved it with her foot, picked up the box, and smiling, handed it back to me. She wore no makeup, and her skin, luminous in the dark, was pale white against her black sunglasses and kerchief, knotted tightly under her chin.

As the movie rolled on and my boredom intensified, I felt her head slowly come to rest on my shoulder. I didn't mind, but I was afraid to move for fear it would awaken this sleepy lady in her nightgown and sunglasses. I stopped eating my candy and sat there, rigid, but then relaxed into the headiness of her perfume, stronger and even more aromatic as she leaned in close to me. I could feel my eyelids drooping, but I was determined not to move. I stared ahead, comfortable in her warmth, and as our heavy heads met, I, too, gave in to sleep.

Somewhere in my slumber, I seemed to hear from a far-off distance a gruff voice saying, "Honey, wake up. We have to leave now; the lights will be up in a minute." I awakened as the tall bespectacled man roughly jostled her. She seemed groggy and didn't gather herself together as quickly as he had hoped. They stood to leave just as the house lights were coming up, and there in the cinema began a wave of "Look — it's them," a murmuring that slowly built among the audience.

The tall bespectacled man hustled the woman quickly toward the aisle, tightly gripping her arm. She looked up and gave me a shy, bewildered smile as she pulled her fur coat close, rushing out, leaving behind only the lingering scent of that mysterious perfume.

2

PINKIE
My Mother

FREUD WOULD HAVE had a field day with my mother. Her birth was greeted with disappointment by her father, who wanted a boy. To his way of thinking, boys become men, and men make money, while girls become women who take care of men and children. Her father did not believe my mother should waste her time or his by going to college. Yet she was fiercely intelligent. She read from morning to night and had a special love of English drawing-room mysteries. She was attracted not to the arts but rather to artists themselves and their bohemian lifestyle, the antithesis of her home life. She sought broader experiences, modeling for painters in her late teens and going to concerts and recital halls, where she met my father.

My father possessed an incredibly artistic spirit. He had an aptitude for painting, singing, and performing, but he lacked the confidence to pursue these talents. He conversed fluently in several languages and mastered both science and math, but the ambition needed to succeed in the business world eluded him. His greatest champion was his older brother Bernie, who, according to my mother, was "dumber than a door-nail and must have fallen on his head one too many times. What else could explain all those cockamamie ideas of his?"

I was a hyperactive kid with enough bottled-up energy to launch a rocket. When my mother wanted to enjoy an afternoon of uninter-rupted reading, she would take me to the park, tie one end of a rope around a tree, then tie the other end around my waist. She would sit on a bench and read her book while I ran around in circles like a carousel pony. On one occasion, her unique form of child care caught the atten-tion of a neighbor, to whose inquiry she tartly responded, "One time he got loose from the tree, and what does Mr. Smarty Pants do? He walks up to me with the rope in his hand and wants me to tie it back around the tree. I always make sure the rope is just long enough to keep him in my sight. So what's wrong with that?"

My parents had a strong political viewpoint. When I begged them to take me to see Mary Martin on Broadway as Peter Pan, soaring across the stage, they instead took me to see *A View from the Bridge*, by Arthur Miller. Why would they encourage populist flights of fancy when they could immerse my eight-year-old mind in the gritty realism of society's downtrodden workers?

Like many intellectuals, my mother was highly political and had great sympathies for the progressive movement of the far left, which supported labor unions, women's rights, racial integration, and economic equality but was viewed by the government as coming dangerously close to com-munist ("red") ideology. Our six-story apartment building had long, echo-ing hallways, alerting everyone to the sound of approaching footsteps. If it wasn't the landlord knocking at our door, it would be two FBI agents look-ing for my mother. Her involvement in political protests had brought her to their attention. I learned early on to differentiate between the knocks: with the feds, it was always a firm, distinct pounding. When my mother heard it, she would run into the bedroom, leaving me to deal with them. Upon opening the front door, I would find standing before me two impos-ing FBI agents, neatly dressed in suits and ties, hats in hand.

"Young man," they would ask, "is your mother home?"

"No, sir," I would reply with an air of innocence.

"You're not lying?" they would ask.

"No, sir," I would lie again.

They would persist. "Can we come in and look?"

"No, sir. My mother does not allow strangers in the house, and if you come in, it's trespassing, and she's afraid of being robbed."

"We're not robbers," they would say. "We're the FBI." This would be stated so loudly that their words reverberated through the hallways.

Nervous by nature, I knew my mother expected me to stay calm. "Sorry, sir. My mother will not allow strangers in the house." I would then quickly close the door, as instructed by my mother. They would linger outside and eventually leave. This scenario played out many times during my childhood, leading my mother's friends to nickname her Pinkie.

Things were financially difficult for us. My mother, despite her politics, perhaps would have been happier if she had married into wealth — the kind of wealth my father had no real ambition to achieve. By default, my mother became the breadwinner of the family after going to college, getting her master's degree, and becoming an elementary school teacher in the neighborhood known as Fort Apache, the roughest part of the Bronx.

As she was getting ready for work each morning, my father would dress in his one Brooks Brothers suit and head out to pretend he was job hunting. As soon as she was out the door, though, he would return, and I, playing hooky from school, would join him in our innocent deception. I would spend the day drawing and daydreaming while he played classical records or read one of the lengthy volumes of history he had on his bookshelf.

We lived in a small three-room apartment on the third floor of a building right across the street from Bronx Park. Crammed into this space were my mother, my father, my sister and me, two Persian cats, a cocker spaniel named Timmy, and a parakeet named Petey Boy (the reason the bird and I had the same name was never explained).

My mother loved to collect antiques, which she would buy for a few dollars at the Salvation Army store. Our apartment was bursting with her finds, and it was an art unto itself to navigate your way around this tight maze of furniture, lamps, vases, and endless knickknacks. My parents slept in the living room on a Castro convertible couch that opened up to a bed, while my sister and I slept in the bedroom on twin beds.

There was one tiny bathroom in the apartment, which we all tried to be the first to use in the morning, taking extra care not to step into the cats' litter box. My mother had no patience for housecleaning, so the putrid stench of that fetid box permeated the whole apartment. From the moment you walked in the front door, it hit you square in the face. The spasmodic retching of the cats, continually coughing up hairballs, also resonated throughout the day. My mother refused to have the cats' nails clipped, meaning that every surface of her beloved antique upholstered furniture was a shredded mess, all covered in cat fur. Timmy, our dog, tried to escape from it all and took up residence in the closet, which was stuffed with so many coats and hats that we ran out of hangers. Anytime we had to hang things up, we opened the closet to the sound of an unhappy growl from Timmy, vocalizing his displeasure at the sudden invasion of his peaceful space. We would swiftly throw in our coats and close the door, leaving it open an inch so that Timmy could get some air.

Paying the rent was always a problem. I can still clearly hear Mr. Talb, our landlord, hammering on our door as he yelled, "Rent! Rent! Your rent is due." Like the FBI agents, he was left for me to handle.

"Gee, Mr. Talb, my mother wanted me to let you know that she'll have it for you in three days."

"Oh, I heard that story three days ago. I need the rent now, or out you go," he would impatiently reply before thundering off.

When a friend of my mother loaned her money to buy a television, it was cause for celebration. In those days, very few people had a TV, and if you wanted to watch something, half the neighborhood would pile into the apartment of the TV owner and gather around the small screen for an evening's entertainment. My mother's purchase, however, was strictly political: She wanted to watch the live broadcast of the McCarthy hearings. There she sat, glued to the screen with the volume blaring, as Roy

Cohn and Joe McCarthy pounded their fists on the table, day in and day out. In the evening, my sister and I had the pleasure of taking over the set.

I could never understand why I was subjected to continual ridicule from my fifth-grade teacher. To avoid her inexplicably sadistic behavior toward me, I would often play hooky. Some mornings or afternoons, I would take the subway downtown, exploring far-off places such as Times Square and Coney Island. Late one morning, the downtown local subway train stopped at the 34th Street station, where passengers were told that they needed to transfer because of a broken water main that was causing a flood at the far end of the platform. This was a time when the local TV stations started showing live broadcasts of events happening throughout the city. Gabe Pressman, the popular news anchor, was always the first to arrive at the scene. Gabe was interviewing subway officials and passengers regarding the unexpected delay. I shimmied my way through the crowd and stood just behind him as he spoke into the camera. To make sure I'd be seen on TV, I jumped up and down, making funny faces behind him. I was soon joined by other truants looking to seize their moment in the spotlight.

When I got home later that afternoon, my mother was knitting on the living room couch, cigarette dangling from her lips.

"Peter, how was school today?"

"Oh, you know, Mom. The same ol' stuff."

"Got much homework?"

"No. I did most of it during recess."

"Can I see it?"

"I left it in my desk."

"What homework was it?"

"Oh, you know. The same old stuff."

"Peter, you're not lying to your mother, are you?"

"Mom, why would I do something as stupid as that?"

"*Stupid* is right! What the hell were you doing standing on the 34th

Street subway station at ten thirty this morning, jumping up and down like a monkey, when you're telling me you were in school? Like when I found that pack of cigarettes in your underwear drawer last weekend. Do you expect me to believe that Mr. Hoffman at the corner store sold them to you by mistake, thinking they were candy cigarettes? Do you really think your mother is that stupid? Jumping up and down on TV like a baboon. What if some of the other neighbors saw you acting like an idiot and not in school? Don't argue with what I saw with my own eyes!"

"But Mom, you do wear glasses. And why would I be stupid enough to stand in back of Gabe Pressman, knowing I'd be seen on TV?"

"Now, Mr. Smarty Pants, you just incriminated yourself. Who the hell said anything about Gabe Pressman being there?"

At that moment, Max, one of our two Persian cats, threw up right next to the couch where my mother was still feverishly knitting.

Saved once again, this time by a hairball.

Pistol Pete…Age five with my mother and sister

3

PLAY YOUR HUNCH
My Father

Mᴀ ꜰᴀᴛʜᴇʀ ᴡᴀꜱ always a mystery to me. A brilliant and sensitive man who lacked formal education, he was a ferocious reader and a stickler for elocution who took great pains never to adopt a New York accent, speaking as though he were raised in a grand manor.

Growing up in Harlem, he somehow became fluent in many languages, but Italian was his favorite because of his love of opera.

As a young man he won a scholarship to study with one of the great vocal masters in Italy. Unfortunately, it was during the Depression, and he felt it was his duty to remain in New York and help support his family, which consisted of two older brothers, an older sister, and his parents. He answered an ad for a singer in a vaudeville troupe, and at the age of fourteen, he left home to become a member of the Shubert Advanced Vaudeville organization, traveling all over the country. He often described to me, in great detail, the train the Shuberts owned, complete with a dining car and sleeping bunks, which they used to carry all the scenery and actors to various locations. The train departed from New York City, making its first stop in Hartford, Connecticut, where they would play the local Shubert theater for three days before heading to Springfield, Massachusetts; Boston; Maine; and then out West, where he traveled as far as Houston, Texas.

When he returned home, at the age of fifteen, he found work in an exclusive shoe store near 42nd Street catering to an illustrious clientele, including Al Jolson and Irving Berlin. My father was obsessed with all the talents on Broadway and could rattle off every name. Part of his job was to identify famous customers when they walked through the door, then alert the owner so the patrons could be greeted personally and given VIP treatment.

When my father was in his late teens, his older brother Bernie embarked on a career as his manager and booked him on several episodes of a fifteen-minute show aired by the radio station WQXR. My father, accompanied by a pianist, would sing a medley of popular new songs emerging from Tin Pan Alley; thereafter, he became known as the Boy Baritone. That was the pinnacle of my father's show business career until many years later, when opportunity unexpectedly knocked.

On that occasion, Uncle Bernie called my father. "Allen, I got you the chance of a lifetime. That new young host Merv Griffin has a show called *Play Your Hunch*. Three couples must guess whatever scenario the show might invent. Last week the comedian Jonathan Winters was on, and the three couples had to guess which woman was Winters's wife. Was she contestant X, Y, or Z? Here's what's so exciting: next week, they're going to hire a real singing waiter as a contestant! They want two other people who can also sing to try to stump the couples. It's perfect. You go in there and outsing the singing waiter. What an amazing showcase for your talent."

My father hung up the phone and looked like he'd been hit by a truck.

"Dad, what's wrong? Something happen?" I asked. Clearly unsure, he told me Bernie's plan.

"That sounds great!"

"I don't know, Pete. I haven't sung in so long," he replied, full of doubt and apprehension.

"But Dad, I hear you singing around the house, and you sound fantastic! I think you should do it."

As the date of the program approached, my father spent long periods of time in the shower going through operatic arias in his resonant baritone. My mother, with the ever-present cigarette dangling from her lips, would yell, "Please, Allen. Quiet already! How clean can you get in there? If you don't get outta there soon, your skin's gonna wash right off."

My father also took long walks in the park, singing away and smoking a cigarette through a holder. He was oblivious to the stares of the neighbors, who already thought he was quite odd, with his Bermuda shorts, sandals, and beret.

As he and I traveled by subway to the television studio for the live broadcast, I could see that my father was very anxious. Uncle Bernie met us outside and ushered us into a room where there would be a quick run-through rehearsal. Each of the couples would be sitting at a small café table. The singing waiters would stand behind a curtain atop a raised platform, one marked X, another marked Y, and a third marked Z. Merv Griffin would introduce them as the curtain opened. Each waiter would walk down the platform steps, singing and approaching the tables. The couples would then have to guess who the real singing waiter was.

Backstage, my father nervously paced as a fellow contestant warmed up by singing operatic scales at the top of his voice. We assumed it was the real singing waiter. Before Bernie left the dressing room to sit in the audience with some bigwigs he'd invited, he told my father, "Break a leg, Allen. Go out there and give it all you got! You'll see — you're gonna stump them. It's a cinch." Then he made a dramatic exit with a short tap dance and a triple spin.

Finally it was showtime; the singing waiters were to be the last segment of the show.

A staff member came backstage with a waiter's jacket for my father to wear, a linen napkin to drape over his arm, and a set of silverware to place on the table. The three contestants were positioned on their X, Y, and Z platforms behind the closed curtain.

I scurried to the side of the stage, where I could watch my father, and I kept glancing at a small TV monitor to see how it was looking on air.

Merv Griffin stood center stage as he introduced the singing waiters segment. The curtain opened, and there stood the men dressed as waiters, holding napkins and silverware. My father was standing on the third platform, marked Z.

The first contestant, X, began singing "What Now My Love" as he walked over to the seated couple, set the silverware on the table, and returned to his platform. Next came Y, the man warming up with scales backstage. He was a tenor and had a strong voice — a little too theatrical for my taste, but he was good. He sang an aria from *The Marriage of Figaro* as he triumphantly walked to the second table, placed the silverware, and returned to his platform. Now it was time for my father. Merv announced, "Contestant Z, might you be the real singing waiter?" He then came to the side of the stage, where I was standing, to watch the TV monitor.

My father paused, raised his chest high, and came out with a beautiful note that he held for an impressively long time while he gracefully stepped down from his platform. He stopped just before the third table, still continuing the aria from *Don Pasquale*. He used his hand dramatically, as if he were performing on the stage at La Scala. The full-bodied notes he held, even as he reached up into the top of his range, sounded powerful and magnificent. The audience began applauding. Still singing, my father approached the third couple, and just as he was about to place the silverware on the table, he froze and went silent. Standing still, holding out the silverware, he realized he didn't know the proper way to place it on the table. Merv Griffin, who was standing next to me at the monitor, said to a staff member, "He had them all fooled. It was right in his pocket. What a schmuck!"

The air visibly drained from my father as he walked back to his platform. I wanted to say something to this Merv guy, but he was already out front, engaging with the couples before announcing Y as the real singing waiter. Backstage, I walked into my father's dressing room, where he was sitting quietly, elbows resting on his knees. I could tell he was not only disappointed in himself but also embarrassed. "Dad, you were great! I never heard you sing so well. It was amazing!"

"Pete, let's leave before Bernie or anyone else comes backstage."

There was no need to say more. I helped him on with his coat and hat, and we left to catch the subway uptown. It was a quiet ride home. I don't think I ever heard my father sing again until just before he died. He sang in the choir at the historic Plymouth Church in Brooklyn Heights, performing one of his favorites from Handel's *Messiah*. It was a piece that resurrected once more within him the voice I had always loved.

My father

4

THE TENDER TRAP
Diamonds Are a Girl's Best Friend

Second grade

MY FATHER WAS parallel parking when I first mentioned that I was getting married. I was surprised at how calmly he took the news. He locked the car, then we walked up the front steps of Uncle Bernie's apartment building. My father rang the bell, and when Bernie opened the door, my father announced, "Pete's getting married!"

"Great news!" Bernie said. "When's the wedding?"

My father then suggested that it might be wise for me to get engaged before the wedding. Uncle Bernie agreed.

Being only six years old, I wasn't versed in proper marital etiquette. "What's an engagement?" I asked.

My father explained that before they get married, most people get engaged, and the man gives the woman an engagement ring.

"Where can I get an engagement ring?" I asked. I was in love with Joyce Fortunato. She sat next to me in our first-grade class, and I was mesmerized by her wavy blond hair, the light sprinkle of freckles across her cheeks, her doll-like lips, which looked as if they were perfectly painted on, her long lashes, and her deep blue eyes — well, she just shook me up. Joyce! Oh, Joyce! Why couldn't I just marry her?

"Dad, where can I get an engagement ring?" I persisted.

He shrugged and answered, "We can stop at Woolworths on the way home and get one there."

My dad picked it out. He said it had the best-looking stone and was the most practical, since the band could adjust to any finger size. I spent all night looking at the ring and couldn't wait to present it to my beloved.

The next day, during recess, I told Joyce I had something to give her, but first I asked, "Will you get engaged with me?"

"Why should I?" she snapped.

I reached into my pocket for the ring, all wrapped in fancy tissue paper. I told Joyce I had bought her a diamond ring.

"Let me see it!"

I could sense how excited she was as I handed her the ring, which she tore from the tissue, her smile quickly fading.

"Are you sure this is a real diamond?"

I stammered, "Of course it is!"

"Well," Joyce answered, her nose held high, "I want an ankle bracelet instead." She squirreled the ring away in her blouse pocket.

This wasn't the reaction I hoped for, but still, I told her I'd get her an ankle bracelet. I couldn't wait to get home and tell my father, who was sitting on the front stoop of our apartment building with Uncle Bernie, who didn't take the news too kindly. He said carefully, "I feel you did the right thing, but maybe you just have the wrong kind of gal." Then he added, "Take it from me, kid: I'm going to remain a bachelor. I don't want to spend my life committed to only one woman. It's like having the same meal for the rest of your life. I like variety, and I don't use just one spice to cook."

"But Uncle Bernie," I protested, "you don't know Joyce. I'm in love with her!"

"Listen, kid, when it comes to women, there's no better person to advise you than your Uncle Bernie. I've spent time with more women than all the whiskers in your father's mustache."

We returned to Woolworths over the weekend and purchased an ankle bracelet with two small silver hearts dangling from a shiny thin chain. At last, when Monday came around, I got to class early so I could be ready when Joyce arrived. She was late and came in with one of my friends, Lenny Glass. As she sat down, I handed her the bracelet, which she quickly took, pocketing it in her blouse, saying, "In case you haven't noticed." She held her hand out to me, displaying a large diamond ring, then pointed down to her left ankle, adorned with a sparkling bracelet.

"Where'd you get those?"

"Lenny gave them to me and asked me to marry him."

"Are you gonna?"

"I'm thinking it over," she said, then she didn't look at me or speak to me for the rest of the day.

I learned at an early age "the curse of an aching heart."

Joyce and I were in the same class for six years, and it was apparent as time went on that she had no interest in either me or Lenny Glass. A true rebel, she was continually reprimanded by our principal for disruptive behavior, culminating in the memorable moment when she flipped a teacher the bird and called her a "fucking old hag." Joyce was immediately transferred, and she never returned to our school after that.

Several years passed before I saw her again. One morning, late as usual, I was running through the schoolyard to make it in the back door. Joyce, looking street tough, wearing a leather jacket and tight black pedal pushers, was standing against a brick wall by the doorway, flanked by two similarly dressed girls with bouffant hair and spit curls coiled dangerously on their painted faces like vipers. A lipstick-stained cigarette dangled from Joyce's ruby lips. "What's your rush?" she asked. At the sight of this enticing trio, I was at a loss for words.

"Joyce, I'm late, but it's sure good seeing you."

"Yeah, good seeing you, too," was her reply, which really took me by surprise.

"I quit fuckin' school," she added. "Who needs it?"

She flicked away her cigarette and said, "You know, I owe you something." Suddenly she put her arms around me, pressed her soft chest into mine, and gave me one long, unforgettable kiss. Looking into my eyes, she said, "That's for the diamond."

5

THE FIRST LADY
Eleanor Roosevelt

A T SCHOOL I was considered a terrible student. My unpredictable coordination ruled me out of sports. In the classroom I couldn't concentrate, and reading was difficult. Much later, I was diagnosed with what became known as dyslexia. Because I came from a musically gifted family, it was not a stretch to assume that I, too, would easily learn to play an instrument. But after I struggled through piano, guitar, and violin lessons, my attempts to develop any real skills left me completely frustrated. I was resigned to performing the slight and seldom ting-a-ling of the triangle in the school band.

Then one day, as luck would have it, I was chosen to be a spotlight assistant for my junior high school's production of Thornton Wilder's *Our Town*. On the night of the performance, the student in charge of the spotlight didn't show up, so the job landed in my hands. I loved it. I became absorbed in reading the script and following the cues. Thereafter I became the spotlight person for every school production.

I also became a full-time member of the public address squad. Our responsibilities involved setting up microphones for the principal's daily morning announcements over the PA system as well as for weekly school assemblies and occasional guest speakers in the auditorium. Our principal, Miss Selkow, was a stern, humorless disciplinarian with no interest in interacting with her students. Tall and thin, with unnaturally red hair worn in a tightly wound bun that sat atop her head like a pillbox hat, she looked as if she had walked out of a previous century. In her fitted jackets with padded shoulders, a cameo brooch on the lapel, and her ankle-skimming dresses, fire-engine-red lipstick, and rimless glasses magnifying her hawklike eyes, she stalked the hallways like a terrifying bird of prey. A stickler for cleanliness, neatness, and obedience, she was affectionately known by the PA squad as "the bitch." Next to her office was a small glass booth where each morning she gave her address to the students and faculty.

The PA squad leader's job was to set up and test Miss Selkow's microphone. My selection for that role was again a result of chance: the student in charge of the PA squad was hospitalized for tonsillitis, and he would be out of school for more than a week, so I was chosen to fill in.

I reported to Miss Selkow's office on my first morning, making it a point to be extra early.

"Where is John? Why is he not setting up my microphone?" Miss Selkow asked.

"Miss Selkow, John has tonsillitis and will probably be out for the rest of the week."

Obvious displeasure creased her face, and she made no effort to hide her dislike for me, which I assumed was because of my rather shabby appearance.

"Well, that's very disappointing news, because this Friday, I'm hosting a luncheon for the New York Educational School Committee, and there will be a guest of honor addressing our assembly. I want to make sure that everything — I mean everything — is just perfect for the committee and, of course, for our guest speaker."

With her microphone set up, she began her address. "Faculty and students, I am so very pleased to announce that a former first lady, Mrs. Eleanor Roosevelt, will be addressing our school assembly this Friday morning at ten sharp. For this most special occasion, I am making certain that all students are properly dressed: formal skirts and blouses for the girls, suits and ties for the boys. The girls' glee club will perform, along with the school band. After Mrs. Roosevelt addresses the assembly, she and the committee will tour several of our classrooms, and I am sure the students and our esteemed faculty will present to her only the best that Junior High School 135 has to offer."

In my household, the names Franklin and Eleanor Roosevelt were as revered as the names Washington and Lincoln. My mother, who had very few positive words for anyone, especially politicians, often said, "If it wasn't for the Roosevelts, this country would be in the shithouse!" She especially adored Mrs. Roosevelt and religiously read her weekly column. When Mrs. Roosevelt was interviewed on the radio, the entire family could not speak for fear my mother might miss a word.

Friday arrived, and Miss Selkow gave her morning address to the school and faculty. Student artwork and welcome signs were hung throughout the hallways, and I was in the auditorium setting up two microphones — one for Miss Selkow at the far side of the stage and the other center stage for Mrs. Roosevelt. By 10:00 a.m., every seat in the auditorium was full. The committee members accompanied the guest of honor, who sat beside Miss Selkow in the front row. Everyone stood as the band played the national anthem, followed by the girls' glee club, who sang "America the Beautiful" and "Stars of the Summer Night." Miss Selkow stepped up to the stage and proudly announced, "We are so honored to have as our guest speaker this morning someone who needs no introduction to our faculty and students — former first lady Mrs. Eleanor Roosevelt."

Everyone in the auditorium stood and applauded as Mrs. Roosevelt climbed the steps and walked to the center of the stage. She motioned for everyone to be seated. Not realizing how tall she would be, I had the microphone set up for someone my height. In this awkward position, Mrs. Roosevelt tried bending down toward the microphone, placing her hands on the stand, but as soon as she started speaking, loud, ringing feedback buzzed throughout the auditorium. Miss Selkow glared at me, and I ran up to help Mrs. Roosevelt.

As I stood next to her, she seemed to tower over me. I adjusted the microphone stand while she looked down from her immense height and gave me a warm smile of gratitude. She waited until I left the stage and resumed her greetings to everyone assembled. Yet around three minutes into her talk, the microphone stand began to slip lower. Mrs. Roosevelt bent down along with it in an effort to continue her speech. Miss Selkow gave me her most sinister death-ray stare, and I ran back onstage and tried to adjust and tighten the microphone stand. Again, loud feedback filled the hall, and some older students in the back could be heard giggling. Mrs. Roosevelt calmly waited until all was back in order, and with her broad, famously toothy smile, she thanked me for coming to her rescue as I shook her extended hand. Walking back to my seat, I could not miss the heated glare of Miss Selkow, made even more threatening through her intensely magnifying lenses.

After Mrs. Roosevelt finished her speech, Miss Selkow dismissed the students for lunch break. Then she approached me. In the manner of a military officer commanding a firing squad, she said, "You are to put away the microphones. I am dismissing you immediately from the service of our honored PA squad." As I stared at her in disbelief, she added, "I have never, in all my years as a principal, been so embarrassed and humiliated by a student." With that, she turned, her heels clacking up the aisle, and left the auditorium.

Near the end of the school day, I gathered the equipment as instructed and put it in the broadcast booth next to her office. It just so happened that the day before, I had purchased the newly released 45-rpm recording of "I've Had It" by the Bell Notes. I was still carrying it in my notebook. I took the record out and placed it on the turntable inside the glass booth. I flicked the switch to activate all the speakers throughout the building. I turned the volume up as high as it would go, placed the needle on the record, and blasted the Bell Notes into every hallway and classroom. Then I put the turntable on repeat mode, locked the PA booth, threw the keys under Miss Selkow's desk, walked out a side door and into the street, and headed home. My mother, although surprised to see me back from school early, eagerly asked about Mrs. Roosevelt.

"She was a very nice lady, Mom. You'd like her, but she's really, really tall."

6

SATCHMO RISING
Louis Armstrong

IT BEGAN ON one of those Saturday afternoons I always relished, traveling downtown with my father to replenish the stock for his short-lived book and record store, the Mary Elizabeth Shop, so named in an effort to sound British. Our first stop, Diamondstein's Book Distributors, was for the latest bestsellers, then on to the King Karol record store on 42nd Street, where my father made his monthly order of new releases. Every record company, from the major labels to the independents, had its own salesman, and I admired the easy rapport my father had with each of them.

We would end the afternoon by visiting my father's brother, my uncle Bernie, in his "office" at the automat, a cafeteria-style restaurant with little glass cubbyholes filled with ready-made sandwiches and desserts. Bernie's talent-management roster had grown to include a wrestler, a champion baton twirler, a live gorilla rented out for events and circuses, ventriloquists, the world's strongest man, plate twirlers, magicians, comedians, puppeteers, and, of course, my father. Bernie was in his element, the latest issue of *Variety* tucked under his arm and a half-smoked cigar in hand, talking with an assortment of oddball characters who were magnetically attracted to his table.

On this particular afternoon, before heading home, my father said, "Pete, I have a special treat for you. It's incredible luck! One of Bernie's clients, a ventriloquist, just sold me two tickets. I can just about afford them, but it's worth it. I'm taking you to see somebody you may not appreciate now, but one day you might thank me for this opportunity."

"Who is it, Dad?"

"I want you to see for yourself the man who, in my opinion, is the father of jazz. This gentleman is so important, and he's performing his final night at the Roxy Theatre. It's a sold-out show, and I got us two front-row tickets. I want you to witness one of the greatest musicians in history doing what he does best."

We were off to see the one and only Louis Armstrong. In my excitement, much of what my father told me went in one ear and out the other — about the importance of New Orleans, Armstrong's journey to Chicago, the various bands he was part of, and the idea that if jazz could be traced to one important source, it would be Armstrong.

The Roxy was a grand theater, with golden ornamentation swirled around the edges of the banisters and plush red velvet covering every other surface, from the curtains to the seats. My father made sure we were front-row center, having paid extra to the ventriloquist so his son could experience, up close, the majesty of Louis Armstrong.

After the newsreels and featurettes were over, the curtains closed. I could hear instruments tuning up. At last an announcer came out and said, "Ladies and gentlemen, welcome to the Roxy Theatre. Tonight we're proud to present a sold-out performance by the one and only Louis Armstrong and his all-star band!"

The excitement level built to a crescendo. My father, worried that I wouldn't see every nuance of Armstrong's playing, insisted we sit high up in our seats. Armstrong greeted the audience, and within moments, the stage slowly began to rise. The band started playing, and the stage continued to rise as Armstrong played his first notes. Higher and higher still, like Jack's beanstalk, the stage soared upward. Our heads followed its ascent, our necks craning, until it was far beyond our line of sight. Just barely visible was the gleaming rim on the bell of Armstrong's trumpet. With our heads tilted so far back, we had a view of only the clear expanse of the ceiling. It was then we realized why the ventriloquist was so eager to sell the tickets.

In spite of this, I am grateful to have had the privilege of experiencing the magnificence of Louis Armstrong and his playing. But my father and I learned a valuable lesson: never trust a man who works with a dummy.

7

THE WIND
True Love Ways

Edie, high school, 1962

EVEN AT AN early age, I was addicted to drawing. Every surface in my parents' apartment, from books to walls, became a sketch pad. Nothing escaped my doodles. Bomber planes, cowboys and Indians engaged in fierce battles, arrows, swords, trains, cars, sailing ships — this continual circus traveled throughout the rooms and along the hallway. One summer we lived in Lee, Massachusetts, where my father was employed singing with the Robert Shaw Chorale at the Tanglewood music festival. He would often drop me off at a local artist's studio while he ran errands. The artist, a thin, kind, bespectacled man, was very friendly and told me that he, like my father, had a son named Peter. Knowing that I liked to draw, he supplied me with limitless paper and pencils, but what I enjoyed most was watching him work. His name was Norman Rockwell.

* * *

It was the summer of 1959 when I was selected to attend an East Bronx summer arts program comprising twenty-five students from various junior highs around the borough. To gain acceptance, students had to submit artwork to a panel of instructors who chose the students they deemed the most promising. The group met twice a week for a month in a local elementary school. Our first assignment was: "Draw the person sitting beside you." I was seated in the middle of the room but noticed, toward the back, someone sitting all alone. That was the moment I first saw her. She was different from everyone — tall, with brown hair arranged in a high bouffant and a face possessed of a calm and natural beauty to rival that of a Vermeer or a Botticelli.

On occasional afternoons the class would venture to Bronx Park, where we would draw landscapes in pastels and watercolors. Even outside, she always sat alone. During break time, she socialized with the only two Black students in the class. One afternoon, while turning around to catch a glimpse of her, I noticed that she had dropped her eraser. Just as I was about to rush down the aisle to gallantly retrieve it for her, she grabbed it. I couldn't stop staring. During the final week, with just two classes remaining, I vowed that I'd move to the back row and sit in the seat right next to hers. Unfortunately, she never showed up. I asked another student about her, but all I found out was that she lived in a housing project.

New York City had three specialized public high schools: Bronx High School of Science, Brooklyn Technical High School, and the High School of Music and Art (not to be confused with the High School of Performing Arts of *Fame* popularity; that school didn't have the same academic standards and requirements as the three other schools). I can't remember who encouraged me to try out for Music and Art, as it was called: the school was said to accept only those students with very high grades, and the entrance exam was known to be difficult. My report card had such bad grades, ferociously marked in red ink, that it looked as if it were splattered with blood.

The day of the exam, my father drove me to the school, located in northern Harlem. He took the opportunity to thoughtfully remind me that tests are not really an indication of intelligence or talent. "Pete, do you know that Albert Einstein failed math as a young student? Van Gogh never really sold a painting...and I know you love van Gogh. Imagine his feelings, knowing no one wanted to buy even just one of his works. Do you know how many great composers' compositions were laughed at when they were first presented to the public? Mahler, Stravinsky, and even Beethoven — yes, even Beethoven's works were ridiculed. I know so many successful and talented performers and artists who have never so much as picked up a book. These kinds of schools have certain criteria, but not everyone does well at exams. A person's potential can easily be overlooked, so don't invest too much in the results." My father was gently preparing me for what would surely be the most predictable outcome.

It came as a surprise to everyone, especially me, that I was accepted. This sudden and dramatic change put an end to my idle days in the Bronx. It meant close interactions with students from all over the city, from a variety of economic backgrounds, all well educated and gifted, leaving me feeling dubious about what lay ahead. My daily journey from the Bronx to northern Harlem was a lengthy and complicated excursion involving buses and subways, followed by a steep mountain of steps to climb through St. Nicholas Park, to the very top of the hill, before at last I reached the great cathedral-style oak double doors of the high school. This distinguished Gothic revival building, with its grand bearing, was right out of Victorian England. On the first day of my journey I felt like Dickens's Pip, leaving the comforts of his brother-in-law's blacksmith shop, off to the big city, with all the great expectations that lay ahead.

On the morning of the second day, already exhausted from the prospect of the arduous journey ahead of me, I boarded the train and stretched out on an empty seat, trying to keep from falling asleep. My eyes would close and open as the train stopped at each station. It wasn't until the 145th Street stop that I realized she was there, sitting opposite me like an apparition, as if born of the sea, blown there by the winds, pure and perfect as a pearl. With her signature bouffant hairdo, she sat serenely, hands folded in her lap, giving no indication that she recognized me. When we reached 135th Street, I realized that perhaps she, too, was a new student at the High School of Music and Art.

Every morning thereafter, I looked for her on the train or on the long climb up the dozens of steps in St. Nicholas Park. A smoker by age eleven, I endured my daily workout only by hoping I'd bump into her. Although I'd pass her in the halls, there was never an appropriate opportunity for any interchange between us.

A whole year went by before I finally found the courage to approach her. At the start of my sophomore year, I noticed her on the subway platform after school, heading back up to the Bronx. I tossed my cigarette, walked up to her, and asked, "Is this the platform for the uptown trains?" She smiled and pointed upward, where directly above us, a large UPTOWN sign was hanging. I remained standing next to her and quickly asked, "What stop do you get off at?"

"The last stop."

"Funny — that's my stop, too!" (That wasn't true at all; the last stop was much farther from the school than mine.) "Mind if I sit with you?" I asked, finding the courage I had lacked for so long. I kept thinking of all sorts of things to discuss, trying to make a somewhat positive impression, relieved to discover that she wasn't hard to talk to. She was relaxed and engaging, with a disarming naturalness that put me at ease.

Her name was Edith Marie Hasselman. At the last train stop, she'd take a city bus to the Edenwald Houses, where she lived with her family.

The notorious Edenwald housing project — an Eden it most definitely was not — was built in 1953 by the New York City Housing Authority under the control of the infamous city planner Robert Moses, who cut right through the communities of the South Bronx to create the Cross Bronx Expressway. Like Sherman marching through Georgia, he ordered the demolition of entire neighborhoods, uprooting the predominantly Black and Puerto Rican residents. Edenwald had only one bus in and one bus out, which took residents to a subway station twenty blocks away.

To help racially diversify this newly created community, the city offered low-rent incentives to white families. Yet Edenwald did not welcome outsiders, and it was a place the police liked to ignore. Many considered it akin to living in a war zone. But as my friendship with Edie grew, it began to feel like a Technicolor musical heaven. Approaching the projects, I could hear multirhythms from timbale and conga players, Latin music, and the latest soul tracks blasting from windows.

Edie had friends of all colors and nationalities and was the least critical or judgmental person I knew. But if you lost her trust, the steel door closed fast and hard.

Before Edenwald, Edie's Dutch father and Baltimore Catholic mother lived with Edie and her two siblings on Manhattan's West Side. Money was short, so they were forced to live in what was known as Hell's Kitchen. At fourteen, Edie was playing with friends in a small playground surrounded by dilapidated tenements when two Puerto Rican gang members known as the Capeman and the Umbrella Man entered the park. Spotting a group of young men sitting on a bench, and assuming they were members of a rival Irish gang, they blocked the park's entrances, preventing anyone from leaving, then stabbed and beat two young men, murdering them both and beating a third almost to death. This happened just several feet away from Edie and her friends. Even in a crime-hardened city, this event horrified the public, becoming front-page headlines in every city newspaper for weeks. It was then that Edie's family jumped at the opportunity to move to Edenwald. Musician Paul Simon, many years later, wrote a musical called *The Capeman* based on this tragic and violent incident.

Edie and I took the train home together every day after school. Wherever we went, Edie's beauty turned heads. Our first date was an

afternoon at the Museum of Modern Art. Even there, among the mas-
terpieces, all eyes were on Edie. Sometimes physical beauty is a puzzle
that can be more compelling than any painting. She was, however,
entirely unaware of her effect on people. Her beauty was not conven-
tional, yet she had an indefinable charisma and natural grace. While
standing in front of a large Franz Kline, she asked, "What is it that you
particularly like about this painting?"

I was explaining the Asian influences, the speed of the strokes, and the
correlation between the white and black spaces, but as I spoke, she rested
her elbow on my shoulder, and I suddenly felt her body pressing closer to
mine. It occurred to me that Edie had things other than art in mind. We
ended up back on the train to Bronx Park and the springtime blossoms of
the New York Botanical Garden. Lying on the cool grass, staring up at the
sky, I was still nervously chatting about paintings, movies, and books when
Edie turned to me and asked, "Do you like kissing?"

Every morning at school, students who traveled in from all five boroughs would gather in clusters outside, eager to squeeze in one last smoke. One day, just as I was about to light Edie's cigarette with my trusty Zippo, her face took on a look of utter surprise. She said calmly, "I don't want you to move. No matter what, stay right where you are." We watched as eight teenage Puerto Ricans in trench coats came toward us, looking like something straight out of *West Side Story*, holding dangerously pointed slim umbrellas. One of them was carrying a baseball bat. Edie approached the obvious leader, a handsome, slick-haired, razor-thin mustachioed tough guy, the one who carried the Louisville Slugger. They exchanged heated words. I realized he must be Raymond, Edie's former boyfriend from the projects.

He pointed at me, cursing loudly in Spanish, holding up his bat, and giving a menacing swing in my direction before spitting out, "Motherfucker, I'm gonna kill you." Yet as soon as the words left his mouth, there was a loud slap — the sound of Edie putting Raymond in his place. She pulled him away from the group as the bell for class began ringing, but everyone stood transfixed by this drama, waiting to see how it would be resolved.

Raymond handed the bat to his comrade, and Edie summoned me over. She introduced us, confidently, while Raymond glowered, staring me down. Edie scolded him and surprised everyone assembled, including me, by insisting that Raymond shake my hand. From that point on, my encounters with Raymond at Edenwald were almost cordial, with an acknowledgment that, for the benefit of Edie, he would hold no feeling of malice toward me.

Edie's fearless nature was as strong as her sense of fairness. On Christmas Eve, her mother gave me the first wallet I ever owned: buttery soft leather into which her father had tucked a dollar for good luck. On my way home that night, I was viciously mugged, thrown to the ground, and beaten by a gang of street thugs. But that good-luck dollar must have worked. I had just managed to roll away when I heard one attacker say, "Let's stab the motherfucker!"

Somehow I pushed my way through their feet and started running. I remember feeling rain dripping down my face. I waved my arms for help at every set of approaching headlights, but no one stopped, so I had no choice but to hobble the remaining blocks to the elevated train station. I ended up in the emergency room, bruised and bloodied, with a broken nose.

When Edie discovered what had happened, she arranged — without my knowledge — to meet with a gang leader known in the projects as King. When she described the gang and the violence of the attack to King, he agreed to take care of it. At Edie's insistence, overseen by King, I later returned to Edenwald, where my attackers apologized, saying they mistook me for just another outsider. King assured me that I would be safe thereafter.

I was always warmly welcomed at the Hasselmans' apartment, where music was the glue that bound Edie and her siblings together. The turntable was always alive with their vast collection of records. Her music tastes were deep and eclectic. She introduced me to such rarities as Dizzy Gillespie's *Live in Paris*. We argued when she played me the Miracles' "Shop Around," because I refused to believe that the voice of Smokey Robinson did not belong to a girl.

Edie was a true music lover. Once she even scavenged through the rubble of a burned-out neighborhood chicken shack, rescuing one record from the remains of the jukebox: "Heartbreak" by Little Willie John, which she gave to me. I still have it.

Edie channeled music with a connection to the rhythm so pure and natural that her body in motion was a song unto itself. When Edie danced, the room stopped. Once, during a concert, the great Wilson Pickett spotted Edie dancing in the crowd. He brought her out of the audience and onto the stage, pulled up a chair midsong, and just sat there mesmerized, watching her dance.

One snowy Monday night, Edie, my sister, Nancy, and I went to an open hootenanny at Gerde's Folk City, where I, true to form, borrowed money from my sister and knocked back one too many rum and cokes — and any other drink I could lay my hands on.

After a few hours of my obnoxiously bumping my way through the crowd, they both decided to call it a night and begin the trek home to the Bronx. I was drunk and belligerent, wanting to stay, but they knew better than to continue the evening. Walking toward Washington Square Park through the snow, Edie and Nancy trudged ahead, arm in arm, as I staggered behind, loudly vocalizing my displeasure at being pulled away from the club. I began cursing them out. Trying to be as creatively lewd and reprehensible as possible, I hurled one too many insults for Edie to take. She stopped and marched back to me, saying, "Time's up, buddy," and punched me square in the jaw. It was a powerful hook, and I twirled hard and fast, hitting a snowbank. Nancy was mortified, but before she could help me, Edie took her firmly by the arm, saying, "He had it coming to him. Let's go."

They walked away, my sister nervously glancing back, unsure what to do, while I lay there, still cursing and covered in snow.

There were never deep fractures between us.

Through everything, she always knew how to deal with me. I loved and respected her for this. First love is a powerful thing, but more rare is one that goes the distance.

One night we were dancing in Edie's living room, as we very often did, holding each other tight. This night, though, was special. Edie approached the phonograph with a 45-rpm record, "The Wind" by the Diablos, and took it from the sleeve. There was something ceremonious in the way she placed the needle on the vinyl. As the opening sound of low chimes began, she draped her arms around my neck, letting her long brown hair fall against my cheek as she whispered into my ear, "This is our song. Our song forever."

Edie entered college in Vermont, and I began a journey to find my place in the world. We always felt like our future lay together and that no matter what roads we took, we could always find our way back to each other.

I moved to Boston and, once there, slowly made the transition from art school to joining a band. Edie finished college, and with both of us broke, we moved into a tiny Cambridge apartment together. A special treat was dining out at a Chinese restaurant that served up a dollar combo-plate special.

Gigs were hard to come by. We supported ourselves by working in the basement shopping arcade of the Brattle Theatre. I worked in the candy and candle shop, and Edie worked in the hipster clothing store, Truc, selling high-fashion imports from London's Biba and New York's Paraphernalia boutiques.

Music and late-night DJing on the radio station WBCN started to take off for me. Edie began teaching at an all-Black girls' school in Dorchester. Her job, in a deeply segregated neighborhood, gave her a renewed sense of purpose. She related to her students, their lives, and their struggles, and they, in turn, appreciated Edie's focus and understanding. It was, for her, a reclaiming of her childhood growing up in the projects.

As the Geils band began to take off, Edie and I spent more time apart, since I was often on the road. Even though we explored other relationships in short-lived dalliances, we never doubted our future together.

With Edie and Doc Hodgins

When I was coming off the road, we sometimes had difficulty getting reacquainted with each other. For me, adjusting to the normality of domesticity exacerbated my moodiness, but Edie remained supportive and loving and did not take to heart my insular moments.

It is difficult to acknowledge the strain my burgeoning career may have placed on her. I was trying to make a name in the music world, while Edie sought a more spiritual direction, searching for deeper meaning in her life. Her adventurous spirit led her down many paths. In the summers, when school was out, she used time away from teaching to explore the world, traveling to idyllic Greek islands, Europe, and the Mediterranean. Edie was a natural bohemian, breezing through the markets of Marrakech, then coming back home to Cambridge. She was present in every moment of her life, never dwelling in the past but always in the now.

Although there would be no other relationship that came close to the depth of ours, our time apart increased.

I was on tour with the Geils band when, late one night, I was surprised by our drummer knocking on my motel-room door. Ashen-faced, he entered with a seriousness entirely out of character for him.

"Pete, I want you to sit down. I have terrible news. Edie has been killed in a car accident."

I can't remember the flight back to Boston with the band.

I do remember sitting with Edie's mother in the small office of a funeral home as the owner, a cruelly garish woman, tried to guilt her into buying the most expensive funeral package the home offered. It was sickening to witness, especially considering that Edie's family was still living in the low-income projects and had no real savings to speak of. I couldn't bear it any longer and expressed my fury at the funeral director's exploitation of our grief. Edie's mother quietly asked for nothing more than a pine box, with no trimmings, no floral arrangements — just a hearse and a limo for the immediate family and a notice in the obituaries section of the newspaper.

* * *

My life thereafter was empty, so I threw myself full-throttle into the band. I often felt as if I was just simply going through the motions. Alive, performing, hanging out, but hollow inside, as if a great chunk of who I was had died along with Edie.

I was back at our Cambridge apartment, alone, listening to music, after months spent on the road, when a knock came at the door. A man in his early forties, balding, wearing a wrinkled, sweat-stained suit with a shirt open at the collar and no tie, was standing in the hall holding a small box.

"Are you Mr. Wolf?" he inquired.

"Yes. Is there a problem?"

"No problem, sir. This delivery is for you. Just sign the sheet to confirm you have received this package."

I signed the sheet; he offered his condolences and left. I stood there, listening to the sounds of his footsteps retreating down three flights of stairs. *Condolences?* I shut the door and got the box cutter. The package came from Crescent Place in Yonkers.

I opened the box and took out a round metal tin around the size of a standard coffee can. Enclosed in the box was a business envelope, and inside, a typewritten document.

EDITH MARIE HASSELMAN
BORN AUGUST 11, 1945
DIED JULY 22, 1972
CREMATED JULY 30, 1972, AT CRESTVIEW CREMATORIUM

Doug, a friend and former bandmate, was able to borrow a boat located off the coast of Cape Cod — in North Truro, near Provincetown. With Edie's sister, Margaret, we took the boat out on the calm, lavender-hued waters. In the tradition of New Orleans musicians, we toasted her life with songs and champagne. It was the artistic and spiritual goodbye

Edie would have wanted. I brought along a portable cassette player. To the sounds of some of Edie's favorite songs — Billy Stewart's "I Do Love You," Jimi Hendrix's "Little Wing," and the haunting soundtrack to the Roger Vadim film *Et Mourir de Plaisir* — we honored her memory, then scattered her ashes as I played the final song, "The Wind" by the Diablos.

The waves took her out to sea, brushing against the boat like her hair against my cheek when we first danced to our song.

> *And even until the heavens above can no longer shine,*
> *Even until then I shall still love you.*
> *I know she is gone but my love it lingers on*
> *In a dream that the wind brings to me.*

8

SIMPLE TWIST OF FATE
Bob Dylan

M Y ADVENTUROUS TEENAGE spirit, always seeking art and music, found its home in Greenwich Village, where Washington Square Park was a magnet for artists and musicians. The artists exhibited their works — abstracts, landscapes, celebrity caricatures, sad-clown paintings, and those ever-present big-eyed Keanes — along the outer fence of the park, while the musicians, playing guitars, banjos, fiddles, mandolins, washtub basses, and harmonicas, congregated in the center.

Mostly these players came in from suburbia, performing generic folk tunes like "Freight Train" and "500 Miles." I soon found my way to the area between MacDougal and Bleecker Streets, where various coffeehouses, bistros, clubs, and other venues supported the talented (and sometimes not-so-talented) musicians who were playing jazz and folk music rather than the formulaic pop sounds of the day. These alternatives carried an anticommercial ethos that appealed to the hard-core Village crowd — and to me. My parents, who first introduced me to the Village, were "fellow travelers," a term used to describe people with left-wing beliefs.

To gain admission to the Village coffeehouses and clubs, all you usually needed to do was pay a small fee or just drop a tip into a passed hat. The main gathering place and resource for the folk musicians was a destination called the Folklore Center, located one flight up on MacDougal Street. This small, narrow record shop was famously captured on a Dave Van Ronk album cover and was owned and operated by Izzy Young, a friend of my father who shared his political and musical tastes.

Beginning in 1961, I would spend hours in Izzy's shop. He could be a moody character and didn't have the patience to suffer fools gladly, yet he never made me feel unwelcome. There was a warmth to the man, with his strong New York accent and thick-lensed glasses constantly in need of cleaning. Izzy's imposing appearance seemed even more massive within the narrow confines of his store. He had a permanently disheveled look, as if he had just rolled out of bed, which most likely was the case. His perpetually untucked shirttails hung out and flapped up and down as he rushed around the shop.

I was browsing through a record bin one afternoon when I heard a voice that caught my ear from behind the thin half-closed curtain separating the front of the store from the back. I walked up to Mel, a banjo player working at the front desk, and asked, "Hey, who's that singing in back?"

He stopped playing his banjo and gave a quick listen. "Oh, that's some new kid, friend of Izzy's. He just rolled into town."

I went back toward the curtain to listen more closely, attracted to the unusual style of this voice. The singing continued for quite some time, followed by chatter amid the closing of guitar cases. After the singer and two other young men left the shop, I asked Mel, "That guy sounds really good — does he play anywhere?"

Mel, more interested in his banjo than my questions, shrugged. "Oh, he's just hanging around the Village here and there. Ask Izzy — he'll probably know."

"What's his name?" I asked.

Mel, still picking away at his banjo, said, "Bobby. Bobby Dillon."

I rushed down the steps to see where they were headed but couldn't spot them. I had, however, been overcome by this voice and was determined to hear more.

Hoping to speak to Izzy about this mysterious new singer, I returned to the Folklore Center many times, but Izzy was always off on errands or at the printer's. Although Mel later told me that Bobby might be playing at Cafe Wha? or the neighboring Gaslight Café, I couldn't seem to find him anywhere.

Once, when I happened to go to an open-mike night at the Gaslight hosted by Dave Van Ronk, I saw Bobby there, sitting at a crowded table. I asked the club manager if Bobby would be playing and, to my amazement, he said yes. After several artists had taken their turn, Dave announced him to a good round of applause. As Bobby settled himself onstage, he accidentally jostled the harmonicas on the adjacent stool, sending them clattering to the floor, then joked, "My harmonicas are always ready before I am," to which the crowd responded with laughter. He fiddled with his cap, talked about soaking his harmonicas in water to help them sound better, and wondered whether they would sound drunk if he put them in red wine. His natural rapport with the audience seemed effortless. He performed three numbers — an original talking blues, a Woody Guthrie song, and "Gospel Plow." When he left the stage, the place erupted in sustained applause. I was, perhaps, the one clapping the loudest.

Not long afterward I was at the Folklore Center, and Izzy mentioned that Bob Dylan — not Bobby Dillon, as I had thought — would be playing at Gerde's Folk City along with blues great John Lee Hooker. This double bill was a double treat for me, for I would get to hear two favorites in one night.

Since the drinking age was eighteen and I was underage, I had to go with my older friend Paul Fury, who was home from the navy. The club was crowded at least three deep at the bar, and there seemed to be anticipation for Bob, who was opening for John Lee. When Bob took the stage, people were yelling out songs for him to perform. He responded, "Some of those I can't remember too well, but here's a new one I just wrote." That night, each song he sang was introduced with an amusing ad-lib. The crowd roared its approval when he finished his set. The crowd also went mad for John Lee from the moment he walked onstage, and it proved to be one of those nights I'll always remember.

Three years later, I became friends with John Lee. I asked him, "Do you remember the time you played with Bob Dylan at Gerde's?"

"Remember?" said John Lee. "Man, that guy would come up to my hotel room, asking me a million questions about my playing and the techniques of other blues players I knew. He always brought along his guitar. Then he'd start drinkin' from my bottle. Man, that Bob. I sure liked him, but he was kinda a funny one."

I asked him what he meant by funny. John Lee said, "He wasn't like the other young blues players that came around. He just was different — not strange or weird, just different, trying to find out every little detail he could."

Bob was always playing and trading songs with other musicians, and this exposed him to a wide array of influences, including Appalachian mountain music, Elizabethan ballads, and the songs of Hank Williams, Hank Snow, and Blind Lemon Jefferson. I came to learn that this voracious curiosity was typical of Bob. Whether I heard him at the sparsely attended concert that Izzy hosted not long afterward in a recital space at Carnegie Hall or in the back room of the Folklore Center, where I began to find him on a regular basis, he always seemed to be doing something new, expanding his taste and his repertoire. Hearing these backroom jam sessions firsthand and being exposed to the tremendous variety of styles he and the other musicians played had a major effect on broadening my musical knowledge.

One afternoon when I was painting at a little studio in the

basement of a friend's house, next door to my parents' apartment building, I had the radio playing in the background, and a show called *Folksinger's Choice*, hosted by Cynthia Gooding, came on. To my surprise, Bob was featured as a special guest. Immediately after the show finished, I called the station, WBAI. Ms. Gooding answered, and I asked her where Dylan would be playing next. She replied, "Hold on; I'll ask."

Several seconds later, surprisingly, Bob himself came on the phone. I told him how much I enjoyed his music and that I was a painter. "Oh, a painter! I love paintings — love to see your work someday."

"I'm in the Village all the time," I said, "and I'm a good friend of Izzy's. I'd be more than happy to show you some of my paintings."

Bob hesitated, then gave me an address. "Sometimes you can find me there," he added, then quickly hung up.

I couldn't believe my good fortune. I hurriedly gathered some paintings and drawings into a portfolio and rushed to catch the downtown train straight to the Village, heading right to the address Bob had given me. When I arrived at the brownstone apartment building, there were several performers I recognized sitting on the steps out front, including Mark Spoelstra and Patrick Sky. I looked for Bob's name on the apartment buzzers. "Who you lookin' for?" Mark asked me.

"Bob Dylan," I answered.

"Oh, we've been waiting for him for over an hour. Just grab a step."

A few minutes passed, and John Herald of the Greenbriar Boys bluegrass group passed by and said, "If you're all waiting for Bob, he's hanging out at the Kettle of Fish."

Like the Pied Piper, John led us to the bar, where we found Bob seated with a group of people at a large round table littered with half-empty pitchers of beer, wineglasses, and ashtrays stacked with high hills of cigarette butts. I approached Bob and hesitantly said, "Hey, Bob. I'm the guy you spoke to on the phone a while ago...about seeing some paintings?"

He was holding a wineglass and turned, giving me a real long stare. It was the first time I realized he had blue eyes that could cut right through you. After emptying his glass, he turned away from me, saying, "Paintings? I don't wanna see no damn paintings." Then he drank another glass.

I was taken aback, but at that very moment, John Herald mentioned there was a good party happening over at Annie Bird's apartment. Everyone drank the last of the beer and wine, then got up to leave. As they headed out the door, Bob turned to me as if motioning for me to follow. The group walked together amid shrieks of laughter, and I trailed behind them, lugging my unopened portfolio. When Bob entered the party, he began a conversation with a willowy brown-haired girl in a tight black turtleneck and miniskirt. Realizing that I wasn't going to accomplish my objective — showing Bob my paintings — I drowned my disappointment and nervousness in endless glasses of red wine from the several jugs that were scattered around the apartment.

Bob's first album, *Bob Dylan*, came out soon afterward, and I immediately bought it. When my sister saw the cover, she said, to my surprise, "I met him when I was at college in Wisconsin. He was playing the piano with a harmonica attached by a wire to his neck. That's him on the cover. It was at a gathering in the room of my guitarist friend Danny Kalb." (Danny Kalb went on to become a member, with Al Kooper, of the group the Blues Project.) My father, hearing me playing the album, looked at the cover and said, "That's Bobby, Izzy's friend. What a character that guy is. He's a hoot!"

"Dad, you know Bob Dylan?"

"Sure. I met him lots of times when I'd visit Izzy. We even had lunch across the street, and one time we were joined by this really wild character who called himself Tiny Tim. When you're down in the Village again, ask Izzy where Tiny Tim is playing. I thought I knew a lot of songs from the early days, but that fella seems to know almost every song that was ever written from the thirties on back."

First my sister; now my father. And there I was thinking Bob was my own personal discovery.

Late one evening, I stopped in at a nearly empty Gaslight Café. Sitting together were Dave Van Ronk and, as I recall, singer Buffy Sainte-Marie and performer David Blue. Someone mentioned that Bob was supposed to come down and play that night. It was getting near closing, which for New York was pretty late, when finally, in walked Bob. I overheard him say to Dave that he had just been writing, and Dave asked Bob if he'd like to sing a few. Bob got up on the small stage and seemed to have difficulty tuning the guitar that someone handed him, so Dave tuned it for him. Bob tried several keys until he found the one he wanted.

I was sitting alone at the table nearest the stage. Bob played one song, then began singing, "Oh, where have you been, my blue-eyed son? / Oh, where have you been, my darling young one?" The song had many verses, and each line was as compelling as the one before it. Bob was totally absorbed, as if he were channeling every word. It had the form of an Elizabethan ballad but with imagery like nothing I'd ever heard before. He finished the last chorus, repeating, "And it's a hard, it's a hard, it's a hard, it's a hard / It's a hard rain's a-gonna fall."

When he stepped off the stage, there was complete silence. We were spellbound by what we had just heard. I don't know if that was the first time Bob performed the song, but it certainly was the first time I heard it, and that might have also been true for the small crowd gathered at the Gaslight. In one seismic moment, he had brought us into new and unexplored terrain, just as Picasso helped radically reshape the landscape of modern painting with *Les Demoiselles d'Avignon*. My mind was filled with so many images from the song that as soon as I got home that night, I headed to my small studio and began a painting I called *Hard Rain*.

My next sighting of Bob was at the Monday hootenanny night at Gerde's Folk City, where established musicians as well as recent arrivals in town signed up to perform. Tom and Jerry, who became Simon and

Garfunkel; Judy Collins, in a formal dress and high heels; blind Puerto Rican José Feliciano; comedian Flip Wilson; and a long list of other notable performers — they all made appearances there. You paid a dollar at the door and got a free drink card.

Bob would usually show up, but he rarely played on these nights. He'd stand by the bar, order red wine, and hold court. I always tried to stand next to him to hear what he might be talking about. One evening, he was telling a guy that his producer, John Hammond, had given him an amazing record that came in a simple plain white sleeve. It was a 1930s recording of Robert Johnson. Bob was over the moon about it, and he couldn't stop telling the guy at the bar just how great the recording was.

That night, I had used my drink ticket for a glass of 151-proof rum and Coke, which had certainly given me quite a buzz. I didn't want the feeling to fade, but I couldn't afford another drink. Bob, with his back to me, was still talking to this guy about Robert Johnson when I noticed his half-empty glass of red wine just sitting there next to me. I quickly drank it. Several minutes later Bob turned around, saw his glass was empty, and called the bartender over for a refill. He took a couple of sips, put the glass back on the bar, and continued his conversation. As I had with the first glass, I emptied most of the second. Bob was telling this guy, "I can look into people's eyes and see truth in them. Robert Johnson had truth, a truth that only a few singers are capable of capturing." Again Bob turned for his wineglass, saw it was almost empty, and ordered another. This went on for several more rounds, but never once did he suspect that the young squirt standing next to him kept guzzling his wine before he had a chance to finish it.

As Bob's fame grew, I saw every major show that he played in New York, from Town Hall to Carnegie Hall. I didn't attend the Newport Folk Festival, but I did see him perform at Forest Hills Stadium, and that, like Newport, turned into a chaotic and somewhat scary evening. The crowd was loud, and many folk fans booed Bob when he started his electric set. People began running onto the field in front of the stage, and one guy even made it onto the stage itself before he was dragged off.

In October of 1964, I moved to Boston to study at the School of the Museum of Fine Arts. I was still planning to be a painter, not a musician, but I did join a band made up of several art students. We weren't the greatest players, but we sure had attitude. Over time we talked our way into performing with some major artists, including John Lee Hooker, Muddy Waters, the Shirelles, Howlin' Wolf, Sun Ra, and even the Byrds, whose cover of Bob's "Mr. Tambourine Man" had just been released.

Bob's right-hand man at the time was Bobby Neuwirth. I knew Bobby partly because he was a close friend of the lead guitarist in my band and partly because he had studied at the same art school. He got us tickets to Bob's sold-out concert at Boston's Symphony Hall and invited us to the after-party in Cambridge. It seemed like the entire folk community was there: Jim Kweskin and the Jug Band, Jim Rooney, Eric Von Schmidt, the Charles River Valley Boys, Leon Bibb, Tom Rush — the place was packed. Paul Butterfield and most of his band came, since they were also playing in town that same night at Club 47.

Bob was in the kitchen surrounded by a large crowd, mostly ladies, all asking him to sing. Maria Muldaur handed him a guitar, and he launched right into one of the top hits at the time, Martha and the Vandellas' "Dancing in the Street." Nobody else could have made that song so surprisingly enjoyable for such an orthodox traditional-folk crowd.

Back in New York City later that year, I was walking uptown on Sixth Avenue, having drunk a few too many Bacardi 151s at the White Horse Tavern. I was teetering along, feeling no pain, when I spotted Bob in front of O. Henry's Steak House. He was sitting alone at a café table, reading the *New York Times*, wearing a black Spanish-style hat reminiscent of Zorro's, dark Ray-Ban sunglasses, and a fitted leather jacket. Anxiously tapping his slimly denimed leg, he spotted my approach and

raised the newspaper to hide his face. Too late! Uninvited and undeterred, I sat down at his table.

"Excuse me, Bob, I don't mean to bother you." (People often say
these words upon encountering celebrities, then proceed to do exactly
what they say they're not going to do.) "I don't want to interrupt you, but
I wonder if you can tell me... uh... tell me... what is truth?"

Bob sat still. He didn't move. Then very slowly, he lowered his newspaper and gave me a long, hard stare. I could almost feel those steel-blue
eyes blazing right through his dark Ray-Bans. If my memory serves me
well, to paraphrase the bard himself, this was his response.

"You mean you want ME to tell YOU what truth is? You want ME
to explain to YOU what is TRUTH? You see that tree behind you?" I
turned and looked and acknowledged, yes, I saw the tree. "How the
FUCK do you know it's there? How do you know it's not some sort of
APPARITION? Have you touched it? You believe it's there because you
see it? Do you BELIEVE everything you see is the TRUTH? What
about what you DON'T SEE? Is that the UNSEEN TRUTH? Do you
believe EVERYTHING you hear? How do you KNOW I'm going to
be truthful if I DO try to tell you what I think truth MIGHT be? How
do you know what I say ain't nothing but ONE FUCKING BIG LIE?
Lotsa people BELIEVE lies! What's the difference between TRUTH
and a LIE? Is the time on your watch the truth? You want ME to tell
YOU what TRUTH is? Have you ever read T. S. Eliot? Ezra Pound?
Jack Kerouac? Socrates? Plato? Aristotle? Ovid? Virgil? Dante? The
ancient scriptures? The Talmud? The book of Revelation? The book of
Numbers? You just casually come up to ME, as if I SHOULD REVEAL
TO YOU what I know or don't know? Why should I tell YOU ANY-
THING? You think I'm some kind of PROPHET? You think I've been
encountering ALL the mysteries back beyond thousands and thousands
of years before the time of the PHARAOHS and the PYRAMIDS?
You just want an EASY ANSWER! You just want ME to pass along to
YOU some ancient secret that I might have discovered! Truth, if it exists,

is something YOU have to search for YOURSELF! So I ain't gonna waste my time EVEN ANSWERING YOU! The REAL TRUTH IS, I just wanna finish drinking MY coffee and read this newspaper and be left ALONE!"

Leaving the table, I realized that for a guy who said he wasn't going to waste his time answering me, he sure did pack a lot of truth into everything he said.

In 1981, after *Freeze-Frame* became the Geils band's most popular release, we were invited to tour, as special guests, with the Rolling Stones.

Our first date took place at the Los Angeles Memorial Coliseum. I was hanging out after our set in Keith Richards's dressing room. There was still some time before the Stones took the stage. At one point the door opened, and Ronnie Wood brought Bob in to chat with Keith. While Bob and Keith talked, I hung out to one side, still in my stage clothes, wearing custom-made zebra-print shoes. Bob sized me up and down, then asked, "Hey, what did you have to kill to get a pair of shoes like that?" It was too good a one-liner to even attempt a reply.

The years passed, and via a mutual friend, Bob and I came to know each other through our shared interest in painting and literature. He also dropped by the studio during the recording of my first solo album, *Lights Out.* His visit meant a lot to me and gave me confidence at a time when I truly needed it.

I started going to his sound checks, and it intrigued me to see how Bob continually rearranged his songs. I would always bring him books that I thought might interest him, and he sometimes did the same in return. Since painting was a frequent topic of our conversations, several times he shared some of his latest artwork with me.

It was during one sound check that I noticed Bob was wearing an especially sharp pair of black leather pants. At the end of the sound check, after complimenting him on these finely tailored trousers, I jokingly added, "What did you have to kill to get a pair of pants like that?"

Almost a year later, I received a large box in the mail. Inside was a stunning pair of lightly worn black leather pants, custom-made by Manuel of Nashville, who apprenticed to the famed rodeo tailor Nudie of Hollywood. There was no enclosed note, and I was confounded, though I recognized the return address on the box as Bob's New York office. I called his chief coordinator and asked, "What's the story about the pants that just arrived?"

He answered, "Didn't you once tell Bob you liked his pants?"

Puzzled, I said, "Yeah, but that was a really long time ago."

"Well, Pete, Bob must have remembered, and he wanted you to have them."

Rolling On

"THERE'S A BIG WIDE WORLD I WAS BORN TO SEE"

9

HAVE THUMB, WILL TRAVEL
David Lynch

M Y HIGH SCHOOL graduation was held at Carnegie Hall. As our names were called, we walked from the audience onto the stage to be presented with our diplomas. When it was my turn, I was instead handed a plain manila envelope, inside of which was a handwritten note: "If you want to know why your diploma is missing from the envelope, please come see me in my office at your convenience. Signed, Louis Wechsler, principal of the High School of Music and Art." I never considered it convenient to see Mr. Wechsler, therefore I never actually graduated from high school.

In order to graduate, I would have had to attend summer school. I had once endured this torment and swore to myself that I'd never go through it again. I dreaded climbing the steps to some randomly chosen high school, feeling like there was a big bubble over my head with the word *loser* floating within it. Instead, I found a part-time job in the want ads. I planned that by the time fall arrived I'd have enough money saved to hitchhike around the country and visit my friends who had graduated and were attending various universities.

The job I found was in the main showroom of an interior decorating firm. The day began with designers searching for inspiration by riffling through endless swatches of fabric, which they casually dropped to the floor. It was my responsibility to pick up the swatches, fold them, and place them neatly onto the correct shelves, over and over again. The manager was a short, thin man, with shiny, greased-back hair and a very narrow face, onto which he drew a tiny mustache with an eyebrow pencil. He always wore an outlandishly colored ascot and favored a strong rose-scented cologne that lingered long after he was gone. One day, he called me into his office. "Peter, you can have a great future here at Stoman-Loman, but you need to tidy yourself up — a nice hair trim for a start. Any way I can be of assistance to you, please don't hesitate to seek my guidance," he said as he slid my weekly pay envelope across his desk.

During my lunch break, I headed over to the hot dog wagon that was always parked alongside St. Patrick's Cathedral. As I waited in line, paperboys farther up the block began shouting, "Kennedy shot, Kennedy shot!" People were clamoring for news, gathering in clusters, looking for any information, craning their necks over the shoulders of those reading newspapers, desperate to know what had happened. I stood in the midst of the pandemonium of Fifth Avenue, unable to digest this terrible news, having no sense of where to go or what to do. I walked to 42nd Street and took the subway shuttle to the West Side, where I walked onto the entrance ramp of the Lincoln Tunnel, stuck out my thumb, and, without rhyme or reason, headed west.

On every ride I caught, the drivers were glued to the radio. At rest stops, people gathered in front of radios and televisions in somber silence. The journey seemed to pass in slow motion as I made my way to the University of Wisconsin, where my sister, Nancy, was enrolled. When I finally arrived, I saw students gathered around the television in the main campus lounge — and we all witnessed Jack Ruby suddenly shoot Lee Harvey Oswald. After a few days, I headed back home. I felt an imperceptible change within me, as if the ground had slightly shifted and somehow I needed to find more stable footing to keep from feeling further adrift.

I returned home, painting with more fervor than ever before. After a year, I made the same trip, but this time with an agenda. I visited a number of colleges and universities, pretending to be enrolled as an art student. I sought out old high school friends who attended the colleges, slept on their dorm-room floors, ate in the student cafeterias, and, most important, attended the art classes and gained access to the schools' art supplies.

Some institutions were easier to penetrate than others. Three that proved to be tremendous windfalls were the University of Chicago, the University of Wisconsin, and the real bonanza, Brandeis University, in Massachusetts. Brandeis had recently built a new art center, and I showed up so frequently — far more than any other art student — that the visiting instructor put me in charge of the keys to the painting studios and the fully stocked supply cabinets. I didn't feel like an impostor because I was in search of knowledge, not credentials.

Masquerading as an art student and sleeping in the Brandeis student lounge, I couldn't always avoid the campus security. They caught me several times. It was uncomfortable, but the campus police, fortunately, preferred to handle their problems internally, without involving the city police.

It was during one of my later visits to Brandeis, after a long day of painting in its studios, that I lay stretched out on the campus lawn, drinking a bottle of Tango — a mix of vodka and orange juice — when I heard the sound of Chuck Berry guitar riffs coming from a nearby dorm. My curiosity piqued, I got up to investigate. As I entered the dormitory building, I saw three students playing on the lounge steps. The lead guitarist was the most enthusiastic of the bunch, and I complimented him on his playing. "Hey there, King, you sure can play that guitar of yours." He seemed to like my Elvis reference and introduced himself as Jon. I told him I was an art student on campus and asked if he and his band were playing anywhere. He mentioned he was signed up to play an acoustic set the next evening at a hootenanny in the campus coffeehouse. I told him I played harmonica and suggested we play a duet. The following night we sat together at the rear of the small club. I was really looking forward to playing, but when Jon's name was called, he turned to me as he took his guitar from his case and said, "You know, I think I'm going to play alone tonight." I guess that was Jon Landau's first managerial decision. We remained friends, and years later, he went from being a rock critic for *Rolling Stone* to managing Bruce Springsteen during the making of *Born to Run*.

The University of Chicago was a wellspring for my artistic needs. I loved the city. It was cheap, easy to get around, and had a fine art museum, grand architecture, and, of course, excellent music. The first high school acquaintance I contacted at the university wasn't exactly a friend at the time: Leon Botstein. He was probably one of the smartest and most accomplished students who graduated from my high school. He was class president, editor of the student newspaper, head of the debate club, and first violinist in the student orchestra. His father was a prominent oncologist.

There had been a party for Leon at his family's stately home in the posh Riverdale section of the Bronx. My girlfriend, Edie, was invited, and I tagged along as her date. I felt very out of place and wished I hadn't come. After knocking back several cups of refreshment from a large punch bowl on the dining room table, I decided to pick up the whole bowl and drink it down. Leon's brother, mortified by my behavior, pulled me away from the table. Punches were thrown, and we ended up rolling down a flight of stairs. Edie also indulged in too much drink and threw up into the shrubbery. She and I were both driven home by Leon's father, who seemed amused by our behavior.

My visit to Leon in Chicago would be our first encounter since that evening. I walked into his dorm room smiling, a cheerful look on my face, and exclaimed, "Leon, what a wonderful surprise!" I was the last person Leon wanted to see, and knowing that, I had to be quick and to the point. "Leon, I was staying at the University of Wisconsin, working as an apprentice for the art classes. Now, with my duties fulfilled, I'm heading east and thought I could perhaps stay here for a bit. I assure you I'll keep out of your way, and you won't even notice I'm here." Leon wanted none of it, but another student, as luck would have it, was in his room and offered me a place to stay. My new friend's name was Rainier, from Iowa. He was studying philosophy and religion. He was not very tall, and he had closely cropped brown hair and a round face framed by a neatly trimmed beard. During one of our many late-night discussions, he revealed that his father was a high-ranking officer in the Luftwaffe during World War II. For reasons unexplained to Rainier, his father had been brought to this country in secrecy.

Rainier, an ascetic, believed in having as few material comforts as possible. He felt his true calling would be in the ministry. He gave me his bed and slept on the floor. He also gave me some of his food tickets, since he believed in having only one meal a day. If he passed by someone in need, he would always try to give that person something. Rainier enjoyed theological arguments, and between us, they were never in short supply.

Leon, eager to get rid of me, suggested that I join him and some other students for a long weekend visiting friends at Harvard. Like someone trying to shoo away a stray dog, he encouraged me to have a look at the city's art schools. He was offering me a free ride there and back. I wasn't so sure about the reliability of a return trip, but Boston, with its abundance of universities and colleges, interested me. I threw some paintings in the trunk of his car, and once there, followed Leon's advice and, just for the hell of it, applied to the Boston Museum School of Fine Arts. I borrowed the $18 application fee, lied and said I was a high school graduate, and traveled to Providence and looked around Brown and RISD. I missed the return ride, but I hitched back to Chicago, much to Leon's disappointment.

Chicago soon began to feel a little constricted after the East Coast. Rainier was then in the middle of a hunger strike, protesting the

61

Vatican's refusal to speak out against the escalating war in Vietnam. During one of my weekly calls home, my mother said a letter had arrived from a Boston museum school. I asked her to open it.

"Peter! Are you sitting down? It says your application was approved, along with a grant if you choose to accept."

With news of this unbelievable good fortune, I gathered my meager belongings. As a final act of gratitude for my host, I managed to persuade Rainier to eat before I headed back to New York. When I told Leon I was finally leaving, he was unable to hide his joy.

I arrived in Boston the day before classes were to begin. I had enough money to stay just one night at the nearby YMCA, a short distance from the school. In those days, the Y was only a step or two up from a flophouse. The small, thinly walled gray rooms had frayed yellow window shades and beds so worn that the mattresses almost touched the floor. Throughout the night, you could hear endless hacking coughs coming from the other rooms. With almost no money left, I spent the next day trying to find a place to sleep for free. I went to Harvard, hoping I might stay for a night or two at an old high school friend's dorm, but he was not keen on the idea. I had no choice but to spend my second night sleeping alongside the Charles River next to the Larz Anderson Bridge, where Quentin Compson, the main character in William Faulkner's *Absalom, Absalom!*, commits suicide. (There once was a brass plaque on the bridge marking the exact spot.) But the weather for another night by the river was not in my favor, so I was determined to find a halfway decent indoor option.

The school had a long wall next to the front entrance where students posted notices. "Can't keep my cat"; "Selling chairs and a hot plate"; "Roommate wanted to share loft — no heat"; "Need an easel?" As I anxiously browsed the wall, I heard a male voice behind me.

"Are you looking for a roommate?"

I turned to see a pleasant-looking student with thick light-brown hair. He was dressed in a sport jacket over a neatly pressed shirt and tie. "As a matter of fact, I am," I quickly replied, wondering if he were miraculously sent from heaven.

"Gee, that's good. I have an apartment, and I've been looking for a roommate, too. My name is David."

We discussed the financial details, and I went to give his place a look, even though I was prepared to take him up on his offer no matter what.

The apartment was a third-floor walk-up a short ten minutes from the school on a street that was mostly inhabited by students at various colleges. It was a freshly painted, cramped two-room space with a tiny kitchenette. The small bedroom had a bunk bed, and the living room walls were covered with his paintings. David was very accommodating, and we both seemed glad to have satisfied our mutual need. Although both of us were young men with a headstrong artistic temperament, as roommates we were an odd couple. I would compare our differences to those of Gauguin and Van Gogh, but ours were of a more mundane nature.

There is an internal and external part to everyone. David seemed to come from a world of fraternities, proms, and double dates. Being the buttoned-up, neat, and tidy guy he was, he appeared to be in his natural milieu. I, however, was a mess. I rarely showered and hardly changed my work shirt and jeans. We both smoked cigarettes — he Marlboros and I almost three packs of pungent Gauloises a day — so we always had to keep a window slightly open. The girls David dated were a particular type, some with virgin pins primly placed at the necks of their fluffy cashmere cardigans. We were also in different orbits regarding painting: I loved Soutine, Beckmann, and the German expressionists, but he leaned toward abstraction.

Early one evening, along with some other students, we were chatting about being underage and not allowed to buy beer, because the drinking age was twenty-one. I came up with the bright idea that if we drove to New York, a trip that took four hours, we would arrive around 10:00 p.m., and since the drinking age there was eighteen and the bars didn't close until 4:00 a.m., we could surely quench our thirst in that period of time. We climbed into a friend's truck and headed down to Katz's Delicatessen, on Houston Street, where the beers were only fifteen cents. We drank until the joint closed. It wasn't until we began the long drive back to Boston that we realized how wasted and tired we were. Thankfully, we crashed at my parents' apartment, in the Bronx, rather than into the East River.

David's staid demeanor never altered except for one night, when I was half asleep in the upper bunk bed and I heard him give a bloodcurdling scream from the bathroom. He was brushing his teeth, and as he was putting more toothpaste onto the brush, he realized that part of a cockroach was caught in the bristles. The remainder was surely in his mouth. I like to imagine that this helped inspire the surrealist aspects of many of his defining films.

I was constantly late paying my share of the rent, and David was understandably becoming more and more agitated with me. I started asking around, hoping to find a cheaper place to live, and finally I did. I came back to collect my belongings, including my beloved records, and to my surprise, I discovered that David had changed the lock. His patience, after chasing me down for the rent so many times, had finally run out.

I thought I would outsmart him by having Peter Laffin, a sculptor and my new roommate, drive me over to David's place in his orange ex–highway maintenance truck. There was a narrow alley in the back of the building where the fire escapes were located, allowing me to climb to the third-floor apartment window that we always left open. Peter, in order not to block the alley, planned to wait for me on an adjacent street. I would pack up my things, then Peter would drive around and help me load up the stuff, and we'd be off on our merry way in victory, like brave Odysseus sacking the city of Troy.

As I was making my final descent and my foot was just about to touch the ground, however, I heard several loud clicks, and a blinding light erased the darkness of the alley. A spotlight, along with several flashlights, made an approach toward me with the loud command

"FREEZE! Hands up. Lie slowly on the ground, facedown, with your hands and legs spread far apart!" I did as they ordered.

"That him?" a cop holding a flashlight asked.

"Naw. Some punk doing a B and E," a plainclothes-man answered.

"Shit, after all that waiting," said another.

"So Hoppy, what you up to?"

"Nothing, Officer. I'm moving stuff from my apartment. I live here and just forgot my key."

"Yeah, and I'm Ted Williams," said the cop.

"Officer, these are my records and my paintings. My name is on them."

"Got any ID, kid?"

"Yes, sir, in my back pocket."

An officer took it from my pocket, then shone a flashlight on my records and paintings.

"Those your paintings?" one of them asked.

"You call that painting? My fuckin' goldfish can paint better than that," contributed another.

"Leave him alone. Call headquarters and tell him he ain't the Strangler."

"Strangler?" I asked, bewildered. "The Boston Strangler?"

"Yeah, and be glad we didn't shoot first. Now get this shit outta here."

After that, whenever I would see David walking through the halls at school, we always politely acknowledged each other. He grew a beard and began to look scruffy, but he still always had his shirt collar buttoned. Eventually he left Boston to study at the Pennsylvania Academy of the Fine Arts, in Philadelphia, where he formally began his film career.

Decades later, I was filming a music video for the title song from my album *Come As You Are*. My grandmother had always gone to the movies on Tuesdays, no matter what was playing, and I often tagged along. I vividly recalled the MGM musical *Small Town Girl*, which has long been forgotten. It contained a choreographed scene that completely mesmerized me from the moment I saw it, when I was eight years old. A character joyfully jumps through the streets of a small town, never stopping once, greeting every passerby he encounters, continually jumping, his amazing endurance never letting up.

I thought it would be a great idea to re-create this energetic scene for my video. I chose the director Edd Griles, who was known for Cyndi Lauper's "Girls Just Want to Have Fun" video. He agreed once he saw the archival footage and discovered that the set where the original movie was filmed still miraculously existed on the Universal Studios Lot. After green-lighting the idea with my record company, we started the arduous job of preproduction. I knew the stamina needed for continually jumping was going to take some preparation, but I never fully grasped the physical commitment required. I hired a personal trainer a little too late. He tried hard to get me in shape, but after around ten minutes on the treadmill each day, I was too damn bored and out of breath to continue. The day before shooting, Edd and I did a walk-through of the set. Edd asked me to start jumping on the sidewalk, and after two minutes I was exhausted. "Pete, you trained for this, right?" he asked as I was struggling to catch my breath.

"Oh, sure, Edd," I claimed. Edd seemed worried, though, and I was overcome with anxiety, seeing the huge area through which I needed to jump bright and early the next morning. Edd said nervously, "Go to your hotel and get a really good night's rest, Pete. You're going to need it for tomorrow." Little did he know that telling a lifelong insomniac to get a really good night's rest is a surefire way to induce an anxiety attack. I was panicked and knew sleep would be an impossibility. I had heard about a fast-acting sleeping pill, Halcyon, that worked when others failed, leaving little or no hangover the next day. So I called a friendly LA doctor, picked up my prescription, and tried for an early night, to be ready for a 5:00 a.m. wake-up call.

* * *

I have no recollection of my trainer, along with hotel security, forcing open the chain on my hotel-room door. Apparently, not being able to fall asleep, I took one pill and then another. The next thing I do remember is being in my trailer on the set, asking Edd, "When we gonna start filming?"

"Peter, are you okay?"

"Sure, Edd, why?"

"Because, Peter, you've been jumping all morning. It's a wrap."

Halcyon didn't last too long on the market, thanks to one of its side effects: severe short-term memory loss.

The cinematographer of the shoot was a gentleman named Fred Elmes. Fred shot *Blue Velvet* for David and was meeting him for dinner later that night. When I first saw *Blue Velvet*, it was quite a surprise to see that Kyle MacLachlan, who portrayed the lead character, Jeffrey Beaumont, had so many of the qualities of the David I knew back then. I sent someone on the production team to purchase a copy of *City of Nets* by Otto Friedrich, one of my favorite books about Hollywood and the dismantling of the studio system. I wrote a note to David congratulating him on all his success and asked Fred to give it to him with the book at dinner. The following day Fred handed me an envelope with a note inside:

Peter —

So good hearing from you after all these years. Thank you for the book, but I must remind you that you still owe me thirty-three dollars and forty cents.

Best,
David

10

DIAMONDS AT YOUR FEET
Muddy Waters

M Y INTEREST IN blues dates back to my late teens. I would often take the subway to Times Square, where there was an abundance of specialized independent record stores that stocked some otherwise hard-to-find music. One day, while hunting through a shop's record bins, I came across an album called *The Best of Muddy Waters*. The artist's name, along with a photograph of him in profile on the cover, instantly captured my attention. I bought the record without having any idea what the music inside would sound like and raced home to listen to it. For hours on end I played that album, staring at the photograph, until every song became etched deeply into my brain, like lines in the palm of my hand. From that day forward I was a devoted Muddy Waters fan.

The first time I saw Muddy in person was at the Apollo Theater as part of an evening of blues artists that included Jimmy Reed, Jimmy Witherspoon, Bobby "Blue" Bland, and B.B. King. The evening kicked off with an introduction from the flamboyantly dressed Apollo emcee, announcing, "Welcome, ladies and gentlemen, to the world-renowned Apollo Theater. Let's give a real warm Apollo welcome to Mr. Big Boss

Man himself, the great Jimmy Reed." Reed walked onstage, a little unsteady, as if he may have had one too many, but his soulfulness shone through.

Things switched gears altogether when Muddy's band took the stage and opened with several instrumentals spotlighting the harmonica master James Cotton and piano virtuoso Otis Spann. Muddy then walked out to thunderous applause. After so many hours spent staring at the record cover, I was mesmerized at the sight of that familiar face come to life. His playing and singing were even more powerful onstage than they were in his recordings. He brought the audience to their feet several times.

The excitement continued with amazing performances by Jimmy Witherspoon, followed by the dynamic Bobby "Blue" Bland and B.B. King, the closing act. His set was sailing along smoothly until he began a rap about "being down home in the hot southern sun pickin' cotton. You all know what I mean: that's one way we get the blues, pickin' cotton." Some young city hecklers, obviously of the Motown generation, were seated in the balcony and didn't want to hear about the hardships of rural folk. They began shouting, "Hey, we don't pick cotton up here in Harlem." Undeterred, B.B. continued with his tale of days spent in the hot Mississippi sun. The shouts from the balcony increased, becoming louder. "Hey, man, we said we don't pick no cotton up here in Harlem." B.B. ignored their catcalling and kept right on rapping. The interruptions from the balcony kept up, too: "Why don't you go back down South, Grandpa?"

Unwilling to ignore them any longer, B.B. finished his set but soon returned to the stage, this time joined by all the performers, for a blues number directed straight at the young balcony hecklers. The verses they sang kicked off with B.B.: "Listen, come on back in the alley and we'll show you what a bluesman can do."

Witherspoon chimed in: "Come on back in the alley and we're gonna make a mess out of you."

Bobby was next: "Come on back in the alley; we don't care if you're three, four, or five."

Muddy finished it off, singing, "I'll put the hoochie coochie on you; you'll be lucky if you walk out alive."

At that the hecklers in the balcony were silenced, and the crowd went wild. My first introduction to a blues concert had turned into an unforgettable evening.

The next time I had a chance to hear Muddy Waters was after I'd moved to Boston, and I saw a flyer advertising his appearance at the prestigious club the Jazz Workshop. Having just formed my first band, the Hallucinations, I knew this was something I couldn't miss. Although you had to be twenty-one to be admitted, and I was underage, I managed to borrow someone's ID, and I went with my bandmate Paul Shapiro.

We sat as close to the stage as possible, right in front of the amplifier used by Muddy's dynamic harmonica player, James Cotton. Since I was teaching myself blues harmonica, the spot couldn't have been better. As they did at the Apollo concert, the band kicked off with a few instrumentals, then Cotton sang, followed by the piano player Otis Spann, after which out walked the charismatic Muddy Waters. I was just a few feet away, hearing each inflection of his pitch-perfect voice, believing the truth of every powerful word he sang. When he played the slow-tempo numbers, the musicians swaying from side to side in unison, my body felt so in tune with the rhythmic rocking and pulsating that it became an almost sexual slow grind.

During intermission, the band eased over to the bar, and Muddy went into the dressing room. I said to Paul, "Let's check out James Cotton's harmonica amp and see what he's got behind there that helps create his sound." Cotton, like all blues harmonica players of the time, was continually trying to imitate harmonica virtuoso Little Walter's sound. From the audience we could see there was nothing in the front of his amp, and there was only a simple bullet microphone on top. That couldn't be the secret, so it had to be something behind or inside the amp. We stepped up onto the low stage and had started poking around when we heard a voice behind us. "What the hell you guys doin'?" We turned around, and there was Cotton himself, giving us a menacing stare. "Get off the stage and stay the hell away from my gear." To show us he meant business, he added, "You try that again, and that will be the last thing you guys ever touch."

Chastised and embarrassed, we took our seats. As soon as the second set began, I forgot the humiliation and got lost in the music. Being in such close proximity to Muddy in this oddly intimate setting, with clouds of cigarette smoke swirling around our heads, the sticky scent of liquor in the air, and women at the tables nearby swaying to the beat, gave me a taste of what it must have been like to see Muddy, Howlin' Wolf, and Sonny Boy Williamson playing in the clubs on the South Side of Chicago.

As members of a new band, Paul and I realized we weren't even touching the tip of the magic Muddy and his band were creating. Walking home afterward, we talked about how Muddy controlled the dynamics of the band with just simple movements of his hands, like a regal king, so that every player's contribution added to the emotional meaning and gravity of each song. We sat up all night talking about the show, playing old 78-rpm blues recordings. I pulled out my Muddy album, looked at the picture on the cover anew, and went over each of the songs in my head even more intensely than before.

When Muddy next came to town, in 1966, I was living just a few short blocks from the historically important folk venue Club 47. I was there so often that I'd gotten to know the managers, who were musicians themselves, and they usually let me in without charge. Because it was a folk club, the usual performers on the bill were musicians in that genre. So I couldn't believe my eyes when one day I spotted Muddy Waters on the club's calendar of events. He and his band were booked for an entire week. I counted down the days until their arrival.

On the day of the first show, I walked over to the club early, eager to see my idol arrive. I waited for hours until a big black Cadillac drove down the street, followed by a station wagon. The Cadillac slowly pulled up to the club, and there on the passenger side sat Muddy Waters. Muddy's huge driver and assistant, Bo, came around and opened the door as two perfectly shined black dress shoes touched the pavement and an incredibly handsome, elegant man emerged.

I rushed over to Muddy and said, "Mr. Waters, welcome to Cambridge and to Club 47." Seeing that he nodded agreeably in response, I asked, "Any way I can help you?"

"Yeah," he said. "You can carry that amp." I picked up the amp, pleased that he seemed to believe I was an employee, then waited for the rest of the band—James Cotton, pianist Otis Spann, bassist Bobby Anderson, guitarists Sammy Lawhorn and Luther Tucker, and the great drummer Francis Clay—to get out of the station wagon. I walked in with them, put the amp down, and ran back out to Bo, who told me what piece of equipment to bring in next and where to put it. The band began setting up as the manager of the club, Jim Rooney, came out to talk with Muddy and show him to the tiny dressing room. I was very careful to stay away from Cotton because of the incident at the Jazz Workshop and was glad he didn't seem to recognize me.

When I went into the men's room I overheard a conversation between him and Otis Spann. Cotton, annoyed, said to Spann, "Man, this place is a coffeehouse!"

"So what's the problem?"

"It's just a coffeehouse. They don't serve any booze, just damn coffee," Cotton said.

"What do you mean they don't serve booze? What kind of club is this? Where the hell we gonna get some booze?"

Recognizing an opportunity, I volunteered, "I can get you guys booze." Startled, they both looked at me. Otis, clearly suspicious of my intentions, asked, "How much will it cost?"

"Don't worry about money. Just tell me what you want, and I'll get it for you." They were both taken aback, but figuring they had nothing to lose, they asked me to get a pint of scotch for James and a pint of gin for Otis. I left the club and headed down the street to my apartment. I didn't have much money, but I grabbed whatever I had and ran to the liquor store in Harvard Square, where I had to wait outside for a while before I could find a customer willing to buy alcohol for me, since I was still underage. Once the purchases had been made, I ran back to the club, where I proudly presented the bottles to Otis and James and was gratified by how appreciative they were.

I was sitting in the back of the room, watching them as they set up their instruments and tuned up, when I saw James Cotton walking toward me, giving me that hard look I'd seen when I was checking out his amp at the Jazz Workshop. I was nervous, wondering if I'd mishandled his gear as I carried it in. Prepared for the worst, I was surprised when he said, "Man, I wanna thank you for the scotch. You're a lifesaver." But then he added, "Aren't you the young fellow that was checking my amp out the last time we were in town?" I was embarrassed to admit that it was me, and I wondered how he'd react — but he was quite friendly, as it turned out. "Let me tell you," he said, "there ain't no tricks involved. There ain't no machines involved. It all comes from inside the mouth and listening to the right players and listening really hard, understand?"

I was encouraged enough by this generous response to tell him that I was trying to learn harp myself. And when he looked interested, I was emboldened to add: "I live right down the street. I've got a lot of blues records — all of Muddy's and even the first record you made on the Sun label."

"You're kidding me," he replied. "I haven't heard that in years and would love to hear it again and play it for some of the guys."

"Well, you and anyone else in the band are welcome to come over."

James went into the dressing room to talk to Muddy, then returned and asked, "How far is your place?" I told him it was less than a ten-minute walk away. He yelled up to Otis and the drummer, Francis Clay: "Come on. We got a place to hang before the gig." I led the way to my apartment with three men whom I'd spent years admiring in tow.

I didn't have much furniture in my apartment, just a futon, a little spinet piano, and a record player, with piles of albums leaning against the wall next to endless stacks of 45s. I wondered if the band would be appalled by these modest digs. But they didn't seem to notice. As soon as we arrived, I put on James's record, which he was so thrilled to hear that nothing else seemed to matter. After we listened to it, Otis made a beeline for the spinet and began playing; then James pulled out his harp and started blowing, saying to me, "Go grab a harmonica, let me show you a couple of things. You know anything about tongue blocking?" I replied that I didn't, to which he said, "How in the hell can you play blues if you don't know nothing about tongue blocking? You gotta learn." He proceeded over the next hour to teach me about blocking, wobbling, and the correct way of bending notes, all while the bottles of booze were opened and passed around.

When it was time for the band to return to the club, I led them there and then hunted down a friend from whom I could borrow enough money to buy another bottle of gin for Otis and another bottle of scotch for James. By the time I arrived for their set, the place was packed — not an empty seat in the house. As before, I stood at the back of the room listening, only this time it felt different, like I belonged there.

During intermission, Muddy remained in the solitude of the tiny dressing room. But once again, the band headed back to my place for more drinking and playing and to mellow out before the second set.

The next day, Muddy had an afternoon interview, so the band arrived at the club early. James walked over to me and asked, "Would you mind if Muddy and the band came over to your place to hang out?"

My jaw dropped as I asked, "Muddy, too?"

"Yeah," he said. "Muddy don't wanna hang in the club, and we don't wanna hang at the hotel, so I told him that you got this place with stacks of records, and it might be nice for Muddy to stretch out and relax before the show." When Muddy was done with the interview, Big Bo drove him to my apartment as the rest of the band walked over together, following me.

Once inside, Muddy took off his shirt, revealing a muscular physique under his sleeveless white T-shirt, and tied a do-rag on his head, clearly ready to unwind. He stretched out on the futon while I brought out more bottles of whiskey and gin for the band. James asked me to put on some music, so I chose a single of Muddy's that I treasured: "Just to Be with You," with Little Walter on harmonica.

"Man, I haven't heard that one in forever," Muddy exclaimed. "That Walter — man, can he play." I asked Muddy how he first met Little Walter, and he said, "Walter made a name for himself down along Maxwell Street, where everyone played" — "everyone" being Muddy and Walter and Howlin' Wolf, among many others. This gave me an opening to ask Muddy endless questions about his early days. He gladly reminisced as we hung out in my little two-room apartment, waiting until it was time to leave for the club.

As Otis continued tinkling on the piano, Bo, Sammy, and Bobby relaxed, staring into space, and James dutifully washed the dishes. Muddy closed his eyes and drifted off. I just took it all in. Here was a man of great distinction, one whose talent brought him from the rural woods of Clarksdale, Mississippi, into the juke joints of Chicago, one of the bestselling recording artists for Chess Records, quietly lying on my futon, napping. These visits were a sacred time in my life.

During that evening's performance, they tore it up. Muddy was much looser than he had been the night before, and he really worked the room. On "Got My Mojo Working," he began dancing. The audience went crazy. Most people there, except for a few die-hard blues fans, had never seen or heard anything like it before. I couldn't believe this was just the second of five shows, with three more to come.

Once I found out that James and the rest of the band were staying at a hotel that they had to pay for out of their earnings, I worked up my nerve to invite James to stay at my place. And to my surprise — and delight — he accepted.

After that he was generous in offering to teach me whatever I wanted to learn about the harp and blues in general. Once, when the topic of Little Walter's playing came up, James gave me a sideways stare. "Man, there's no disputing Little Walter's a great player. But for me the greatest is my teacher, Sonny Boy Williamson. Sonny Boy brought me up and taught me everything about the harp."

He then launched into a story about the first night he played with Muddy. Having carefully studied everything about how Little Walter played, he was in the midst of accompanying Muddy on a slow ballad when, "out of nowhere," Walter himself "jumped up onstage and brought the house down. I mean, he just started playing, and then he went into his big hit, 'Juke,' and the place went crazy. I walked in the back toward the bar, totally humiliated. I heard a familiar voice call out my name. 'James, get over here.' I turned around, and it was Sonny Boy, rip-roaring mad. 'Man, how could you let that guy embarrass you like that?' 'But Sonny,' I said, 'that's Little Walter.' He came back at me: 'I don't care who the hell that is — didn't I teach you how to play? Didn't I show you how to make that harmonica moan?'"

Sonny Boy then sent James out to get a large locked wooden box of harmonicas he kept in the trunk of his car. After Walter finished playing, Sonny Boy got onstage, called out one of his hits, "Fattening Frogs for Snakes," and started playing.

"Peter, by the end of his solo, he had three harps all going at once, one on each side of his mouth plus one he was playing through his nose. By the time he finished playin', the place was goin' wild. When he walked over, he looked me straight in the eye and said, 'Don't you ever forget the lesson I just taught you. Don't ever doubt yourself. We come from the country, and you just keep playin' that country style.'"

Edie and I became close to James during his stay at my apartment. Together we would sit at the cafés in Harvard Square, which for James was like entering a new world. He met all sorts of people — writers, painters, poets — far removed from his isolated life on the road. Edie took James shopping in Cambridge, and they would return home with bags full of groceries that James would cook up into amazing southern-style dinners with all the fixings. Every day, Big Bo drove Otis and some of the other band members to my apartment, where they sat around and relaxed and ate the meals James had prepared.

Muddy would arrive later, and he, too, enjoyed those meals and seemed to feel right at home. He liked when I DJed, playing selections from my blues collection. And given that he was one of the greats and I was just one of his many worshippers, he was extraordinarily appreciative of even small acts of kindness. One day I saw a glowing review of Muddy's show in a local paper that I thought he'd enjoy reading. But when I passed it to him, he gave it only a quick glance, saying, "Oh, man, it looks good." Since I wanted Muddy to hear all the positive things it said, I read it out loud, and I could see how pleased he was. "Thank you, Little Wolf. That was real nice." After that he started to call me Little Wolf. Another time I asked Muddy to sign an eight-by-ten photograph of himself that I had taken off the wall at the Jazz Workshop. As I watched how slowly he formed the letters of his name, taking quite a while to commit his signature to the photo, it finally dawned on me that Muddy, like John Lee Hooker and many of the other bluesmen who came from poor backgrounds, had had little in the way of schooling. After that I was always careful not to give Muddy anything to read. If there was something I wanted him to know about, I read it to him.

Muddy may not have been a reader, but he was a great storyteller. I loved listening to him talk about his early musical experiences, including the first time he heard Robert Johnson play, surrounded by a crowd of people so deep that Muddy had to stand on top of a car to see him. He spoke about his life growing up on a plantation, playing in juke joints, and finally moving out of Mississippi to Chicago. When Muddy mentioned that he used to perform country and western songs, I was amazed.

"Yeah, man, we listened to all the different blues shows on the radio and the Grand Ole Opry. They had some mighty good pickers on them shows. I even played songs like Gene Autry's 'Back in the Saddle Again.'"

He talked about the players who inspired his guitar work, the most influential being Son House, who lived near where he grew up. "Man, I'd play for dances; I even started my own little juke joint where I sold moonshine. Come Saturday night, I'd be shaking up the joint."

Muddy's stories were so intriguing that I asked him if I could record some of them, but he didn't seem enthusiastic about the idea, and I didn't want to make him uncomfortable. As much as I would have loved to preserve his recollections, it seemed like it might inhibit the conversations between us.

Once, when I was hanging out with Muddy, I mentioned that I had recently met Howlin' Wolf when we opened a show for him. During a break, Wolf and I were sitting together in the club's dressing room when a photographer walked by the doorway and snapped a picture, saying, "What a classic photo — two wolves sitting together." Without missing a beat, Wolf growled, "There's only one Wolf in this room."

After the show, Wolf, a commanding presence at well over six feet and at least three hundred pounds, along with his longtime guitarist,

With the Howlin' Wolf

Hubert Sumlin, who looked like a thin branch next to Wolf, spent an afternoon at my apartment between sets. That night after their show, Wolf was hungry, so we walked to a twenty-four-hour cafeteria nearby in Harvard Square. Wolf sat down at a table with a trayful of food. He noticed three Harvard students sitting next to him. Their table was covered with books and notepapers. They seemed to be cramming for an early morning exam. That piqued Wolf's curiosity, so he asked them in his low, gruff voice, "Hey, what you guys studying over there?"

One formally dressed student wearing a blue blazer with gold buttons and a Harvard tie answered, "Environmental agriculture, sir."

Wolf said, "Man, why you'd be studying for that? Out in the boiling hot sun, working in the fields all day . . . man, that shit don't take no damn studying."

The students at the table looked over at this huge man dressed in overalls and obviously didn't know what in the world to make of him. Muddy laughed when I told him that. Then I added, "Wolf mentioned that he had a big fancy liquor store on the South Side and that some guys recently burned it down to the ground."

Muddy laughed even harder. "Liquor store? Man, Howlin' Wolf never had no liquor store. Stay away from that man. He's too strange to get close to."

A couple of years later, on April 4, 1968, Muddy was booked at the Boston Tea Party, and I made sure my band, the Hallucinations, was the opening act. Whenever Muddy came to town it was a special event, and he came often in those years, but this time it was even more special because the date happened to fall on his birthday. I planned a party after the show next door at the Diplomat Hotel. It was a down-and-out, anything-goes kind of place in the red-light district, but it was where Muddy's band always stayed, as did a lot of other bands, because it was cheap. To help make it a celebration, I bought a cake and champagne, Muddy's drink of choice, and bottles of scotch and gin for the rest of the band. Even though it was an early show, we played our set to a packed house. Then I watched Muddy and his band from the side of the stage.

During the third number, the club's manager began frantically waving to get my attention. I hurried down the steps to see what he wanted. He whispered in my ear that Martin Luther King Jr. had just been shot. I froze in disbelief. I knew someone needed to tell Muddy, but I wasn't sure it should be me. I walked over to Otis Spann's wife and whispered the dreadful news in her ear. She covered her mouth to block her scream and said, shaking, "You gotta tell Muddy; you gotta tell him." In shock, she kept repeating that phrase as I waited until Muddy finished his song. Then I walked onstage and told him that something horrible had just happened, that Martin Luther King had been shot.

Muddy stood stock-still, trying to grasp what I had just said. He gave me a long, hard stare, then turned to the band and called out for a very slow blues instrumental. In the middle of the number, he abruptly stopped the band, raised his hands for silence, and spoke: "Young people, listen to me. I want everybody to listen. I have very sad, sad news. Martin Luther King has been shot. Please, please, everyone, quietly leave the building." You could hear a collective gasp as the shock and horror registered throughout the crowd. In as calm a voice as he could muster, Muddy continued: "Stay together, be careful, and get home safe."

The crowd did as he instructed, silently. Everyone onstage began to clear out, too, packing their equipment as quietly as possible, barely speaking. I went with Muddy and his band back to their hotel. Muddy quickly retired to his room, and the rest of us gathered in Otis Spann's room. Everyone sat numb, listening to the sound of sirens in the distance. I began to wonder about the unpredictable repercussions of King's assassination. The birthday cake and liquor now seemed out of place, but everyone felt we should at least acknowledge Muddy's birthday. Muddy's assistant, Bo, volunteered to get him while I lit the candles on the cake. Muddy entered the room, a solemn look on his face. Otis said, "Make a wish, Muddy." He walked over to the cake, paused in front of it, leaned forward, and blew out the candles, his expression never changing.

As the sirens grew louder outside, it wasn't hard to imagine what his wish was.

Muddy thanked me for the cake, then placed both his hands on my shoulders, looked at me with great concern, and said, "Be real careful gettin' home — real careful." Then he went back to his room.

Although he didn't say this, he was probably worried about my walking through a Black neighborhood at such a volatile moment. In those years, Boston was an extremely segregated town. The Italians lived in the North End; the Irish lived in Southie; Newton and Brookline were mostly Jewish neighborhoods; and the hotel was in the predominantly Black part of town. I left there, running through alleys to avoid the main streets, as cop cars spread widely, sensing that the city could explode at any minute.

Muddy's show the following night was canceled, but James Brown was still scheduled to play the Boston Garden. The city considered canceling the sold-out event, but officials were afraid of what would happen if they did. The mayor, Kevin White, negotiated with Brown to allow the public TV channel to videotape the show. Brown agreed, and the concert was shown live and rebroadcast throughout the night. This became a historic musical event unto itself. It kept Boston from experiencing the rioting that was occurring in other major cities across the country.

Besides James Brown at the Garden, the band Cream, which at the time was one of the most popular rock bands, was in town, playing the Back Bay Theatre. Muddy's music was a big influence on the members of Cream, and they had recorded several of his numbers. I felt bad that Muddy's show had been canceled and thought it would be great if Muddy could appear onstage with Cream. I ran it by Otis, and he agreed and persuaded Muddy to do it. Road closures and a heavy police presence meant that getting to Muddy's hotel was not an easy task, but a friend drove me, and we were able to pick up Otis and Muddy. When they emerged, they were dressed to the nines. Muddy, as always, looked immaculate, wearing a beautiful suit with a diamond stickpin in his tie, his hair meticulously coiffed.

Without passes, I wasn't certain we would get in, but the formidable impression Muddy made granted us instant entrée to the backstage area, where we found Jack Bruce, Ginger Baker, and Eric Clapton sitting on a couch in their dressing room. Given that they were big fans — especially Eric, who was known to idolize Muddy — I was stunned by what little reaction they had to meeting him. They just stared, acknowledging him with the faintest of nods. Soon a crew member entered to tell them it was time to go on, and we followed them out, watching from the side of the stage. Although they did a version of Muddy's "Rollin' and Tumblin'," they made no mention to the audience that Muddy himself was right there, standing stageside, despite the fact that this would have been the perfect moment to honor his presence. Mortified by their lack of respect, I quickly agreed when Muddy turned to me and said, "Maybe it's best we get back to the hotel."

My good intentions had resulted in a disastrous evening, about to be made even more humiliating for Muddy and Otis by the fact that, in the aftermath of King's assassination, it was almost impossible to get a cab to stop to pick up two Black men. The few that did stop refused to take us once they heard where we were going. We finally secured a cab, and during the long ride, each of us was lost in our own thoughts. When I dropped Muddy and Otis at the hotel, I apologized profusely for dragging them out that night, but Muddy was gracious, as always: "Man, don't you worry, Little Wolf. You just get home safe."

Decades later I was invited to Keith Richards's fiftieth birthday and tenth wedding anniversary party, where I was seated next to Eric Clapton. During all those intervening years I had wondered why he had barely acknowledged Muddy at that Cream concert, and toward the end of the evening I finally asked Eric about it. He looked at me with complete surprise when I recounted what had happened. "I can't believe it," he said, clearly stunned. "I have no recollection of Muddy coming backstage, but what you're telling me makes sense, because during that period, Peter, we were so high, taking so many drugs, that it's not a surprise I don't remember. I loved and respected Muddy so much; he was such a hero to me. In a way I'm glad you told that story, because hearing something like that helps me remain sober."

Over the years I got to play and tour with Muddy many times. Whenever he came to town, I was only too happy to continue to act as his personal valet. I would take him for a bite to eat after his show, and then we would head out to the airport in the early morning to wait for his flight. By then he flew to mostly all his gigs because a bad car accident had left him unable to endure long drives with the band. The last time I saw him, we sat together all night under the harsh glare of the fluorescent lights at Logan Airport. When it was time for him to board his plane, I walked him to the gate, and it was as if he knew we might never see each other again.

"Little Wolf," he said, "Peter the Wolf, thank you, thank you, thank you, my friend." He repeated it once more, and then, with that regal bearing that never let you forget you were in the presence of a king, he walked down the Jetway, turning just once to wave before he disappeared from sight.

11

MOON OVER ALABAMA
Ed Hood and Andy Warhol

EVEN THOUGH I was at least a block away, the glinting shock of silver hair in the distance was unmistakable. "Hey, Andy," I said, smiling and approaching him. He was snapping Polaroids of a well-dressed elderly woman wearing a wide-brimmed black velvet hat, a vivid orange cashmere waistcoat, and enough jewels to be a walking advertisement for Harry Winston. She was gripping the leash of her restless dachshund, who was just as extravagantly outfitted in a neon tartan vest.

It was the corner of Madison Avenue and 63rd Street, and I was having a typically innocuous chat with Andy Warhol, whose presence was always monochromatic, in distinct contrast to his iconic brightly colored artworks. "Oh, hi there, Peter. God, it's so great to see you. Are you still in Boston? God, it feels like years since I've been up there."

"Yes, Andy, still there." He aimed his Polaroid at me, snapping several photos. But the conversation took an unexpected turn when Andy asked out of the blue, "Peter, how exactly did Ed die? I've been thinking about him a lot."

I was taken aback. Although I didn't know Andy terribly well, I knew that death was a topic he didn't dwell upon. After all, he was once quoted as saying, "I never think that people die. They just go to department stores."

"Andy, I thought Donald Lyons would have told you."

"Oh, Peter. Donald won't talk about it at all, and I've got to know."

The Ed we were discussing was Edward Mant Hood Jr., a literary scholar born into a prestigious southern family in Birmingham, Alabama, with its own darkly gothic history. The Hoods' real estate holdings were vast, and his upbringing groomed him for Birmingham's high society. Young Ed took to reading the classics and the Romantic poets, but his father, an investor, disapproved, saying, "Only sissies read poetry." Ed's mother, a friend and classmate of the famed writer Eudora Welty, was more tolerant, having literary interests of her own.

As Ed's homosexuality became more apparent during his teenage years, it was considered downright scandalous not only by his father but also by most of his tony Birmingham community, which viewed it as unacceptable. Prior to his graduation from high school, his prom date was future actress Louise Fletcher, the daughter of an Episcopal priest. Louise went on to win an Oscar in 1976 for her role as the authoritarian Nurse Ratched in *One Flew Over the Cuckoo's Nest*.

Ed and his prom date, actress Louise Fletcher

Ed left the South to study at the University of Minnesota and later joined the staff of the literary journal the *Southern Quarterly*, corresponding with such eminent poets as Robert Frost, e. e. cummings, Robert Penn Warren, Ezra Pound, and T. S. Eliot. He finally ended up at Harvard as an assistant professor, working on a doctorate about the use and definition of love in the works of William Shakespeare. He lived off campus in an apartment complex called the Craigie Arms, a historic four-story Georgian revival brick building located just outside the shadows of Harvard Square. The complex covered almost an entire block, and each of its four sides had its own entrance. It was here, when I moved into a cramped one-bedroom apartment, that I first made Ed's acquaintance.

I had only a few belongings — art supplies, a minimal amount of clothing, and my treasured records — but at $50 a month, my apartment was a palace to me. In the empty bedroom when I first walked in I found a copy of Howlin' Wolf's *Moanin' in the Moonlight* along with a beautifully carved red velvet Victorian armchair; I felt both were good omens.

While exploring my new neighborhood, I became aware of the friendly communal interaction among the many eccentric residents of the building. One particular tenant caught my eye. He seemed to leave and return to his apartment at all hours, several times even stopping to give me a long look and a welcoming nod.

He appeared to be in his early thirties, balding, not too tall, strong in build, and always dressed in a dark narrow-lapelled suit with a tie and a well-starched white dress shirt. His walk was slow, with perfect posture, and under his arm he always carried several books.

I was coming out of my building one afternoon when I spotted a tall, willowy beauty with dark brown shoulder-length hair, her long legs encased in tight black leather, wearing a sheer, loosely buttoned white gauze blouse. Later, as I was browsing the shelves of the Mandrake Book Store, a well-known gathering spot for Harvard's literary-minded folk, she approached me, introducing herself in a sultry voice. "Hello, I'm Andrea. I live in your building. I know you're a musician, and I'm trying to expand my blues collection. Do you have any suggestions for what I should buy? Or, better yet, if you're not already occupied, can you come up to my apartment later and see what, um ... I might need?"

Hoping curiosity wouldn't kill this cat, I asked, "What time is good for you?"

"Oh, anytime, really," she replied. "Let's say eight tonight." And off she slithered.

At eight o'clock sharp I knocked on her door. The sound of a Junior Wells record and the thick aroma of incense filled the hallway. There was a slight delay before I heard her heels clacking toward the door. It opened slowly. She wore the same outfit, except with a blouse that was even more transparent. Her eyes were outlined in heavy black liner, reminiscent of Elizabeth Taylor's in *Cleopatra*. "Please come in. I like a man who is on time ... if you know what I mean." The darkened apartment was ceremonially lined with rows of burning candles. Moroccan tapestries hung on the walls, and the floor was covered in large velvet pillows.

She pointed to a small record player and a few stacks of 45s, saying, "Oh, check out my records and let me know what I might be missing." I was playing DJ when she asked, "Want to smoke some opium with me?"

I had never tried opium, but there was no better time than the present. She squirted brown goo onto a spoon, held a match under it, leaned in close, and told me to deeply inhale the vapors. We did this several times, then Andrea lay back on one of the pillows as if she were in some dreamlike state. I, however, didn't feel a thing.

Suddenly there was a knock at her door, followed by a persistent pounding. It kept getting louder, and a voice shouted, "Andrea, let me in!" Was it a boyfriend? She told me to ignore it. The voice persisted, louder and louder, repeating, "Andrea, open this door. I know what you're up to!"

Andrea, finally out of her haze, screamed, "Get the hell out of my hallway!" The door seemed to be rattling off the hinges as Andrea leaped up, opened it, and yelled, "He's mine, you fuckin' queer!"

There he stood — the intriguing stranger I always noticed, only now carrying not only books but also a bottle of bourbon. Several highball glasses were sticking out of his suit-jacket pocket. He strategically pushed Andrea aside, held out his hand to me, and announced with a firm grip, "Hood here."

Andrea was livid. "Ed! I got to him first. Now beat it!"

He was having none of it and proceeded as if Andrea weren't even in the room. "Welcome to the Craigie Arms. I think we should all adjourn to my apartment, which is far more suitable for a diverse and intelligent conversation than this dark den of foolishness. Why, there are so many things to know and learn, and I, Edward Mant Hood Jr., can provide you with every bit of knowledge a young man like you should possess. All it will require is your full attention."

Andrea huffed her displeasure at the intrusion and lit a cigarette. I felt like I was caught in *The Maltese Falcon*, in the scene where Mary Astor and Sydney Greenstreet argue over who has the rights to the precious black bird.

Ed sat down on a pillow and began to recite. "One of my favorites and possibly the most curious of Shakespeare's sonnets, number 94: 'They that have the power to hurt and will do none, / That do not do the thing they most do show, / Who, moving others, are themselves as stone, / Unmoved, cold, and to temptation slow.'"

"Ed, you damn faggot, get the hell out of my apartment!"

"Now, Andrea, is that the way a proper lady talks or acts? Pardon me, darling, but maybe I was assuming too much of you." Finally, when two friends of Andrea and Ed arrived, the party did move to what Ed described as "my salon — as used by the French, not by hairdressers."

"How would you know, you bald-headed cantaloupe?" Andrea snapped. It was apparent that she and Ed allowed each other liberties that only good friends can get away with.

Ed's apartment looked just as I imagined a room at the Ritz would look. It didn't seem as if it was even in the same building as mine. You entered through a small hallway, passed a kitchenette, and proceeded to a Regency-style living room. Tastefully framed prints hung on pale-yellow walls, and long, heavily lined flowered curtains draped the two living room windows. This home was obviously that of a well-traveled aesthete: walnut furniture, Persian rugs, and leather-bound books tastefully arranged on gleaming walnut shelves.

Ed was the perfect host, supplying everyone with their drink of choice from a well-stocked bar cart, complete with a shining silver ice bucket. Each drink was delivered by a young Irishman whom Ed introduced as Patrick. He had dark brown eyes, neatly combed brown hair, and a face with chiseled features, even though his nose seemed to have suffered from one or two bar brawls. His engaging smile revealed one missing tooth. He was short, with the muscular build of a Triple Crown jockey, and he was dressed in a tie, white shirt, and black suit that had been dry-cleaned so many times it had a metallic sheen on the shoulders.

An immigrant runaway from Barryroe, County Cork, Patrick had little to no schooling. When Ed first saw him, he was an assistant gardener pulling the weeds in Harvard Yard. Thereafter Ed became his benefactor, while Patrick became Ed's somewhat reluctant manservant. Although Patrick often scowled when Ed summoned him to chores with the ringing of a brass bell, their bond was unbreakable.

Prior to meeting him, I had often seen Patrick around the Square, always dressed in the same suit and tie, sitting at the outdoor cafés in front of the famed Brattle Theatre. Patrick was easygoing, well known and liked even by the street squatters and buskers who huddled around the Square in those days. Though Patrick couldn't read or write very well (a situation, along with Patrick's teeth, that Ed was determined to correct), he was very musical, playing a good accordion, and he could recite and sing epic-length Irish ballads. I came to discover that Patrick was a generous person, too — good-hearted. If someone needed something, he was quick to share what little he had.

Patrick continually answered the door as yet more guests arrived, one of whom was a friend of Ed's from New York, Gerard Malanga, who worked closely with Andy Warhol at the Factory. The evening rolled on, with drinks served and joints lit and passed around while a Stones record played in the background.

The following afternoon, Ed spotted me across the street, and he crossed over so we could talk and walk together.

As we were chatting, he stopped and asked me, "Do you read?"

"Sometimes," I replied.

"What did you last read?" he asked.

"*Catch-22.*"

"Did you like it?"

"I enjoyed it, yeah."

Then he asked, "What classics have you read?"

"Classics? I'm not sure what you mean by 'classics.'"

He said, "You know — Melville, Flaubert, Homer, Dostoyevsky, and Dickens, for starters."

"Well, I read *A Tale of Two Cities* in high school."

"Did you enjoy it?"

"No, not really," I replied.

"Well, there's better Dickens than that. I would highly recommend *David Copperfield* or *Great Expectations*. What about poetry?"

I replied, "I read some Ginsberg, Carl Sandburg, and 'O Captain! My Captain!' I think that was by Melville."

He quickly responded, "No — Whitman. Walt Whitman. Any Pound, Eliot, Frost, Tate, or Lowell?"

"No, I don't think so."

"You don't think so? If you ever read Eliot or Lowell, I think you'd surely remember. Are you interested in learning about literature? Fine, important, and meaningful literature for the ages, like Bach, Beethoven, and Mozart are for music? Works that can become as enjoyable and significant to you as Elvis, Dylan, and the Stones? If you're interested in learning, I can teach you, but only if you really want to learn. I can teach you more than you can ever learn as a student at Harvard. Come by this evening if you want to get started."

That evening I went over to Ed's, where Andrea also awaited my arrival. He seemed quite serious.

"So Peter, you want to explore the world of literature."

"Well, sure, I'd like to learn some more about it."

"Good; let's start now."

Ed went into his bedroom, covered wall-to-wall with books. He came out holding Graham Greene's *Brighton Rock*.

"We'll start you off with this. I don't care how fast or slow you read it, as long as you make a concerted effort."

He sat down on the linen sofa, emptied his whiskey glass, and asked me to pass him the grand brass cigarette lighter from the marble coffee table. Very dramatically and ever so gracefully, he lit a cigarette. Smiling, he turned to Andrea and said, "Honey, what I can offer our new friend here is something those long leather legs could never provide."

"Fuck off, Ed!"

He puffed a flurry of perfect smoke rings in her direction.

I devoured *Brighton Rock*. Several days later I was back at Ed's, thanking him for the recommendation. He asked what I liked about it, whether I understood the symbolism of the characters and the sense of good versus evil, and followed with a long disquisition about the life of Graham Greene.

Ed was a masterly reader. When reading out portions of *Brighton Rock*, he gave it even more power and depth, teaching me not only what to read but also how to read. Greene was followed by Christopher Isherwood's *Berlin Stories* and *Prater Violet*. We dived into poetry, beginning with *The Oxford Book of American Verse*. Ed savored Robert Lowell, with whom he had studied. From there we went backward: Dickinson, Whitman, and Poe. Then on to the Brits: Tennyson, Keats, Shelley, and Yeats (okay, Irish). Ed's poetry books all contained meticulously handwritten tiny notations in blue pen, like ancient hieroglyphics, alongside every line of the poems.

Ed's seminars would go long into the night, and even far into the next morning, such was his desire to instill knowledge. One evening, as I went through his record collection, I was surprised to find a worn copy of *Hank Williams' Greatest Hits*.

I asked, "Ed, you like Hank Williams?"

"Do I like Hank Williams? That's like asking me if I think Elvis is a hot hunk. Peter, if you think you like Hank Williams, you might hear the music, but believe me, you don't *know* the music. You've got to understand Alabama and the whole South in general. Know and feel the heat of it, the dust on the unpaved streets, the sweat, the poverty, the gentry versus the rednecks, the rednecks versus the Negroes, love versus hate, Christ versus

Ed Hood at the Craigie Arms, Cambridge, MA, 1964

the devil. Damn, there are parts down there that still refuse to accept Lee's surrender. Until you absorb all that, you can't really understand the music."

He disappeared into his bedroom and returned with a stack of books, from which he read me Faulkner's short story "A Rose for Emily." "Now, that's real southern gothic — the same roots that Tennessee Williams and Capote come from, then Walker Percy and Flannery. It's in the water, in the air. Like Hank's music, it runs deep in our blood.

"You must read this book next — Faulkner's *Light in August* — then Katherine Anne Porter's collection *Pale Horse, Pale Rider.*"

He went over to the record player, put on *Hank Williams' Greatest Hits,* then filled a tall glass with ice and poured it full of straight Kentucky bourbon. He closed his eyes, remembering the hot Alabama sun on that cold Boston night.

If you were lucky enough to be allowed to borrow a book from Ed, he made you fill out a blue index card with the date, your signature, and a written promise to return it in a timely fashion. I was returning *The Heart Is a Lonely Hunter* one day when Patrick opened the door and I was pleasantly surprised to find standing in the kitchen, refreshing a drink, one of Ed's closest friends, Donald Lyons. Donald was perhaps the only person Ed considered to be even more intelligent than he; Donald, of course, disagreed and valued Ed as the superior intellect. Donald had graduated from Fordham University and throughout his student life was advised by the Jesuits to enter the priesthood; with his intellectual brilliance, he could surely become a cardinal in the Vatican. He and Ed would enter into explosive arguments over which translation of Homer was better or which poet or writer was of greater importance. Then there were their lists, written on Ed's blue index cards: the all-time top ten movies, the twenty most important books, and the most desirable movie stars (on the screen or in bed).

As I walked into the living room that night, there came an even bigger surprise. Seated on Ed's couch were Andy Warhol and an equally transfixing Edie Sedgwick.

I knew of Andy's controversial works, since they were the topic of many debates at the Boston museum school: Is it really art? Can't anyone just copy a Campbell's soup can or a Brillo box? Is he just imitating Duchamp?

In person, Andy's white hair and somewhat pasty skin seemed otherworldly. Wearing black sunglasses and dressed in a white suit jacket with a black shirt and pants, he sat as still as a mannequin, hands folded on his lap. Alongside him was a shimmering vision. Edie Sedgwick's cropped marble-streaked hair, eyes thick with black liner, and fabulously long legs in black tights and black patent-leather heels were spellbinding. She was sitting on her blue-and-yellow striped jacket, so close to Andy that it almost looked like they were supporting each other.

It was Donald who first introduced Andy to Ed sometime earlier. Now Donald and Ed were in high gear, jovially performing for the two honored guests, who seemed to be in their own private bubble. Donald and Ed tried to outdo each other, mimicking some of their favorite movie actresses: Conchita Montenegro as Lola Montes, Dietrich in *Shanghai Express*, Crawford in *Mildred Pierce*. The real showdown came with their Bette Davis impressions. The entire party then moved up the street to the Casablanca, the only highbrow semigay bar in town, with jukebox selections featuring Marilyn Monroe's "Heat Wave" and "Diamonds

Are a Girl's Best Friend," Dietrich's "The Boys in the Backroom," and, from the soundtrack of *Casablanca*, Dooley Wilson's recording of "As Time Goes By." It was there that I experienced the full effect of Edie Sedgwick, who dazzled everyone. When she became the center of attention, she seemed to glow brighter. She was singularly enchanting.

Later, in New York, I would encounter a who's who of the underground scene in the back room of Max's Kansas City. It seemed the entire group of Warhol Factory habitués were scattered around the room, with Andy listening intently while Ed and Donald held court — something that was hard to do in a roomful of personalities who were craving attention, especially Andy's. I sat with another friend of Ed, Danny Fields, who was just starting to work in the music business, and Lou Reed, whom I knew from double bills when the Velvet Underground and my band, the Hallucinations, performed together in Boston. It always surprised me that the Velvets had a far more loyal following in Boston than in New York. In Cambridge, the Velvets would camp out at Ed's apartment, so I got to know the band quite well. Sterling Morrison and Ed would discuss literature, while Lou and Ed had a close relationship that centered on poetry. Mo Tucker was quiet. John Cale, who later married clothing designer Betsey Johnson, crashed elsewhere.

Lou would often stop by my apartment to go through my 45s. I was surprised to discover that we both shared a love of Dion when Lou fell head over heels for a rare recording of him singing the Howlin' Wolf–Willie Dixon song "Spoonful."

Ed made several screen tests for Andy at the Factory, and he starred in two of his most well-known films, *My Hustler* and *Chelsea Girls*. In Boston, during a screening of *Chelsea Girls*, I was sitting up toward the front row with Ed and Patrick. As Ed's scene came on the screen, he stood up in the darkened hall, turned to face the audience, took out a cigarette, and held his lighter under his face so everyone could see that he, the star, was there.

After graduating from college in Vermont, my girlfriend, Edie, came to live with me. She and Ed became close friends. When I was performing on the road, the two of them became inseparable. I believe Edie and

Ed knew more about each other's secrets than I did. But the few times they had blowups, they were near-nuclear explosions.

During one evening gathering at Ed's salon, Patrick ushered in an attractive collegiate woman in her early twenties whom Ed was delighted to see. She, however, seemed uncomfortable with all the pandemonium in the apartment, as did her date, a stiffly formal but exceedingly hand-some Harvard letterman. Ed made introductions, then insisted that one of Gerard Malanga's friends give up his seat for the new arrival, Rosie Blake. She had studied at Radcliffe College, became a model photo-graphed by Avedon, and appeared in the film *What's New Pussycat?* Rosie also wrote a novel called *Made in Heaven*, of which Ed always had several copies stacked around his apartment. With her intelligence and Ali MacGraw good looks, she was the most sought-after belle of the ball among the elite of Harvard students.

One night Ed, eager to read poetry to Rosie, called to invite her over. She had recently moved back into her parents' large home in Brookline, a suburb close to Cambridge. When Ed phoned, it was already past mid-night. "No, Ed, it's too late for me to come to Cambridge. Plus, my par-ents are both sleeping, and I'm about ready to turn out the lights." Ed was persistent and kept calling until Rosie finally took her phone off the hook. At that point, even more determined to give his reading, he gath-ered some books and a bottle of bourbon, called a taxi, and headed off to Rosie's parents' home.

The gate was locked. He tried throwing coins at Rosie's bedroom window, but when there was no response, he decided to climb over the garden wall. With books and bottle in hand, he almost made it — but he lost his grip and fell to the ground, books scattering and bourbon bottle broken, along with his leg.

After a night in the ER, and with the help of Patrick, he returned to his apartment with crutches and a large cast on his right leg. He notified his family's lawyer about the medical bills the estate would soon be receiving. The lawyer then informed Ed's mother, who decided to see for herself exactly what kind of mischief her son had gotten himself into.

Ed was thrown into a panic. It had been years since his mother last came north, and his apartment had to be in tip-top shape. He enlisted Patrick, me, and Edie in this mission — dusting, washing sheets, buying new hand towels for the bathroom, and putting away photos of him arm in arm with his many amours. Ed pleaded for us to stay until his mother arrived. When the front-door buzzer rang, he dourly said, "Here comes the grand duchess herself."

Edie opened the door to Mrs. Myrtle Watts Hood, straight from the rolling hills of Birmingham, Alabama. She had the taxi driver bring in her finely stitched brown leather suitcase along with a square white vanity case. She was an attractive woman in her early sixties with an expressionless face and tastefully conservative makeup. She wore a small oval hat covered in tiny white dots and a three-quarter-length mink coat. In one gloved hand was a white patent-leather handbag; in the other, a fancy cane with a mother-of-pearl handle.

She was cordial. With a deep southern drawl, she asked us, "Where is he?"

Ed appeared from the bedroom wearing a blue robe, the crutches under his arms, hopping on one foot. "Mother, thank you so very much for coming and making such an arduous journey to visit your wounded son." His sarcasm seemed to go unnoticed.

"Edward, where am I to sit?"

"On the couch, Mother."

"That? I won't sit on that mess. It's a sad excuse for a proper couch. No! I want a new one delivered here immediately. Young lady," she said to Edie, "can you direct me to a fine furniture store where I can pick out something far more suitable?" With that, the women left. Ed poured a stiff drink, his hands shaking. "Oh, Lord, this is going to be one hell of a visit."

Miraculously, a new couch was promptly delivered — one that, I must admit, was quite an improvement.

The next afternoon, as I was walking past Ed's window, I heard yelling coming from inside. I ran to his door and rang the bell. He shouted, "It's open," and I went in only to find him on the kitchen floor with his mother standing over him, hitting him on the head with her cane. "Edward, where did you hide my bottle? Where is it? I want to know now, or you won't be getting off that floor until I have it!"

"Mother, when you give me back the bottle of mine that you hid, then I'll give you back yours."

Mrs. Hood stayed two nights at the best hotel in Cambridge, and she kept her visit brief. As she was leaving, Edie and I helped her into a waiting taxi as Ed waved to her from the window. He quoted lines from a Marianne Moore poem: "My father used to say, / 'Superior people never make long visits.'" With that, she was on her way back down South. Mother and son never saw each other again.

Both Ed's grandfather and, later, his father fatally shot themselves with the same pistol. Ed grew up fearing that suicide ran in his blood. There was also a long history of alcoholism in the Hood family.

After the death of his mother, the substantial Hood fortune was left to Ed, the sole heir. By this time, during those turbulent years of Ed's life, I was often away touring with the Geils band. Ed no longer wore natty suits and ties and had been evicted from the Craigie Arms for causing one too many disturbances. It was heart-wrenching to see Ed so disheveled, living in a shabby apartment with none of the charm and style of his previous salon. I encouraged Ed to buy his own brownstone or a house in Cambridge, where Patrick could live and help him out. The idea delighted Ed, and, to everyone's surprise, he joined AA and gave up drinking. To support his commitment to stay sober, I accompanied him on Christmas Eve to midnight mass and watched as he took communion. Forgetting that the chalice was filled with wine, Ed took a sip, then discreetly spat it right out into his handkerchief and ran from the church. I found him outside, frantically gargling from a bottle of diet ginger ale, which he always carried with him, hoping that no alcohol ever got back into his system.

He began receiving treatment from a prominent psychiatrist affiliated with Harvard University. Tragically, he was encouraged to participate in a brutal form of conversion therapy. The controversial *Clockwork Orange*–style treatment used electric shocks to try to "cure" men of their homosexuality. Ed was wired up, shown images of nude men, and barbarically blasted with bolts of electricity. After each session he was so out of sorts that his whole body shook, and the pain from the shocks he received exhausted him both mentally and physically.

Ed's unwavering dedication to educating me had opened my mind to the written word. When he attended one of the Geils band's sold-out shows at the Boston Garden, he stood stageside during our performance, silently sizing up the cheering crowd.

He languorously smoked his cigarette, turned to me before the encore, and proudly said, to my surprise, "My student, you're becoming a star."

I couldn't bring myself to tell Andy the details of Ed's death as we stood on the corner of Madison and 63rd. Since we had both been invited to the same dinner party the following night, I decided it would be better to discreetly tell him there.

The dinner was at the home of our friends the society darlings Earl and Camilla McGrath. Andy's escort was Jerry Hall. After dessert and coffee, and before the gathering came to an end, Earl thought it would be interesting if everyone chose a favorite poem to recite. Earl passed around anthologies and started by reading the first part of T. S. Eliot's "Ash Wednesday." I chose Delmore Schwartz's "For Rhoda." Jerry chose Edgar Allan Poe's "Annabel Lee" and read it quite well with her Texan accent, to a round of applause. Andy, sitting on the carpet, was listening intently. When his turn to read came, everyone was curious as to what he might pick, but he just sat there and wouldn't take a book, saying, "Oh, no, I can't. Please don't ask me." Jerry insisted he read something, even a short haiku, but Andy just blushed and shook his head.

"Andy," Earl asked, "what the hell's the matter? Just read something — the phone book, even. Come on, Andy. You *can* read, can't you?"

Andy remained silent, until finally, after much persistence from the gathering, he just moved his mouth without saying a word.

Earl yelled, "I know that one. I love it; it's one of my favorites!"

Jerry Hall quickly snapped, "Oh, Earl, then why don't *you* try recit-ing that poem for the rest of the evening?" Even Andy laughed out loud at that.

Afterward, as guests lingered, I took Andy to a quiet corner and finally told him the sad, strange circumstances of Ed's demise. It was straight out of one of Ed's beloved southern gothic tales.

Donald Lyons had arrived in Cambridge from New York to spend the weekend with Ed. When he found no one home, he asked the superin-tendent to let him in, and they found Ed lying facedown, dead on his bedroom floor.

I was the only friend in attendance at Ed's funeral, in Birmingham. At the cemetery was a small gathering of Ed's distant relatives. I was greeted politely with a curt southern formality that was devoid of any real sin-cerity. Many of the assembled hardly even knew Ed other than through rumors of what they perceived as his scandalous lifestyle.

I was the last mourner remaining by his grave, watching as the work-ers shoveled dirt over his coffin. There was so much we shared together, so much I owed him. He was one of my dearest friends and one of my most important teachers. He fulfilled his promise of unlocking the rich world of poetry and literature as we navigated those all-night sessions.

At a barbecue following the service, Ed's name was hardly men-tioned. I was introduced to the lawyer who was handling Ed's estate. He informed me that in Ed's will, I had been named the executor of all the belongings in his Cambridge apartment, which included his entire library, correspondence to and from many eminent writers and poets, published and unpublished manuscripts, paintings, and furnishings.

I couldn't spend another sleepless night in Birmingham, and my experience of the archaic world Ed had escaped so many years previously made my departure and the return trip north even more poignant.

A detective from the Cambridge police precinct contacted me well over a year after Ed's death. A local priest had come to the station accompanying a young woman. She was there to tell the police of a crime that her former fiancé may have been involved in. They were due to be married on New Year's Day, and the night before their wedding, her fiancé consumed a large amount of alcohol and confessed something that had been haunting him.

A year prior, he had met Ed at a bar and went back to his place for some drinks. When Ed left the room, the man stole a $20 bill from his wallet, but Ed caught him and yelled, "If you want something, just ask, don't steal!" Ed went to grab the bill. The young man pushed him, and Ed fell to the floor, flopping around like a fish on a hook. The young man poked Ed with his foot, but he didn't move. Panicked, he ran to a window and made a quick exit down the fire escape. Later, he saw in the papers that a man had been found dead in that apartment. His fiancée begged him to confess, but such was his burden of guilt that he fatally shot himself that night.

The distraught girl told all this to the priest, who suggested she tell the police. To compound the tragedy, the police informed her that her fiancé had nothing to do with Ed's death — it was caused by a status epilepticus seizure.

Andy listened intently, his hand covering his mouth. When I finished, he seemed depleted. He was a man of few words, but now there was even less to say.

In the silence, a line of Faulkner's that Ed once quoted came to me. During a reading session, when he noticed I was tired and my attention was beginning to fade, he snapped his fingers and shouted, "Wolf, stay alert!" Then he recited, with perfect diction, "The reason for living was to get ready to stay dead a long time."

12

IF IT'S IN YOU, IT'S GOT TO COME OUT

John Lee Hooker

THE WEATHER FORECAST predicted a cold night in the low teens, wind speeds of twenty miles an hour with a slight possibility of snow, and on that November evening in 1965 they were right: it was positively cold in Boston. Bandmate Paul and I stood shivering for well over two hours by the steps of the Odyssey, a large coffeehouse and performance center. We were early, hoping to be first in line for the best seats to see one of our favorite blues musicians, John Lee Hooker.

Paul was older than I was, in his twenties, already married, with one son. He was a dedicated painter and played lead guitar for the new band we had just formed, all of us art students. We called ourselves the Hallucinations or the Hallucination — we never could decide which. Paul had a handlebar mustache, dark piercing eyes, and jet-black hair. He had earned a black belt in martial arts and was exceptionally fit. He walked tightly coiled, with a cold eye and ready hands in anticipation of an ambush.

The show started at eight, but it was almost seven, and no one else was waiting. Like many of the well-established blues artists, he arrived in a sleek black Cadillac, which pulled up to the curb. Sitting in the front passenger seat, wearing a narrow-brimmed gray fedora and dark wrap-around sunglasses, was the star of the night, Mr. John Lee Hooker. I approached the car, and his electric window slowly lowered. Excitedly, I welcomed him to Boston. In a deep voice, with a bad stutter on certain words, he kindly thanked me. I called Paul over, and we told him we were in a band that played a lot of blues, including many of his songs.

Hallucinations out on Cape Cod

"Oh, yeah? What's the name of your band?"

Paul answered, "The Hallucination."

"Yeah," John Lee replied, "that sounds cool. I'll keep an eye out for your records."

"Oh, no," I said. "We just got together and haven't made a record."

"Well, then," John said, "when you do, I'll check it out."

His driver, also in dark wraparound shades, got out and opened the back door of the Caddy. He was tall, slim, and wore a heavy black over-coat under which was a shiny red-and-gold suit jacket, blue pants, and slick pointed green suede shoes. He took a guitar case from the back seat and opened John Lee's door.

John Lee emerged wearing a black fur-collared cashmere topcoat over a shiny gray sharkskin suit with a red pocket hankie peeking out. A diamond stickpin pierced the collar of his white silk shirt, patterned with pale gray pairs of dice. I was surprised how short and thin he was. He wore his belt high, as if he had no waist. He introduced his driver as Detroit Willy, a relative of the blues singer Jimmy Reed. He told Willy to park the car and he'd go on ahead upstairs to find the dressing room.

Paul asked what kind of guitar was in his case. John Lee said, "Oh, this is a Gibson 335. I just picked it up in Detroit. My other guitar was going out of tune too much an' was starting to bug me. This one plays real sweet an' gives me no headaches. I wish I could find me a nice woman like that."

We offered to carry his guitar, which he handed to Paul. We walked two floors up, where we were met by the club's manager, Dave Wilson. He greeted John Lee and showed him to his dressing room. Thinking we were John Lee's guests, he told us to sit at any table we wanted.

I had seen John Lee perform four years earlier, when a very young Bob Dylan was his opening act. That time, he played alone, with just an electric guitar and a small amplifier. He used his foot to create a unique percussive rhythm.

It was just at the beginning of my interest in authentic blues, and I wasn't too familiar with a lot of John Lee's material or his historic impor-tance. I had records by Josh White, Big Bill Broonzy, and Sonny Terry & Brownie McGhee, but John Lee's music was a darker and somehow much deeper experience. I was unaware that he recorded his first hit, "Boogie Chillen,'" way back in 1948. The popularity of that recording was the envy of many up-and-coming young blues artists like B.B. King and Muddy Waters and even rockers like Bo Diddley. John Lee was an important bridge between country blues and electric blues.

He didn't want to be pinned down to just one record company because of the rampant exploitation artists suffered at the hands of many small, independent blues labels. Also, signing with different labels was a way to get some cash up front. He usually outsmarted the labels by recording under various names — Delta John, Johnny Williams, Texas Slim, Johnny Lee, Birmingham John, and even, during the British Invasion, Sir John.

Paul and I sat at the table closest to the stage as a small number of people slowly trickled in, totaling not more than twenty-five. The club held at least ten times that number. There was, however, enthusiastic applause as John Lee appeared from the dressing room, slowly and gracefully walking up to the stage. He sat in a chair beside the amp, tested the microphone, and softly, with a mild stutter, said, "Thank you all for coming. Tonight I'm going to play some real blues — deep blues and down-home blues."

He started with "When My First Wife Left Me," low and slow. The club was so quiet you could hear the chairs creak. He followed it with the mesmerizing "Hobo Blues." The tempo slowly picked up with songs like "I'm in the Mood," "Crawlin' King Snake," and "Dimples," then he wrapped up with the infectious "Boogie Chillen'." The crowd was riveted. He left the stage to a standing ovation. He returned for an encore, ending the night with "Boom Boom," a cover of which became popular when it was recorded by the British band the Animals. John Lee's singing was soft but commanding, and his guitar playing was primal, rough, and haunting.

As the audience drifted out, Paul and I walked past John Lee's dressing room. I knocked on the door, surprising myself that I had the nerve to do that. I could hear him say, "Come on in."

"Mr. Hooker, you were amazing!" I said as he wiped his face with a hankie, then put on his hat.

"Well, I'm glad you enjoyed it. Wish they had a bigger crowd, but you never know until you get to where you're goin'." It felt sad that such an important artist wasn't drawing a larger audience.

"Mr. Hooker, our band members are big fans of yours, and some of them are coming tomorrow night," I said, then Paul added, "If you let us open for you, I promise we can pack the place."

"You guys a blues band?"

"We do play a lot of blues," I answered, "and between the students in our art school and loads of handmade flyers, we can have this place packed tomorrow night."

"You guys don't play loud?" he asked.

"No," I replied nervously, though most of our audience liked our music really loud. Paul added, "We'll definitely keep it low."

After a long pause, John Lee said, "I can't pay you."

I replied, "No, no, we're not thinking about money. But we'd fill the place and do it for free. Just the honor of playing on the same bill as you means more to us than money."

John Lee responded, "I'll tell you what. You guys come in early and be all set up and ready to play by seven o'clock, and I'll listen and see if it works out."

"Fair enough," Paul said.

The three of us left the club together, and as we walked down the stairs, I asked John Lee where he got his sharp-looking boots.

"Oh, these guys? Eric Burdon of the Animals, he bought 'em for me the last time I was in London. They're made of real genuine horsehair, top quality."

Detroit Willy had the car warming up, so I rushed over and opened the door for John Lee, thanking him for giving us the opportunity to possibly play with him. He got in the car, then lowered the window and repeated, as if we might have forgotten, "Remember — not too loud. See you tomorrow."

Paul and I couldn't believe it. We were floating on air with excitement.

After we said goodbye to John Lee, Paul and I headed over to our rehearsal loft, where Doug Slade, our rhythm guitarist, lived. It was in the South End, then an unsavory part of town. The first floor of the building was a pool parlor, and behind that lived a man known as the King of the Gypsies. It was rumored that his many young sons would walk around nearby neighborhoods and knock dents into fancy cars, after which their older brothers would contact the owners, telling them they could fix the dents for a small fee. The King was always selling something—televisions, clock radios, bicycles, and knickknacks galore. We were on good terms with the King and his large family, and because of this we could safely leave a car full of instruments parked out front.

Above the pool parlor was a soup kitchen, outside of which hung a white neon sign promising JESUS SAVES. Late at night, when we were returning from gigs, drunks would be passed out on the long, steep wooden staircase, and the hallway reeked of urine.

Doug was extremely good-looking in a classic Paul Newman sort of way. He had been the star quarterback on his suburban high school football team and never seemed to be far away from three things: pretty ladies, music, and drugs, not necessarily in that order. Doug never slept. Many nights found him and his friend Magoon, dressed in black, climbing onto rooftops of decaying and mostly deserted brownstones, salvaging copper ornaments, weather vanes, statues, crystal doorknobs, and marble reliefs before returning at dawn, laden with forgotten treasures to sell to their own syndicate of antiques dealers and decorators.

Doug's loft was inhabited by far-gone acidheads, meth freaks, Hare Krishnas, nodding heroin addicts, bikers, and junked-up jazz musicians jamming day in and day out. To throw one more character into this menagerie, next door was Linda Kasabian, who, after moving away from the neighborhood, ended up joining the Manson Family and taking part in the Sharon Tate murders.

Doug did have one rule he seriously enforced—no drug dealing. You could carry and use as much as you wanted, but if you tried to sell it to anyone inside the loft, you were immediately thrown out. I witnessed Doug sending someone tumbling down those long, long stairs many times.

We told Doug he had to clear out the usual stragglers and pull himself together for a marathon rehearsal the following day. It was an important opportunity, and we couldn't mess it up.

Tom Baliss, a painter friend of Doug, was stretched out on the couch, listening. We all were fond of Tom and valued his artistic opinion. He was around fifty-five, very thin, missing some teeth, and his hair looked like it was in a perpetual windstorm. Hearing our discussion, Tom piped up and said, "Seems like two greats will be playing in Boston tomorrow. Guess who I'm meeting for an early lunch down the corner at Chandler's: John Coltrane."

"I thought he's in town *next* week!" I said.

"No, man — you got all Hookered out. It's tomorrow."

Tom had been a junkie most of his life, but he was deeply spiritual and philosophical. Back in those days, there was no such thing as drug rehab. If you got picked up by the police, which happened quite frequently to Tom, you got sent to a city jail or a federal prison in Lexington, Kentucky, where many heroin addicts were sent to do time and dry out. Tom was doing a stint there when — or so he said — he became friends with jazz genius John Coltrane, although Coltrane's drug problem was nowhere near the level of Tom's. According to Tom, their friendship developed over long, deep conversations. We were all Coltrane fans, but even though a few of us never knew Tom to lie, some of us didn't quite believe him.

I really loved John Coltrane, and I'd seen him perform a few times in New York. The most memorable occasion was at Symphony Sid's Midnight Jazz Cavalcade at the Apollo Theater. On the same bill were Herbie Mann and Olatunji, who were debuting their album *The Common Ground*; Jimmy Smith, who performed his popular "Walk on the Wild Side"; and vocalist and lyricist Oscar Brown Jr.

After each performer's set, the big red Apollo curtain would dramatically close, a microphone would slowly rise from the floor of the stage, and the emcee, Symphony Sid, would saunter out to introduce the next artist. Coltrane and his group had just released their album *My Favorite Things*, which in no time became extremely popular and marked a major milestone in jazz. As talented as everyone was who performed earlier that night, there was great anticipation for Coltrane. You could feel a buzz of excitement around the audience. But there was a problem: it was getting close to the strictly enforced curfew. At the microphone, Sid announced, "We don't have as much time as we'd like, so without further ado, give a warm Apollo welcome to the John Coltrane Quartet!"

You could hear the audience saying, "What the hell does he mean, not much time?" Wild shouts and applause erupted as the band started playing "My Favorite Things" while the curtain was still opening. They played the main melody several times, then Coltrane suddenly stopped and put on sunglasses as McCoy Tyner took a lead solo on piano.

He played long successions of modal chords that electrified the audience, and it seemed like the more they reacted, the longer McCoy kept playing. Then, again as if by some telepathic signal, McCoy stopped playing, and Coltrane slowly began.

The house lights flashed, letting the musicians know the curfew was about to go into effect. The microphone sprang up, and Symphony Sid ran out from stage right, saying, "Let's hear it for the amazing John Coltrane Quartet." But the crowd would have none of it: they wouldn't allow any interruptions in this holy benediction. Coltrane and the band played on as the curtain slowly closed. From behind the curtain, they could still be heard playing, seemingly unaware of and unaffected by the chaos around them. The audience demanded that the house lights be turned off. Several police officers rushed down the aisle. It was evident that nobody would leave while Coltrane was still wailing. The situation was getting tense, and still Coltrane would not stop.

Finally the curtain opened again, and the house lights went off. The audience roared its approval as Coltrane, unfazed, played one arpeggio after another. McCoy Tyner, his head resting on the piano, suddenly lifted his head, and as if by magic, the quartet resumed playing the familiar melody of "My Favorite Things" in perfect unison. The entire house erupted in a state of sheer exhilaration. It was a transcendent moment for me. I had read a quotation by Coltrane about needing to discipline himself to avoid playing too long in places like the Apollo, but fortunately, any such discipline went right out the window that night.

Back in Boston, early the next day, we got together to rehearse. To our collective astonishment, in walked Tom with Coltrane's drummer, Elvin Jones, along with Coltrane's road manager and famed New England jazz promoter Fred Taylor. I'm fairly certain that Tom invited Elvin up for something that would make his gig that night a bit more mellow. We were thrilled about meeting this jazz great on top of playing that night with another of our idols, John Lee.

In the loft, Edie chatted among a group of friends. She was a devoted Coltrane fan, and she caught Elvin's eye. He took to talking with her, not realizing that she and I were together. Elvin needed to iron his one good shirt for the gig that night, and Edie offered to do it for him.

After rehearsal, the band's equipment was stacked by the front door, ready to load into our station wagon. Doug had Dylan blasting through his oversize theater speakers. Suddenly there was a hard, repetitive banging on the door. A loud voice, as if booming from a megaphone, yelled, "Open the fuck up — or we'll bash this fuckin' door down!" And then they did — *boom!*

The loft was invaded by men in gray suits. The heaviest of the bunch announced, "We're the narc squad!" They grabbed Tom Baliss from the couch and hurled him toward the wall. Elvin said in a panic, "I just came here with a friend. I never met these people before or ever been here before. I'm on my way outta here because I'm performing tonight at the Jazz Workshop."

"Grab 'em," said the heavyset narc, whom the other narcs called Chief.

There were racial slurs hurled at Elvin as he was shoved against the wall. When they threw Edie against the wall as well, I turned around and yelled, "What the fuck are you motherfuckers doing?" That's when a narc landed a sharp blow to my stomach. Another slammed me against the wall. We could all smell something burning — it was the iron still on the sleeve of Elvin's white dress shirt. Behind us we could hear dishes breaking as shelves were tipped over, making thunderous crashes that somehow blended in with the sound of Dylan's *Highway 61*. After a few moments, the turntable was thrown to the floor, resulting in an ominous silence.

"Whose dump is this?" the chief inquired. Doug, who was next to me against the wall, shouted, "This is my place! I live here! I don't know what the fuck you guys are after, but where the fuck is your search warrant?"

The heavyset Chief, with a shoulder holster exposed under his suit jacket, walked over, put his face an inch from Doug's, and shouted, "Here's yer fucking search warrant, ya fuckin' hippie!" He held up a piece of paper.

Doug turned to look, then shouted right into the narc's face, "This is apartment number two, not three!"

Everything stopped.

The chief yelled, "Jimmy, check the number on the door."

Jimmy walked over to the door, now hanging by one hinge, and yelled back, "The front door is just thick wood, Chief. There's no number."

Doug, whose face was still right up against the chief's, said, in a softer voice, but with a biting, sarcastic tone, pronouncing each word very slowly, "The mission below us is apartment number one. This is apartment number two, and above us is the apartment you want — number three. I don't know who lives there. Never seen anyone up there, coming or going. I think you guys made a real big fuckin' mistake."

Doug and the chief stared coldly at each other. No one moved or said a word. Finally, the chief yelled, his face still right up by Doug's, "All right, check the joint upstairs."

We could hear the men charging up the steps and a shout from the hallway: "The door has 'three' marked on it, Chief."

"Be right there!" the chief bellowed. "Nobody leave. Jimmy, you stay here until I come back down."

Soon we could hear a shout of "Open up! Narc squad!" followed by a thunderous crash as another door was smashed open.

The chief and two officers returned to Doug's, far less aggressive than when they first arrived. "An apparent mistake was made."

Doug, playing it safe and eager to get rid of them, diplomatically said, "Look, Officer, it's easily understandable in this building to make that kind of mistake."

The chief reached into his vest pocket and took out several business cards. He handed one to Doug and one to Elvin. Then, in the tone you would expect from a helpful flight attendant, he courteously said to Elvin, "You're free to go. Keep that card. Whenever you're in Boston, if you ever run into any problem here in town, any kind of problem, just call me."

Elvin thanked him, took his shirt, complete with a hole burned into the upper sleeve, and quickly headed out the door and down the stairs. The chief said to Doug that he would have some of his men come back and help put things in order. Doug thanked him and mentioned that we were musicians loading up for a big gig. The chief said, "Sergeant Jimmy here will help you with your equipment. And just for your information, and off the record, the fella upstairs has a chemical lab and has been manufacturing enough meth and LSD to supply the entire East Coast."

According to Tom Baliss, two narcs came to see Coltrane perform that night and were sitting with Elvin during the break, buying everyone in the band rounds of drinks.

After the shake-up with the narc squad, we managed to get to the club early enough. In the middle of our rehearsal, John Lee and Detroit Willy came walking in. I was singing an Otis Blackwell song called "Daddy Rollin' Stone," a recording of which was given to me by my friend and mentor Big John Belmonte, owner of the downtown record store Oldies but Goodies. John Lee smiled as he walked past us toward the dressing room. After fifteen minutes, Detroit Willy approached and said, "John wants to talk with you." I went to the dressing room expecting the worst, but John Lee said, "If you guys can play that soft tonight, things could work out, and maybe just a trio can back me up after I do a couple of solo numbers."

I was elated. "Sure, John. And if you want, I'll introduce you, because I think we're gonna have a full house."

* * *

Our club date with John Lee turned out to be very successful. We did have a full house, and John Lee appreciated the low volume. This became the first of many shows we played together. Years later, he often liked to recall a Boston club we had played, Where It's At, which was rumored to be backed by Mob money and looked like a Vegas show room. It booked national acts such as Sonny and Cher, Chuck Berry, Jackie Wilson, and Jerry Lee Lewis. But the club catered to teenagers. There was no alcohol allowed anywhere on the premises, and proper dress for the young audience was required.

The stern manager was a woman who acted like a Marine drill sergeant. She would enter the dressing room and announce the club's strict policies to John Lee and Detroit Willy and then repeat them to our band. She once spotted a half pint of scotch next to John Lee's guitar and took the bottle, saying she would return it when he was on his way out.

"I can't believe it, man. It seems like I'm in my father's church. My dad was strict, but man, this woman, she's crazy. In all my years playing, I ain't never seen anything like this."

The back door was located near the dressing rooms, so Paul and Detroit Willy snuck out and bought two half pints of scotch and poured them into two empty soda bottles. Before we started the show, one of the stagehands told us, "Look out — she comes backstage while you're performing to check if there's any alcohol around the dressing rooms."

"Man, this lady is really plum crazy," John Lee replied.

We did a set, then backed Detroit Willy, who did a bunch of Jimmy Reed songs, playing guitar and harmonica. After Willy finished his short set, I announced to the audience, "Please welcome to the stage the star of the show, the Boom Boom man himself, the King of the Boogie…put your hands together and give a warm welcome to the blues great Mr. John Lee Hooker!"

John Lee did his slow walk from the dressing room to the bandstand while waving to the young crowd. He carried a glass of scotch and soda, and after every couple of numbers, he would raise the glass to the teenage audience with a smile and take a long, slow drink. Then, with a big grin, he would start singing "My Father Was a Jockey," which contained the lyrics "My father was a jockey / Taught me how to ride / Once in the middle / Then from side to side." The audience laughed hard, and the stern manager never caught on.

Van Morrison was an intense John Lee Hooker fan. Van and I became pretty good friends when he lived in Cambridge in the 1960s. He would come by my house, and we would play the 45-rpm single of John Lee's "Solid Sender" over and over. Once, when John Lee was in town, I arranged a lunch with him and Van at a down-home soul-food restaurant called Bob the Chef's. With John Lee's stutter and Van's thick Belfast accent, it was almost impossible for me to understand their conversation, but they seemed to have no problem understanding each other.

Van asked John Lee question after question. What kind of guitar did he play on "Boogie Chillen'"? What kind of tuning did he use? What's his favorite place to record? Both men became animated when discussing the trials and tribulations of their experiences within the record industry. "Backstabbers!" John Lee said. "Oh, Van, the troubles I had to deal with. Those cats would make millions, and I'd be making pennies. Man, them Bihari brothers, they wrote the book on thievery. When I recorded 'Boogie Chillen" for their label and it became a hit, I'd play all the nightclubs, an' people would come up and congratulate me — they all thought I was loaded and swimming in the dough. Damn! I couldn't even pay my rent. It's all about them grabbing from you all they can. It's just their main motivation, to outsmart you, and taking your monies! Even if you keep your eyes wide open, they'll still know how to sneak into your wallet and grab what you got. If they don't get you coming in, they certainly gonna get you coming out." Van was taking it all in, the devoted student listening to the wise master.

Fortunately, thanks to a young and forceful manager whom John Lee met later in life, he was finally able to get back much of the royalties that were due him. His last recordings sold very well. He became one of the few bluesmen who, as he got older, found that his finances, along with his popularity, kept growing.

* * *

During the numerous times I saw John Lee perform, he seemed to be able to avoid any conflicts or fights with rowdy drunks, hecklers, and overzealous fans. He had a way of defusing any potentially volatile situation. When he performed alone with his guitar, it was magical.

Other than music, John Lee loved women and baseball. He became a loyal Brooklyn Dodgers fan when they signed Jackie Robinson, and he remained loyal even when the team moved to LA.

John Lee always enjoyed entertaining the ladies. He never chased after them; in fact it was often the other way around. While he was sitting in his dressing room, enjoying a scotch and soda, a couple of fans might come back to say hello. If one of them happened to be a lady of interest, John Lee would just light up. "My, my, you sure know how to make that dress look good!" There would be a blush. John Lee's sixth sense would go into action. "What does your boyfriend think of you coming backstage?"

"What makes you think I have a boyfriend?" she might respond.

"Come on — a woman as fine a looker as you? Now, don't be lying to Johnny here. You probably got three or four always hangin' round your door."

Drifters and runaways were attracted to what they perceived to be a freewheeling blues lifestyle like John's. He would often try to steer these confused wanderers away from trouble. He tried to persuade them to return home, and if they needed bus fare, he would gladly give it. One thing he would not tolerate was drug use.

I called John Lee on his eightieth birthday, in 1997.

We reminisced about our days on the road together. With a hint of melancholy, he said, "You know, Pete, I'm eighty years old today. My rollin' and tumblin' days ain't what they used to be, but I still love women. I still like 'em hangin' around me. I'll tell you, if I had two really fine women sitting at the edge of my bed right now, just to be able to look at 'em sitting there and hear 'em talk and smell their perfume — man, that would make me feel a whole lot better than I feel right now. Is there anything wrong with that?"

The charm of his character, for me, is best summed up in an encounter I had early on, when I was first getting to know him back in Boston. I asked him, after a show, if I could hang out with him some afternoon. He said, "Yeah, sure, man. Come by my hotel room tomorrow around four o'clock. I'm at the Lenox Hotel, room 302." I was thrilled.

I went to the third floor and knocked on the door, exactly on time. I could hear John Lee say, "Yeah, come on in, it's open." The room was dim, the shades pulled way down. The only light came from a TV. There were two beds, and John was lying on one, wearing wraparound shades, boxer shorts, a Brando-type white T-shirt, knee-high black silk socks, and a kerchief on his head. On the night table between the beds was a bottle of Ballantine's scotch, a pack of Kool cigarettes, and an ashtray stacked with butts. On the other bed, decorously spread out with all its luscious curves, was his gleaming red Gibson 335 guitar. This was the typical domain of a Mississippi bluesman — tough, rough, and traveling light.

Midnight jam with John Lee Hooker

"Hey, man, pull up one of them chairs an' sit down." I did so, realizing that John Lee was watching the TV with his full attention. I followed his gaze, and to my amazement, the man who sang "Don't mess with me 'cause I'm bad, I'm mad, I might shoot ya, I might stab ya, I can cut ya, I'm bad like Jesse James" — that man was watching...*Lassie!* With hands clasped behind his head, he said, "Man, let me tell you, Pete. That Lassie, he sure is one motherfuckin' smart dog."

He died peacefully in his sleep at eighty-three years old. John Lee lived his life just as he sang in his first hit, "Boogie Chillen'": "I heard Papa tell Mama / Let that boy boogie-woogie / 'Cause it's in him and it got to come out!"

13

RAINBOW '65
Van Morrison

Interviewing Van Morrison, WBCN, 1968

M Y EARLY YEARS in Boston included a stint as a radio DJ. My show
was on WBCN from midnight to 5:00 a.m. There was an unusually sensual element to being a late-night disc jockey, broadcasting alone
in a small, dimly lit studio, the city sleeping and closed till morning. I
never knew who, if anyone, might still be up in the wee hours, perhaps
just one mysterious listener somewhere off in the distance, far away, tuning in because perhaps they needed me as much as I needed them.

Except for maybe one or two classical-music programs on the FM
dial, my show was the only game in town during those hours. I was
building an audience slowly, after the TV went off the air at midnight
and the national anthem played, followed by the crackling sound of
static "snow." Cambridge was like a ghost town after midnight, and Boston, during the 1960s, wound down by 1:00 a.m. Every store, subway,
bar, and bus line was closed, the streets dark except for the glow from
traffic lights and lonely all-night diners.

I began receiving intriguing postcards at the station. The front would be emblazoned with the black-and-white eroticism of Aubrey Beardsley and on the reverse would be delicate feminine handwriting stating, "I love your show... Please play more Van Morrison."

I was a fan of Van's music at a time when very few people knew his name. The postcards kept arriving, always Beardsley, complimenting my musical choices — Sonny Boy Williamson, John Lee Hooker, and Muddy Waters — and concluding with the request "Please play more Van Morrison."

My on-air moniker was Woofa Goofa. Between songs, I slipped into my fast-talking radio persona:

> Riding through the motions of the oceans,
> Having fun until the midnight sun.
> Yamma gamma gooma looma.
> This is the Woofa Goofa Mama Toofa.
> We gonna get things movin',
> Keep things groovin',
> Kickin' it high an' lettin' it flow.
> Turn it up, turn it up, an' let your lovelight show.

One evening, my band, the Hallucinations, was rehearsing at the Boston Tea Party, then known as the Moondial. This cavernous hall also hosted the Film Collective, which held screenings of avant-garde movies, often the showcase for many of Andy Warhol's early films. We were the house band, preparing for a gig later that night. I was going over our set list when a young man walked in, looking lost and uncertain. He was sturdily built, not very tall. He approached me, asking in a slightly abrupt foreign accent that I could not place, "Do you work here?"

When I answered no, he quickly asked, "Where's the manager?"

I didn't know, but the neediness I sensed from him compelled me to want to help.

"I'm looking for gigs," he hurriedly explained, and I replied, "What kind of gigs?"

"Yeah, you know, I'm looking for gigs, just looking for gigs."

I couldn't quite understand his accent because his words were spoken so rapidly, so I offered to find the manager if he was willing to hang around and wait. He asked if I was in a band, and when I told him yes, we began a conversation about what kind of music we played. The more we talked, the easier it became to understand him. Then he asked if I listened to the "Wulfa Gulfa radio show, with this old Black fella...Man, he plays lots of great stuff, even early Bobby 'Blue' Bland."

His pronunciation of my moniker made me laugh, and he asked, "What's so funny?"

I told him, "I'm the Woofa Goofa." He was understandably perplexed, maybe even thinking I was putting him on, until I launched into my radio patter.

> With a yamma gamma gooma looma,
> Slippin' and slidin' with a real moe-giin'-gator,
> Doing it to it,
> And getting right through it.

Hearing my rap convinced him, but the real unmasking came when he added, "I dig all that stuff you play, even when you slip in one of my records."

"Your records?"

He could see the confusion on my face, so he said, "I'm Van. Van Morrison."

It was like coming across some ancient mariner long lost at sea. In that moment, Van literally came out of the mist. His song "Mystic Eyes," recorded with his group, Them, defined the vibe and sound my band had been aiming for. When I first heard it, I couldn't believe the energy that poured from the recording. Now here he was, standing in front of me, looking for a gig, even though his first solo release, "Brown Eyed Girl," was being played continually on the radio. After the rehearsal, Van and I walked back to Cambridge, talking all the while. That is where our friendship began. I would come to learn that Van, like Dylan, always had a sense of his own destiny.

Van's decision to move to Cambridge was forever shrouded in mystery. At first he said it was to check out the music scene there, which was vibrant, with many folk, rock, and jazz clubs.

He hardly ever talked about his days with the group Them, which he formed in his hometown, Belfast, in Northern Ireland. Also at that time, he didn't have any kind words to say about the legendary record producer and songwriter Bert Berns, responsible for bringing Van to the United States. When Bert was in London and heard Van perform with Them, he recognized Van's prodigious talents and persuaded him to sign a long-term solo recording and management contract, which gave Berns complete control of Van's career.

As Van told it, once he was living in New York, he wanted to move in a musical direction that was counter to Bert's vision, causing great tension and resulting in a widening creative gulf between them. Van felt he needed to break away or be suffocated artistically. Bert, though, was supposedly involved with the Italian Mafia. "One night these guys from the Irish Mob just came and rescued me and my family from that scene. They took us up to Boston. I was on the run." Through the years, Van told varying accounts about the move, with varying degrees of color, but whatever the reason, he wound up on Green Street in Cambridge, not far from, in Dylan's words, "the green pastures of the Harvard University."

We entered his apartment, located on the ground floor of a small row house. He lived with his wife, Janet, her son, and her and Van's new baby. Janet was a delicate beauty, madonnalike, seated on a chair, breastfeeding. Although the cramped apartment was bare, with a mattress on the floor and what looked like an Ovation guitar in the corner, it had a tired rather than squalid feel. Van introduced me, telling Janet that I was the Woofa Goofa from the radio show, and she excitedly said, "I've been sending postcards asking you to play more Van!" I was at ease in their company, the hours drifting past as we bonded over our shared love of music.

Although I didn't have money to help Van financially, I used the connections I had to introduce influential people on the Boston scene to Van's music. He seemed to be in a perpetual state of crisis, frequently dropping by my apartment to use the telephone for long-distance business calls. He was trying to get released from his recording contract, and the emotional toll it was taking on him was evident.

He had a definite vision of his musical direction and was determined to make it happen. In the time leading up to the recording of his momentous *Astral Weeks* album, a therapeutic escape for us both was to sit in front of my record player listening to Muddy Waters, Little Walter, and John Lee Hooker. It became somewhat of a religious ritual for us. Favorites of ours included Jackie Wilson's first recorded version of "Danny Boy," King Pleasure's "Moody's Mood for Love," and Little Richard's "I Don't Know What You've Got But It's Got Me." A few that were always on Van's request list were my obscure Billy Stewart recordings along with Gene Chandler's live recording from the Regal Theater of Curtis Mayfield's "Rainbow '65." Van would play that record over and over until he had every bit of Gene's vocal inflection memorized. Our listening sessions helped Van forget the legal troubles he was facing.

Sometimes, if he was in a depressed mood, he would perk up considerably when we walked around Harvard Square, got a coffee, or just sat on a bench watching the world pass by.

I introduced Van to many friends, including my literary mentor, Ed Hood. Together, we became a drinking trio. Van responded to Ed's intellectual genius, discussing literature and poets such as Shelley, Blake, and Yeats and the dark fires they inspired.

I invited Van to see the Hallucinations at the Boston Tea Party, not only so he could watch us perform but also so I could introduce him to the club's new management. I was the lead singer and sometimes shared vocals with other band members. On this night, Doug, our rhythm guitarist, sang Van's "Gloria," which at the time was a garage-band anthem across the country. Doug blasted the opening chords at full volume, singing, while I played tambourine and maracas. I noticed Van standing to one side of the stage and thought it would be a real surprise for everyone if I called him up.

Doug finished a verse and chorus, with the audience singing along, before launching into a guitar solo. I signaled Van to join us onstage as Doug, eyes closed, played furiously. Van walked up to the microphone, grabbed it, and started pacing across the stage and scatting the "Gloria" lyrics: "Let me t-t-t-t-t-t-t-t-ell ya about my b-b-b-b-b-b-b-baby, she-e-e-e-e-e c-c-c-comes a-a-a-a-around here." The audience was totally perplexed by the strange singer taking over, performing such a popular favorite so unusually. They began booing. Doug yelled to me, "What the fuck is he doing? He's fucking ruining *my* song!"

"Doug, he wrote the song!" I yelled back, but Doug's amp was so loud that he didn't hear.

As Van got to the final chorus, "Give me a G-G-G-G-G-G-G-G-G-G-G-G-G-G-G-G-G-G-G," I had to grab his mike and shout to the crowd, "Ladies and gentlemen, this is Van Morrison, the man who wrote this song!" The announcement had no impact whatsoever on the audience, still booing loudly.

Van grabbed the mike back and continued, "L-L-L-L-L-L-L-L-L-L, O-O-O-O-O-O-O-O-O, R-R-R-R-R-R-R-R-R-R, I-I-I-I-I-I-I-I-I, A-A-A-A-A-A-A-A-A-A-A," but all the audience wanted to hear was the crowd-pleasing hit "Gloria," not Van's wildly improvised scat. Doug was about to bop Van right off the stage with the neck of his guitar, so I signaled to our drummer to end the song. I called out for an instrumental and walked Van toward the dressing room, where I introduced him to the club's manager, who later booked Van to perform there.

The Tea Party was originally built as a synagogue in 1872. It had a wooden interior and high ceilings, creating rich acoustics. The drawback was that the venue had only one long staircase for the entrance and exit, which made it a dangerous firetrap.

During the middle of Van's first Tea Party performance, smoke started billowing from the large ceiling fan high above the stage. The staff immediately climbed up to the rafters to investigate and found that a fire had indeed broken out. Van, eyes shut, was deep into his song, oblivious to the commotion of ladders and fire extinguishers being hoisted up to the ceiling right above him.

I first heard Van perform songs from *Astral Weeks* at the small, true-to-its-name club the Catacombs. You entered near a ground-floor pizza parlor, then went down a set of rickety stairs and past a pool hall. Three floors below that was the club. It was like entering a pharaoh's tomb, with gold-painted walls covered in Egyptian motifs. At a venue that held two hundred people, perhaps no more than thirty were on hand to witness the unveiling of songs from *Astral Weeks*, a musical turning point for Van.

Astral Weeks was mostly an underground success for him, but it was followed by the huge hit albums *Moondance* and *His Band and the Street Choir*. By then he had moved with Janet to Woodstock, New York, and I was playing with the Geils band. For the *Street Choir* tour, Geils was the opening act, and the first show was scheduled for Boston's Symphony Hall, an unprecedented location for a rock concert.

During intermission, after our set, I was sitting in the audience when Janet came running up the aisle, looking anxious. In a panic she said, "Peter, please, quick — I need your help. He said he won't go on and won't leave the dressing room." Van's band was already onstage, playing an instrumental. I rushed into his seemingly empty dressing room, shouting "Van!," and heard from behind the bathroom door a deadpan reply of "Yeah."

"What are you doing?" I asked.

Casually, he replied, "I don't want to go on."

I shouted back, "What do you mean? You gotta come out of there."

"No, I'm not going on."

"We're at Symphony Hall, and it's a sold-out house. The band's already onstage, and the crowd is waiting for you."

"Just leave me alone."

"No, Van. You're coming out now."

"Yeah, I'm not feeling good."

"Do you need a doctor? Is that what's going on?"

"No. Just leave me alone."

Losing patience, I opened the bathroom door to find Van, fully clothed, sitting dejectedly on the toilet, looking not dissimilar to Rodin's *The Thinker*. I cursed him out, reminding him of all the people waiting for the show and the humiliation of not getting out there onstage. I hoisted him off the toilet and continued my rant as I dragged him out, pushing him straight onto the stage. As he walked out, the crowd broke into thunderous applause. He performed a singularly unforgettable show, his voice and presence as powerful as they were riveting.

Van and I always stayed in touch, even when he moved to Fairfax, California. He followed the winds, wherever he felt the musical vibe was headed, be it Cambridge, Woodstock, or Marin County. When Geils played San Francisco's Winterland, Van wanted me to visit him out in Fairfax, a drive he described as being a quick and easy hop from where I was staying.

After sound check I figured I'd have plenty of time to be back for our show. I had a crew member drive me on what became a seemingly endless journey through hills and valleys until at last we came to his alpine chalet–style home nestled in the woods. The difference between it and the old Cambridge apartment was incredible, a measure of the renown Van had achieved in the intervening years. Janet welcomed me warmly, but I was disappointed to hear her say Van wouldn't leave the basement and was in one of his dark moods. She pointed to a *Billboard* reporter who had been sitting on the porch for the past two hours, patiently waiting for Van's promised interview.

I walked in and yelled down to Van, "You'd better come out. That drive took forever, and I have a show to do tonight."

No response from the basement.

"Van! You said you wanted to play me something. Now get up here."

More silence. But I was not about to have made this long journey for nothing.

"Van, if you're not up here in the next five minutes, I'll come down and drag you up."

I heard reluctant shuffling as he walked upstairs, and then we chatted like old times, as if we had seen each other only yesterday. Van played me the reel-to-reel track of what would become "Wild Night." Hearing this masterpiece, even in its unformed state, and seeing him again made the trek to Fairfax completely worthwhile.

Whenever Van played in Boston, he stayed at one particular Cambridge hotel, and without fail, we would get together for a visit. Van always graciously asked how my music was going — whether I was recording or playing — never behaving like the icon he had become. But on one occasion we argued, and like most arguments, it began inconsequentially but resulted in our not seeing each other for quite a while. Still, I was a fan of his music and live shows, in which his spontaneous unpredictability always created moments of true artistic brilliance, and I never missed a chance to see him perform. In the late 1980s, Van returned to play in Boston, and I caught the show.

Toward the end of the final song, "Caravan," Van suddenly began singing, "Radio radio radio radio radio. I'm calling, I'm calling, FLIP 313, FLIP 313. I'm calling that 313, turn it up turn it up turn it up." For the final verse, he interjected improvised phrases such as "You know, turning on my radio, turning on my radio" before dropping the mike and walking offstage.

Back in the 1960s, my phone number, when spelled out, was

FLIP 313. Many visiting musicians knew that number, and it was passed through the ranks. If you needed a sofa to sleep on, a place to hang out, or a show to promote, you could dial it. Hearing him call it out as he did, I went backstage, hoping to mend fences and renew our long friendship. It was as if no conflict or disagreement had ever occurred.

Van was playing two sold-out shows at the Boston Music Hall, a far cry from the Catacombs, where he first began. The show was Van at his finest. During the ballads, you could hear a pin drop in the five-thousand-seat theater. He mesmerized the audience. The standing ovations just kept coming in waves.

After the show, feeling satisfied with the evening's performance, Van suggested we step out on the town. I acted as tour guide, and we hit one club after another until we ended up back in Cambridge at the original small wooden House of Blues along with blues great Junior Wells, who was opening the shows for Van's tour. Van always had first-rate artists open his shows — artists like Mose Allison, Bobby "Blue" Bland, Solomon Burke, and Wells. I was a huge fan of Junior, who had played harp with Muddy Waters in the 1950s. Junior was good-looking and quite short, hence the nickname. He had a unique harmonica style with an expressive voice to match, but if he got anywhere near gin...look out!

We sat at a back table in the small, narrow club and ordered wine. Junior knocked back several glasses filled to the brim with gin. A local blues band performed that night, doing one slow generic blues number after another. Van leaned over to me and said, "Get up there and get this place jumpin'." At the end of the next song, I went up to the stage and asked the bandleader if I could sit in. I called out a Kansas City–type jump number. As soon as the band started playing, the place came alive. Halfway through the song, Junior walked up, glass of gin in hand, then pushed me away from the mike and yelled, "I'll show you how it's done."

After Junior sang two verses of Muddy Waters's "Got My Mojo Working," Van jumped up to the stage, holding a bottle of wine. He pulled the mike away from Junior and called out to the band to play Bobby "Blue" Bland's "Turn On Your Lovelight." The audience went wild, screaming for more. I tried to keep Junior from grabbing the mike away from Van while he tried to push me off the stage. Fortunately, the house lights came on at just the right moment, putting an end to the chaos. The crowd, still wanting more, had to be cleared out. The club manager locked the door and gave us free rein behind the bar to drink our fill.

In 1998, Bob Dylan and Van did a short tour from Madison Square Garden to the Boston Garden. Ron Delsener, the promoter of the shows, wanted Bob and Van to perform a duet in Boston. The previous night, at Madison Square Garden, they sang a tribute to Carl Perkins, who had recently passed away. In Boston, with no plan for a duet, Ron was nervous. He knew the audience was expecting to hear these two remarkable icons singing together.

Ron and I were sitting in Van's dressing room when Ron told Van he really should do a number with Bob. Van was not sure if Bob wanted to, so Ron asked me to see if Bob was open to the idea. I ran down the hall to Bob's dressing room and knocked on the door. To my surprise, George Harrison opened it. I asked Bob if he was up for a duet with Van. "Yeah, no problem. See what song he wants to sing."

I ran back to Van's dressing room and told him that Bob was fine with a duet but wanted to know what song he would like to perform. I suggested "It's All Over Now Baby Blue," which Van had once recorded with Them, but Van didn't think that was a good idea. Then I suggested "Just Like a Woman," because I knew Van had previously performed it.

"No, no, ain't right!" answered Van.

Ron nervously paced back and forth, looked at his watch, and pleaded, "Van, please make up your mind. They just want to see you both together. Do the Carl Perkins song—that worked fine yesterday in New York."

"No. We did that already," Van replied, sitting and staring into space.

Ron's pacing became even more anxious. "Come on, Van, make up your mind. You're going to give me a heart attack," he implored.

I finally suggested, "How about 'Knockin' on Heaven's Door'?"

Ron shouted, "That's perfect! Brilliant idea, brilliant!"

"No, no," Van said. "It's too commercial."

"Commercial?" Ron exploded. "You think 'Knockin' on Heaven's Door' is too commercial? I can't believe this—a sold-out show, and I'm telling you, you're going to kill me! Do fuckin' 'Jingle Bells,' but do something!"

Van was unperturbed by Ron's rant and sat calmly, almost meditating. There was a knock on the door. I opened it to find Bob standing there, guitar already strapped on, asking, "Hey, Van, wanna do 'Knockin' on Heaven's Door'?" The decision was made.

During Bob's set I was stageside, standing next to George Harrison, who was quietly unassuming. Bob and the audience were connecting so deeply that it was like a form of communion. Then he announced, "We're gonna have a friend come up" as the band kicked into "Knockin' on Heaven's Door." When Van appeared onstage, you almost couldn't hear the music—the crowd was cheering so loudly. I wondered why George wasn't out there singing, too. He and Bob were so close. I said to him, "You should be out there." But George lingered in the shadows of the stage lights, just enjoying the music. Unbeknownst to me, he had been diagnosed with cancer, and the full meaning of seeing his friend Bob perform that song did not hit me until his passing.

The triumphant finale complete, Bob, Van, and the musicians came offstage. Once back in his dressing room, Van declared, "Hey, 'Knockin' on Heaven's Door'—that's not commercial. That's a great song."

It was always an adventure reconnecting with Van whenever he came to town. On one occasion, after a long night of knockin' 'em back, Van called the next day to ask if I'd meet him at his hotel so we could go record shopping. We were both nursing massive hangovers, and because the store was a good mile away, I suggested we hop in a cab. But Van wanted to walk, unaware, as I was, just how sweltering the heat was on that August afternoon. By the time we were halfway there, the punishing glare of the sun was wearing us down. We dragged ourselves on, finally arriving, and just as I opened the record-shop door to the relief of its air-conditioning, Van said, "I don't feel like shopping. Let's head back and maybe grab a bite somewhere."

"You gotta be kidding!" I yelled, but knowing Van as long as I had, I realized it was useless to argue. We passed a landmark Irish pub, the Plough and Stars, named after a play by the esteemed Irish playwright Sean O'Casey. One of the owners was the editor of the literary review *Ploughshares.* "Van, you'll love this place. It's where many writers and poets come to have a quiet glass or two." The word *poets* seemed to catch Van's attention. We opened the shamrock-green door and entered the cool comfort of low lights and subtle Celtic music. Feeling exhausted and dehydrated, like Bogart in *The Treasure of the Sierra Madre* after panning for gold and at last finding it, we gazed up hungrily at the blackboard, looking at the daily luncheon specials and relishing the promise of a cold glass of ale. I called over to the heavyset bartender, "Excuse me. We'd like to order some lunch."

Without turning around to look at me, he yelled back, "Lunch is over today."

"Over? What time do you stop serving?" I asked.

"Two thirty," he said, not bothering to look our way. The big clock hanging on the back wall showed the time: two thirty-two.

"Hey, we're only two minutes late. I'm sure there's something in the kitchen."

"Two thirty: the kitchen closes at two thirty sharp!"

"Listen, can't you just tell the cook we'll take whatever's available?"

Again, he wouldn't turn our way, shouting, "It's past two thirty."

Annoyed, Van turned to me and said, "Let's get the hell out of here."

We made our exit back into the hot sun and walked on, determined to find food and a watering hole. From behind us came the voice of someone calling out, "Van! Van! Come back! We'll serve you whatever you want!" We turned and saw the bartender.

I looked at Van, who said, "Tell 'em to fuck off. Let's keep walking."

I yelled back to the bartender, "Pour yourself a nice, slow pint of Guinness, and at approximately two forty-five, take that pint and stick it right up your fuckin' ass." Van and I howled at that all the way back in the burning heat, slouching toward Harvard Square.

With Van at the Beverly Hills Hotel, 1975

14

BATTLE OF THE POCONOS
Dee Anthony and the Showdown

With "The Big M," Mario Medious

I WAS ENTERING THE elevator in the lobby of the Atlantic Records office in New York when, just as I pushed the button for my floor, I heard the voice of Mario Medious — the Big M — yell, "Hold the elevator, Wolf." Mario was the top rock promotion man at the label and always a sharp dresser: red satin pants, snakeskin boots, fitted waist-length black leather jacket, a blue wide-brimmed fedora, and mirrored sunglasses. From Chicago's South Side via Mississippi, Mario was Black and proud of it. His father was a gambler and hung out at the clubs where Muddy Waters performed, instilling in young Mario a love of blues and jazz. A black belt in karate, Mario was gentle, but when neces-sary, he could kick his foot right through a solid brick wall.

He rushed into the elevator, and I could see following behind him a girl so fashionably dressed it was as if she were coming straight from Portobello Road. She had blue eyes even wider than her smile and wind-blown naturally blond hair. Mario said, "Wolf, meet Angel." As she and Mario got out of the elevator and she gracefully followed him into his office, I couldn't help but notice the tight blue-velvet bell-bottoms wrapped around her figure.

I was at Atlantic to meet with the head of marketing, David Glew, regarding the Geils band's upcoming tour. The drill was that I would ask for something and, true to his name, he *stuck* to the same answer: "No problem, my friend." I knew it was bullshit, and so did he, but that was how it always played out with Atlantic during these necessary, and predictable, rituals.

As the meeting concluded, I headed straight to Mario's office. The moment I walked in the door, Mario said, "She left, and I already know what you're thinking, but get your mind off trying to get close to that walkin' bit of sweetness. She's Stephen Stills's gal, and there'll be nothin' but trouble."

"But Mario," I pleaded.

"Stay your ass away, far away," he warned me.

Just then, Donny Hathaway, a songwriter and singer whose style influenced many younger R & B artists, came into Mario's office. He was short and stocky and was wearing an all-leather jumpsuit and a large floppy leather cap. "Wolf, meet one of the most talented motherfuckers in this building." Donny was having a hard time getting back into the studio to finish his new songs, and Mario was encouraging him by saying, "The cream always rises to the top. These motherfuckers are going to learn one day, all the golden talent they got sitting right in front of them, and Donny, you know Mario don't bullshit nobody."

Donny sat beside me, his head bowed low, listening to Mario's pep talk. Mario paused, which he seldom did, when Donny asked, "Hey, Mario, where'd you buy that slick jacket?"

"I got it at Granny Takes a Trip. My friend Angel works there. She's real cool, and she'll cut you a nice discount if you tell her you and me are tight. Shit, you just missed her. She was —" Suddenly Mario came to an immediate stop, realizing he had just let the proverbial cat out of the bag.

"Wolf, I know what you're thinking, but just leave that lady alone. She's going through enough hell with Stephen, treating her like dirt and messin' with that poor girl's heart. That cat don't know the difference between chicken shit and chicken salad."

I let Mario ramble on, but I was going shopping, and I knew the exact store I'd be stopping by.

Granny Takes a Trip, established in London and considered one of the city's hippest clothing shops, dressed almost every British rock star and had recently opened a small boutique branch in New York, uptown, on Second Avenue.

I headed over on the pretense that I needed to buy a stage outfit. Hoping Angel would be working, I browsed through the racks, but no Angel in sight. I was ready to give up when she suddenly appeared out of the stockroom. "Hey, what an amazing surprise!" I said, mustering as much conviction as I could.

She asked if I needed something special, then added, "Listen, hang around for a bit, because I'm doing the closing up tonight."

I was happy that I'd had the foresight to stop off beforehand and buy a bottle of wine. After locking up, she lit a joint and poured us both a glass. We spent the next hour talking as she dressed me in all sorts of velvets and satins. The price tags were far beyond my reach — painfully so — but Angel had a good eye for what suited me. She was a transplant from Florida and wasn't crazy about New York, preferring a slow, easy-going life with a more friendly southern pace. Music was important to her, and she enjoyed the troubadour lifestyle of most musicians.

We went for dinner at a cozy French bistro nearby, and when I escorted her back to her small third-floor walk-up, she invited me in for a final nightcap.

Thereafter, I tried to see Angel as much as our schedules allowed, even with the Big M always keeping a suspicious, watchful eye on us. We were both in relationships, going through periods of reflection, which helped create an unspoken guardrail that defined the parameters of our friendship.

* * *

I had a meeting with our booking agent, Frank Barsalona, a powerful and respected man in the world of rock. The Geils band had already released two albums, and after several long promotional tours, we weren't making any progress toward bigger things. Frank thought the problem was that we needed a formal manager. My dual role of managing and playing in the band was too much of a load to carry. He suggested Dee Anthony, someone who had already seen the band's live set and was happy to meet with me in New York.

Dee came from an Italian neighborhood in the Bronx, not far from where I grew up. He was short, muscular, and heavyset, with a thick head of wavy graying hair and a well-trimmed beard. He waddled when he walked, but he had an impressive look, along with a certain air of danger. Dee loved the entertainment world and wanted to become part of it in any way he could. After a stint in the navy, he hung around the Copacabana, where some of the great crooners of the day performed — Sinatra, Tony Bennett, Al Martino, Jerry Vale, and Rosemary Clooney. He became a runner for many of the clientele and soon found himself working for Tony Bennett. Yet once the Beatles hit the United States, lounge singers had a hard time finding good venues and were given almost no radio airtime.

Dee, seeing the writing on the wall, became friends with the "king of the agents," Frank Barsalona, who, after working with the Beatles' manager, Brian Epstein, formed Premier Talent. It was the first booking agency that dealt only with rock acts. Dee assisted the groups from the so-called second wave of the British Invasion in the late 1960s. He managed several bands and artists, including Joe Cocker just before he started his groundbreaking Mad Dogs and Englishmen tour, the first large traveling rock event of its kind.

Dee set up a meeting with me in New York, at a small Italian seafood place right in the heart of Chinatown. It was owned by one Mr. B, who collected from all the Chinese bookies and owned several rock clubs, including one in New Jersey and another on Long Island. He was an associate of the ultimate kingpin, Morris Levy, who owned Roulette Records and the jazz club Birdland. Levy was an infamous and connected tough guy. He exercised a controlling hand over some major disc jockeys, jukeboxes, and music distributors, and he had a powerful influence over a good chunk of the recording industry. He would eventually be convicted of extortion, but he died before serving his sentence.

People were coming in and out of the restaurant, surreptitiously dropping off small paper bags with the bartender. There was a low ceiling and flickering neon lights, and the jukebox was playing Sinatra's "Strangers in the Night." I sat by the window and watched as Dee stepped out of his black limo, checked his gleaming gold Rolex, and straightened the cuffs of his gray pin-striped three-piece suit. He waddled into the place, shouting at the bartender in Italian, and ordered us the house special, linguine in white clam sauce with a good Brunello, which they didn't have.

"Where the hell is Mr. B? He's letting this place turn into a shithole! Tell him I came down to have some food and a nice bottle of wine with this young musician here, and even the pasta sucks. It's as limp as your dick." The bartender laughed as Dee threw a C-note on the table. "Let's blow this joint and go to Giordano's."

Giordano's, situated right by the Lincoln Tunnel, was known as a meeting place where, shall we say, certain businessmen from New Jersey came to meet with certain businessmen from the city.

We were greeted at the entrance by the manager, dressed in a tux, who snapped to attention when he saw Dee.

"Mr. Anthony, we are honored to have you dine in our restaurant tonight. Let me escort you to our best table, in the corner, away from the crowd, as you always like."

"Bring us a bottle of Brunello and two Fernet-Brancas to start." Dee turned to me and said, "Let me order. I'll get us a bit of everything. We'll start with some pasta—they make a pretty good sauce. Not as good as mine, but good." Soon the table was filled with plates of food, enough for ten people, and Dee sampled everything. The busboys and waiters danced around, making sure all was to his liking, and our wineglasses stayed constantly full.

"So Frank tells me you're looking for a manager," he said, a forkful of spicy hot sausage in his hand. He began a symposium on his philosophy of show business. "Making good records is not enough. You must have a strong live act. You must create an identity with your audience. They're not coming out just to hear artists sing what they recorded. They want something more, and your job as a performer is to give them that. Stir up their fantasies. Elvis, Sinatra, Garland, even Jagger — they all got that extra something. You got to find what's yours, and once you do, you'll have a good chance of making it big. It's hard work, but with guidance, you can get a shot at it. My job is to help get you the opportunities, but you and the band got to bring it home. I'm like the coach on the sidelines; I can tell you how to make the winning play, but you got to get on the field and do it. Many managers focus on only the records and spend all their time arguing with record companies. Fuck that. I believe you gotta build a fan base first. When you play a club, you might play to fifty people, but then the next time, if you do it right, there'll be three hundred people. If I get you an opening spot on an arena bill, the next time you might be in the middle slot. Then eventually you'll become headliners. You can be a one-hit wonder for a year or two or have a long, sustainable career — you gotta decide."

I was enjoying my evening with Dee. He was entertaining, a charismatic storyteller, and you could still see the Bronx street kid he was, with his napkin tucked into his collar and pasta sauce dribbling onto his jacket nonetheless. His career perspective was like mine. We ended the meal with sambuca and three coffee beans for good luck. "Never an even number," said Dee. "One bean is for health, one for happiness, and the other for prosperity." There were cookies wrapped in thin paper that Dee lit on fire, saying, "If the paper rises upward, it means good luck, and if it doesn't, you got a hex on you." Both our wrappers rose toward the ceiling. Dee smiled. "See? I think that's a good sign."

We met again the following evening in his Park Avenue apartment to discuss the details. In a sitting room decorated with hand-painted Venetian-style frescoes, he lit a Cuban cigar for himself and one for me and began what he called "the business of the day." Puffing away, he said, "Peter, many managers take 20 to 25 percent. The Colonel takes 50 percent from Elvis, so it's all a matter of needs and negotiation of the situation." Dee let this last statement drift in the air alongside the smoke from our cigars as he awaited my reply.

"Dee, how about 10 percent?"

His body jolted, as if he had stuck his finger in a socket. "Ten fucking percent! Are you kidding me? I can see why you need a manager — you're outta your mind. Twenty fucking percent, or let's just shake hands and call it a day." He put out his cigar, squashing it back and forth in the ashtray while staring at me without blinking.

I held his stare and, after a long pause, replied, "Dee, we need a manager, but I'm coming to you as one Bronx street kid to another. When we started, I got the band out of bad management. Then I got us on Atlantic Records and with the best booking agency. I've hustled radio stations, rack jobbers, the press, and promoters. I'm not like those English bands that come over and don't know shit from Shinola. I can handle a lot of the stuff, and we won't be a burden on you like some of your other acts. You meet with Frank, book us some good dates that'll give us the opportunity to move up the ladder, and I guarantee you we'll seize the moment. I've been working my ass off, so let's make it ten percent and shake hands on it. Fuck all this expensive lawyer bullshit. If we become a problem, just call and let me know. Why would we want to work together if it becomes a headache? Let's have a handshake and call it the beginning of a Bronx friendship."

Dee was staring hard at me, but I could sense a smile forming at the corners of his mouth. He took out his wallet, from which he pulled a two-dollar bill. "Sign it, Wolf, and I'm gonna hold on to this. If we have a disagreement, I'll send this back to you special delivery, and that'll be the end of our working relationship." I signed the bill, Dee spit in his hand, I spit in mine, and we shook on it, followed by a bear hug that almost broke my ribs. The deal was done. Dee came out on the road with us, and both he and everyone in the band seemed glad he was on board.

We were scheduled to play a music festival in Long Pond, Pennsylvania, in July of '72. It was a two-day affair held at the Pocono International Raceway and featuring a number of bands. We were billed as part of the evening festivities on the second day, along with the Faces; Humble Pie; Emerson, Lake & Palmer; Edgar Winter; and Three Dog Night.

The other members of the Geils band were installed at a hotel near the festival site on the day of our performance. I was planning to travel up that day with Angel. Dee, who also managed two other acts on the festival's bill, Humble Pie and Emerson, Lake & Palmer, rented a stretch limo for the hour-and-a-half drive from the city and picked us up at Angel's apartment. He was dressed in gold-framed sunglasses, a brown fringed suede jacket, jeans, and sneakers. We stopped at Manganaro's, an old Italian grocery store located on Ninth Avenue, where Dee stocked up on Italian subs, olives, peppers, desserts, and wine. Fully loaded, we sped onto the Jersey Turnpike, Dee on one side, Angel on the other, and me in the middle, with large shopping bags of food and wine at our feet. Dee enjoyed having Angel with us. She was a good listener, and Dee liked to talk. An hour in, Dee fell fast asleep and didn't wake up until we pulled into the driveway of the hotel.

The Geils band gathered in Dee's room, where he passed out the subs and gave us his battle speech, holding a sterling-silver whistle attached to a chain he wore around his neck. "When I blow this whistle, don't walk onto the stage — charge out there! Don't even think about who's ahead of you and who's after. Just hold your own; play like it's your last day on earth!"

With subs in hand, we yelled, "We're gonna do it for Dee!"

We were scheduled to go on at around 7:30 p.m., right after the Faces. I headed over to their room to visit them, since I knew Rod Stewart and Ronnie Wood from their very first days in the States, when they were members of the newly formed Jeff Beck Group and had appeared as guests on my late-night radio show.

Ronnie was friendly as always, and as soon as we saw each other there were big hugs. He was hanging with the Master Blaster, a photographer who was traveling with the band. The Blaster, who hailed from Boston, had helped me on my radio show and given me the nickname Woofa Goofa. Rod, however, was another story. Wearing fur mittens and decked out in scarves, a fitted long velvet coat, and skintight crushed-velvet bell-bottoms, with barely a glance, he walked right past.

His behavior surprised me, because we were often together searching for Sam Cooke rarities whenever he came to Boston. I enjoyed the Faces; they were loose, rocking, had a good time onstage, and Rod knew how to move the audience.

There were ninety thousand presold tickets, and the promoters expected 125,000 people, but by early afternoon, some reports suggested that there were at least two hundred thousand people on their way, creating miles of traffic jams. The weather was turning from good to bad; rain showers started in the afternoon, and heavy storm clouds moved in along with strong winds and fog. In subsequent years, this unpredictable combination of weather and crowds led some to deem the festival another Woodstock. The roads were so blocked with traffic that the

With manager Dee Anthony

promoters used helicopters to transport bands and crews back and forth between the hotel and the stage site.

As dusk fell, even the helicopters were grounded because of the heavy fog. For a brief spell, while the weather held clear, Dee had the foresight to ensure that all his bands got to the site, ready to perform in their allocated time slots. He slipped the copter pilots several C-notes and flew out Emerson, Lake & Palmer; Humble Pie; and the Geils band. Heavy rain started up again, and when it stopped, more than an hour later, the mountain air was cold and damp.

Watching from the makeshift tent area, we saw a sea of people lighting bonfires on the hills to keep warm and dry, looking like Greek armies camped in front of the gates of Troy.

The Faces' equipment was already onstage, anticipating their arrival. Dee spoke with the band's crew chief, advising him to fly the band over immediately before the fog caused further delays. The crew chief resisted, saying, "Just cool your jets. They'll get here when they get here."

The stage was set high, and all Dee's bands and crew were watching from down below. It was getting darker and colder, but I was feeling fairly at ease because Angel and I were snugly wrapped in a blanket to keep each other warm. She, though, was worried that Dee's temper might flare up as he paced back and forth on the stage, yelling to anyone within earshot, "The Faces better be on their way!"

The Faces had pulled this stunt several months earlier at the Mar y Sol festival in Puerto Rico, with a lineup that included David Peel, Elephant's Memory (John and Yoko were to be surprise guests, but John's visa problems kept them both in New York), Billy Joel, Dr. John, the Allman Brothers, Herbie Mann, Roberta Flack, and many other artists. We had played just before the Faces, and we connected with the crowd, even getting two encores. However, the Faces kept the helicopters waiting for almost two hours in an effort to build up anticipation and suspense in the audience.

Back in the Poconos, Dee gathered all his band's crew members together, forming a tight circle on the side of the stage. At least twenty of them surrounded him. Like a coach in a football huddle, he told them, "When I blow my whistle, I want you all to move fast and dismantle the Faces' equipment in the middle of the stage. If you want, you have my permission to even push or throw their damn shit right the hell off the fuckin' stage. Start setting up ELP's equipment. The Faces don't know who they're messing with, but if they don't show up soon, they're definitely gonna fuckin' find out."

The Bronx lurking inside Dee was like a tidal wave, growing larger by the minute as he continually checked his gold Rolex watch. A worried Angel pleaded, "Pete, please go up there and calm him down. He looks like he's going to explode."

"Angel, if I could, I would. There's no way he's gonna calm down unless the Faces show up damn quick or ELP starts playing."

When the rain began pouring down in sheets once again, Dee finally broke. He charged over to the Faces crew chief and screamed at him, "All right! Where the hell are they? I warn you, if they're not on this stage ready to play in ten minutes, it's gonna be showtime!" The crew chief inflamed an already dangerously combustible situation by answering, "Don't fucking give me orders, Grandpa. I don't work for you!"

At this, Dee landed him a punch, right smack on the jaw. As he fell, Dee stood over him and said, "Get up now, kid, and you'll get it twice as hard." Dee took the whistle hanging from his neck and blew it, all the while standing watch over the fallen crew chief.

At the sound of the whistle, Dee's crew jumped into action, pushing the Faces' equipment to the side of the stage and setting up for ELP. Dee walked over to our tent and yelled, "ELP, get up here. Geils, be ready — you're after them, then Humble Pie. We're taking over this fuckin' stage, and I'd like to dare any fucking body that's stupid enough to just try and stop us!"

The Faces' crew chief got up, rubbing his jaw, and stood on the opposite side of the stage. There was nothing he or the crew could do but watch. ELP started playing, and the crowds on the hill cheered in jubilation at the sound of the longed-for music. In the middle of the set, we heard helicopters arriving; the Faces were finally here.

The Faces approached the tented area with their assistants and manager. Their crew chief told them what had occurred, and we watched as he pointed out Dee up on the stage. It was like a scene in a dusty Wild West saloon as the assembled Faces band and crew entered the tent. Rod was truly pissed, and everyone looked accusingly at me, Angel, and the other bands.

What ensued next is a bit of a Rashomon moment.

As ELP was finishing its final song, Dee sent a crew member down to the tent, telling us to be ready to play because we were next. Just then, the Faces' manager and his crew hurried up the stairs to put back their equipment. Dee, in readiness, had our crew rush to set up our equipment. Band crews are like sailors on an old frigate — out at sea on long voyages, eating, drinking, and bunking together. They sometimes might hate each other, but if one member is attacked, there's nothing that will unify them more.

Our truck drivers, two brothers who were ex-Marines, were summoned to the stage by Dee. "Geils is next!" Dee bellowed as our crew went to work. Up the steps charged the Faces' manager, followed by their crew and two of the promoters. Our truck drivers flanked Dee. A promoter approached him and cautiously asked, "Could you please let the Faces play next?"

Dee responded, "Where the hell were you when they were dilly-dallying at the hotel, keeping not one but three of my acts waiting around in this fuckin' rain, in a shit-ass tent to boot? Not one band, not two bands, but three fuckin' bands — and if you fuck with me, I'll pull the other two!" That was a possibility the promoter didn't want to argue over, so he backed away.

When the Faces' manager saw this, he rushed over to Dee and shouted, "Who do you think you are, moving my band's equipment? I'm ordering you to let my band play next. You already robbed them of their given place on the bill!"

Dee replied, "What kind of manager worth his weight lets his band hold up an entire festival?"

"Listen here, Mr. Anthony, you and your people aren't scaring me. The Faces are going on next!" But as he finished this statement, he made the grave mistake of poking his finger into Dee's chest. *Bam!* Down he went, folding over like an accordion.

Between the fog and the rain, the schedule was running hours behind. I remember we went on after ELP at 2:30 a.m., followed by Humble Pie and, finally, the Faces. We could see the crowds on the hills, almost too wet and frozen to move. The band and I flew back on the copter while Dee and Angel, who wanted to see the rest of the show, remained on-site. When Angel returned to the hotel in the early morning, she woke me. "You should get up, Pete. Dee's in the hotel dining room with most of the crew, and you won't believe what happened."

I threw on my clothes and headed to the dining room, where Dee (whom I never saw drink beer) was sitting at a round table full of empty beer bottles. He was in the middle of reviewing the evening's events with the crew, like a general assessing the outcome of a recent battle. "Wolf, where the hell you been? You missed all the fireworks!" he said as he went back to detailing the events of the evening.

A full-on brawl broke out between our crew, the Faces' crew, and even the promoter's stage crew. Equipment was thrown offstage and instruments were wrecked, yet Dee, opening another beer, was as excited as a kid sitting on Santa's knee. He asked Angel to sit right next to him. "Wolf, while you were sleeping, this gal over here, she's a real trooper. She tried to keep people from getting up the stairway to the stage. When a guy pushed her away, Mullin here knocks him back down the steps like he was a bowling pin — hit straight on! You see, there's a lot more to management than just sitting around collecting a percentage."

It was a memorable moment in a year spent endlessly on the road. Angel and I stayed in touch, mostly by phone. She eventually moved back to Florida and ended up where she always dreamed of living, Key West. Ever the adventurous spirit, she met someone who also loved the ocean, and they were happily married. Her husband, Dirk Fisher, was a treasure hunter whose father searched the waters around Key West for shipwrecks in the hope of finding sunken treasure. In 1975 he discovered the wreck of the *Atocha*, which sank in the 1600s with around $450 million worth of gold, coins, and jewels aboard. Angel and her husband were part of the crew involved in the discovery. One night, as they were asleep on the haulage barge, a pump failed, causing it to sink. Both Angel and her husband were trapped and drowned.

Dee continued to manage artists, and when Peter Frampton left the group Humble Pie to go solo under Dee's guidance, he became a superstar, and by 1978 he was one of the bestselling artists in the entire recording industry. Dee was intoxicated by Frampton's success. He soon took on too many artists. In the following years, he was sued by Frampton and several of his other artists who claimed he was withholding money and taking more than his designated share of profits. The Geils band decided to split from Dee because of his overloaded roster and lack of interest in our career.

I met with him in his swank new offices and told him that things just weren't working out, and it would be best for all involved to part ways. However, we did owe Dee $35,000, which at that time was a lot of money for us. We promised to pay it back to him. Dee said he understood and appreciated the fact that I was meeting with him to discuss the matter face-to-face. "Wolf, we always got along. Just tell your band to forget about paying me the $35,000 they owe." He spit in his hand, I spit in mine, and we shook on it.

Although it appeared in later years that greed may have gotten the better of him, the week after we went our separate ways I received a small package in the mail. Inside was the two-dollar bill we had both signed some six years earlier, at a time when it seemed, to quote the title of the Faces album, "A nod's as good as a wink…to a blind horse."

I Rode This Dream

"WHERE I'M HEADED I
CAN'T BE SURE"

15

THE RED SHOES
Dorothy Faye

I REALLY LOVE SAN Francisco—don't get me wrong, Bryn—but whenever I hear that damn 'I Left My Heart in San Francisco,' it makes being here feel even lonelier." Bryn wasn't listening; she was concentrating on rolling a large braided stick of Thai weed with an odor so pungent it permeated the entire room.

Half interested, she replied, "Just have some of this—it'll chill you out."

"Bryn, I can't smoke that stuff. It's too damn strong, and besides, me and pot never seem to agree with each other."

Bryn Bridenthal was a respected public relations rep for *Rolling Stone* magazine at a time when it was still based in San Francisco, where the Geils band had arrived to play the following two nights to a sold-out crowd at the Winterland Ballroom, ending a multicity West Coast tour.

Bryn was in her twenties, thin and lanky, with short hair and straight-cut bangs that fell just above her oversize glasses, much too big for such a small face, but somehow they worked as her signature look.

Sensing my loneliness, she suggested, "Listen, Pete. I'll call a friend to come to the show tomorrow night. You might enjoy meeting her."

Feeling doubtful, I asked, "How do you know her?"

"Oh, we have mutual friends. She's pretty interesting, and speaking of pretty, she's damn good-looking, too."

At Winterland the following night, we made our way toward the stage, and there was Bryn in the swampy green light of the concrete hallway, huddled in conspiratorial girl talk with her friend, who was dressed in jeans, suede boots, a Naugahyde jacket, mirrored aviator sunglasses, and a large-brimmed floppy brown hat pulled so far down that it almost covered not only her curly brown hair but also her entire face. She looked like a Haight-Ashbury hippie, and however much Bryn may have liked her, this brief glimpse did not spark my interest.

They stood stageside, and I noticed the intensity with which Bryn's friend watched our performance. It was a dream audience; they called us back for three exhausting encores. Sweat-drenched, we couldn't wait to change and leave the venue after the show, but Bryn insisted that I meet her friend, Dorothy. We had a fairly innocuous introduction during which Dorothy thanked me for a wonderful show as the band and I made our way back to the hotel. Bryn and Dorothy asked for a lift, and they hopped in the back seat with our drummer. I rode shotgun next to our road manager and driver, Jim D. I glanced in the rearview mirror to see Bryn fast asleep, while Dorothy and the drummer kissed like teenagers in the back seat. We arrived at their destination, a bar where the mysterious Dorothy went off to meet someone else. I couldn't shake the sense that something about Dorothy was strangely familiar, like I had met her before but couldn't quite place where.

The following afternoon at my hotel, before I jumped in the shower, the phone rang. It was Dorothy, looking for Bryn and asking if she could wait in my room.

No problem, I said. I'd leave the door unlocked. When I emerged from the bathroom, half dressed in a robe, towel-drying my hair, Dorothy was sitting in one of the lounge chairs, trying to unknot a tangled bunch of fine silver and gold necklace chains. I just kept drying my hair, barely acknowledging her with an offhand "Hello there."

"I tried calling Bryn, but there's no answer," she said, breaking the silence. "You don't mind me waiting here, I hope?"

"No, not at all."

I offered her a cigarette before lighting mine.

"I must say I really enjoyed watching you work the crowd last night. The ease you have onstage and the stories you tell. Do you write them yourself? Or does someone help you with the dialogue?"

"Dialogue? That's just stage raps. I usually make 'em up on the spot."

"Really? How wonderful!"

"Well, it ain't Shakespeare, but it helps get us through the night."

"I find that fascinating...to go onstage and just wing it in front of so many people."

I thought she was laying it on a bit too thick and felt like quoting Bogart's line to a lying Mary Astor in *The Maltese Falcon:* "You're good. You're very good."

"So how was your night?" I asked.

"My friend at the bar is truly a very sweet person, but we don't really click, so we sort of...parted on friendly terms. But I see it accomplished what I wanted."

"What's that?" I asked.

"I finally got your attention."

That caught me by surprise. She spoke with her head lowered, deep in concentration, intent upon undoing the tangled chains, which gave me the opportunity to closely observe her for the first time.

Small little details I found quite captivating: the graceful way she smoked her cigarette; her casually pinned hair, elegant hands, and perfectly manicured nails; a perfume both subtle and pleasant; and her eyes and lips, so delicately Botticellian. I was wondering how last night's hippie girl could make such a complete and captivating transformation.

No hat, no sunglasses, no makeup, with her hair pulled off her face — it couldn't be. But instantly, I knew it was her.

"I still think it's quite a talent. Lord knows I couldn't do it," she said.

Now fully alert to the fact that I was sitting with one of the world's most alluring movie stars, I commented, "I probably couldn't do what you do, remembering lines, hitting marks, catching the light, take after take. That requires a whole other discipline," I said with true admiration.

"Perhaps, but I am fascinated by watching rock bands, especially yours."

"Who else have you seen?" I asked, curious to discover more about the mysterious Dorothy.

She rattled off a list of current radio favorites.

"They're all really talented, but they ain't what I'd define as my kind of rock-'n'-roll band," I said defiantly.

"Well, how do you define rock 'n' roll?"

"It's gotta swing. It's gotta be blues-based or gospel-based, with a bit of that country twang thrown into the mix. It's gotta move you — well, pardon my French, but move you in the groin. Now, there's a whole lot of rockers out there, and I ain't saying we're on any A-list, but the musicians I like all pretty much share the same roots: Muddy Waters, Howlin' Wolf, Hank Williams, Aretha, Buddy Holly, Elvis, and Otis Redding."

"Honey," she said excitedly, putting down the clump of necklace chains, "now you're speaking my language. I could listen to Otis Redding's *Otis Blue* album every day and not get tired of it — and, by the way, I usually do listen every day. As far as Hank Williams, sugar, I was weaned on Lefty Frizzell, Ernest Tubb, and Kitty Wells. My daddy and uncles were real drinking men. Some were musicians and played in country bands. They'd hit the honky-tonks on weekends and come home all bruised up, and as far as Elvis — me and my friends lost our voices for almost a week from screaming so hard the first time we saw him."

"You saw Elvis?"

"Three times. Mister, where I come from, almost every girl I knew with a beating heart couldn't wait till Elvis came to town. Otis, Sam Cooke, Aretha, Dylan, and Billie Holiday — I might have been raised hillbilly, but I sure didn't stay one."

"I had no idea you were from the South. Exactly where did you grow up?" I asked.

"I was an army brat. We traveled all through Europe, lived for a long time in Germany, then moved around the States. Most of my high school years were in Tallahassee. Don't get me wrong — I love some things about where I grew up, but I knew there was a whole lot more out there, and I wanted to find it."

Hours flew by as we sat talking away the afternoon. She had lived in Boston and received a theater scholarship to Boston University, working as a waitress in bars and restaurants to make ends meet. At twenty-one she moved to New York to study at the American National Theatre and Academy but was spotted by director Elia Kazan for his Repertory Theatre of Lincoln Center. After performing in several productions, she got the leading role in the Drama Desk Award–winning *Hogan's Goat*, written by Boston playwright and poet William Alfred, who remained her lifelong friend and mentor.

Dusk was settling in, signaling time for the band's sound check. She mentioned that she needed to be back in Stockton that night, where she was finishing *Oklahoma Crude*, a film with George C. Scott.

"I wish I could stay; I really do. I don't think I've relaxed and enjoyed myself like this in a very long time. Christmas is just around the corner. What are you doing for the holidays? Why don't you visit me in New York? I'd gladly see you in Boston, but my mother is coming to stay with me."

"Well, that could be a possibility," I was surprised to hear myself say.

"Oh, please come to New York."

And then, out of the blue, we were in the midst of a long, soft, and unexpected kiss.

Back in Boston, I received several phone calls from her, each one gently reminding me of her open invitation to spend the holidays with her in New York.

I took the leap and arrived in Manhattan, checking into the band's old haunt, the City Squire hotel, in midtown. It was an inexpensive place that had once seen better days and now mostly catered to traveling salesmen. In the lobby, unaccompanied painted ladies leisurely sat, waiting discreetly for a new friend. The doorman's last words upon check-in were usually "If there's anything you need, anything, don't hesitate to call. If it exists, we'll find it."

I called Faye and told her I was in the city. When she asked where I was staying, I vaguely said, "Just a midtown hotel."

"Which one?" she inquired. "I love hotels."

"Faye, you won't like this one. It's a bit...on the funky side. You pick a place to meet."

"But Peter, funky sounds intriguing. Please, let's meet there and then we can decide where to go."

I figured she must realize I wasn't rolling in dough, because in Frisco, I mentioned that the band was pretty much in debt, and we were just barely scraping by. There was no sense hiding that fact or pretending. I was reminded of a John Lee Hooker song, "Take Me as I Am."

I gave her my room number, and it wasn't long before there was a gentle knock at the door. As soon as I opened it, she threw her arms around me and whispered how much she had missed me.

"I love this place. The lobby is a real trip — you can tell there's a lot of wild stuff going on down there."

The TV was on, silently. She noticed the beginning of *Gunsmoke* and became excited. "I just love *Gunsmoke*! Could we watch it?"

I turned up the sound.

"Do you mind if I call room service and order a club sandwich? Do you want one?"

I replied no and didn't mention that, thanks to my slightly reduced circumstances, I had never used room service before. I handed her the phone, and she ordered. "I'll have your club sandwich, on white toast, of course, with bacon — please make sure it's done extra crispy — plus extra tomatoes, lotsa mayo, half-sour pickles, and two large glasses full of ice with two bottles of Coke."

Soon she was sitting beside me on the bed, munching on the sandwich, commenting, "This sandwich is fantastic! One of the best I've ever had, and believe me, I know my club sandwiches."

She was totally transfixed, eyes glued to the TV screen.

"You know, Peter, I just love Kitty. That actress Amanda Blake plays her so well. She's one of my favorites. Nobody ever gives her any credit for how talented she is."

It happened to be a *Gunsmoke* marathon night, so we sat in bed, watching episode after episode, and that's how we spent our first date.

The following day, she phoned, asking if I would join her and her mother for dinner at the Russian Tea Room. I knew of this illustrious place but had never been there. It was the kind of restaurant continually name-checked in the Out on the Town sections of newspapers.

"Now, listen," she said. "I'm inviting you as my guest, and it's quite improper for a guest to even think about paying," which was very thoughtful of her, since we were dining in such a grand location, well beyond my economic reach.

The Russian Tea Room was bustling, with waiters darting around in Russian-style dress — white Cossack shirts with puffy sleeves and crimson pants tucked at midcalf into black boots. The red walls were covered with an assortment of paintings in stylized gold frames. As I walked in and headed to the coat check, I was stopped, abruptly, by the assistant maître d', who informed me that there were no tables and no room at the bar. I knew the drill and replied firmly, "I didn't ask for a table or a seat at the bar."

"Then how can I help you, sir?" he replied in a condescending tone.

"First, I'd like to hang up my coat."

The head maître d' appeared, sensing some sort of problem. "Can I assist you, sir?" he asked, joining the blockade of my path to the coat check.

"Sir," I snarled, "you can help me by stepping aside so I can check my coat."

Just at that moment, Faye rushed over from inside the restaurant, took me by the arm, and led me to the table to join her mother.

As I passed the maître d', I lifted my sunglasses and said, in a mock Russian accent, "Please tell this woman to unhand me. This is outrageous. This kind of behavior will ruin my reputation, and while you're at it, can you please check my wrap?" Then I handed him my coat. Faye, leading the way, tossed her head back, laughing. Her stunning looks drew admiring glances from every person in the room.

When we were seated, I noticed her subtle makeup: pale green eye shadow, mascara, and rouge that heightened her already prominent cheekbones. She wore a figure-hugging low-cut blue satin dress. Her hair was pinned up, exposing a seductive neckline that would have driven Modigliani wild. She was picture-perfect, ready for her close-up, looking exactly like what she was, a movie star. I had a hard time realizing that this was the same woman who had watched *Gunsmoke* with me the night before.

Faye's mother was in her late fifties and spoke with a thick southern accent. She had a pleasant face and a heavy build, with hair permed and stiff from hair spray. I tried to engage her in conversation, but most of the night her mind seemed elsewhere, and there wasn't much interaction between her and Faye.

"Listen, Peter, Mother gets tired early. After dinner, why don't you join us back at my apartment, and you and I can listen to some records and have a nightcap or two?" Throughout dinner, Faye ordered us Russian imperials, small carafes of Russian vodka nestled in a silver bowl of crushed ice and poured straight up into thin, extremely cold glasses. They went down a little too easily.

Faye's apartment was in the historic El Dorado building, located at 300 Central Park West; it was jaw-dropping. The apartment spread across the entire twentieth floor and would have been the perfect setting for an Antonioni film. Sleek and contemporary, it had been gutted and redesigned by the famed architect Charles Gwathmey, sparing no expense. The long rectangular windows displayed panoramic views of Central Park West and Central Park South, and there were three large terraces, the smallest of which was bigger than my entire Cambridge apartment.

Faye's mother went straight to bed after we arrived. Faye put on Al Green's album *I'm Still in Love with You* and opened a bottle of champagne. At that point, the night became a scene from a 1940s film in which the camera pulls away toward the smoldering warmth of the fireplace then pans slowly over the skyline's distant lights, twinkling like diamonds on black velvet.

I was awakened in the morning by a gentle knocking on the bedroom door. A female voice with a thick Irish brogue asked, "Shall I bring in the breakfast tray, Miss Dunaway?"

"No, Mary," Faye replied. "I'll take it." I could hear the bedroom door slide open and shut.

"What's that all about?" I asked as Faye got back into bed.

"Oh, that was just Mary, the maid. I called her on the intercom and asked her to make us some coffee and tea. I wasn't sure what you drank in the morning."

"You have a maid?"

"Yes. Mary, dear heart, has been with me for years. She's from Ireland. She's in her late seventies, and she never stops working until she leaves, at five sharp." Faye jumped out of bed, saying, "I'm taking a shower. Why don't you check out of the City Squire and just stay here? Mother's making her famous pecan pie, and it's an all-day affair. You'd be very foolish to miss out on that."

I took her up on her invitation and checked out of the City Squire hotel.

Faye's uncle and his wife arrived from Tallahassee for the holidays. Neither had been to New York before. They were genuine, down-home country folk. One of their worn suitcases even had a rope tied around it to prevent it from popping open. I took an instant liking to her uncle, whom Faye called G.O.

The next morning I was awakened by a noise. I checked the time — 4:30 a.m. Faye was fast asleep, so I crept out of the room to find G.O. standing in the kitchen, wearing trousers with suspenders, an undershirt, and socks, one toe poking through. I asked him if there was something wrong.

"Oh, no. Hope my stirring around here didn't wake you. I'm an early riser; it's a habit from growing up on the farm." He shook coffee grounds into a saucepan, added around three inches of water, and set it on the stove to boil. Then he poured the mixture into a cup, grounds and all. From his back pocket, he took a half-pint of Jim Beam and sloshed a decent amount into the cup, then shot it straight down. "Mercy! Now, that's how we do it on the farm, and I'm telling you, it's the best way to get yourself up and at 'em. Care for one?"

"No, thanks, G.O. I'm gonna try to get back to sleep. I was just checking in on you."

"Son, got a minute?" He didn't wait for a reply. "Now, listen here. I got friends that work in the vice squad down in Tallahassee, and I'm sixty-three, and you know what I'm gonna do in two years, after I retire? I'm going straight into vice. That's right — straight into vice! I got it all figured out — who to cut in and who to cut out. It'll be legit, too: credit cards, the whole works." With that pronouncement, he took another swig of bourbon, then proceeded to sing a song he wrote when he played guitar in a country band.

> Come on, you fine young fellas,
> An' listen to my song
> About a red-haired woman
> She'll always do you wrong…

Uncle G.O. was just getting started. I lasted for five verses.

Faye's birthday is in January, and that year she wanted to celebrate in Boston, not only to be with me but also to visit her beloved mentor, William Alfred. It was an opportunity for me to spend time with this renowned man who was held in high regard by many of my friends. I had had brief encounters with him previously and looked forward to getting to know him better.

I was a little nervous about Faye seeing where I lived after being in her luxurious New York apartment. Located on the top floor of a red-brick three-story walk-up, my place was in a building that housed mostly musicians, writers, painters, and other eccentric characters. The rent was cheap, and the atmosphere was funky, with kitchen floorboards painted a bright Shaker yellow and framed posters, photographs, prints, and artwork covering the walls. The rooms were stacked with guitars and amplifiers, and there were curved bay windows, a working fireplace, and a Victorian-style red-velvet couch. Faye seemed immediately taken with the place. I guess for her, it felt like being in a garret in Montmartre in the 1920s. Our reunion was comfortable from the moment she came through the door.

When friends dropped by, Faye was a generous hostess, putting everyone at ease. There was always music on the turntable or visiting musicians playing in the living room. She let her hair down and once again became the Dorothy Faye who attended Boston University and worked six nights a week as a waitress.

She, Bill Alfred, and I celebrated her birthday at the Athens Olympia restaurant, located in the heart of Boston's theater district. It was frequented by actors, playwrights, and visiting poets and was known as much for its superb Greek cuisine as for its exquisitely made gin martinis. Bill Alfred was a rare gentleman indeed, the living embodiment of Mr. Chips. The evening and conversation were as fulfilling as I had hoped, and after we sent Bill home in a taxi, Faye and I went dancing at the rough-and-tumble Hillbilly Ranch, a western-themed roadhouse in Boston's combat zone, right alongside the Trailways bus station. We danced for hours on the sawdust floor, and I discovered that this country girl sure knew how to move.

During the day I would rehearse with the band while Faye and Bill went through the script of her new project, *The Three Musketeers*, an all-star remake of the film based on Alexandre Dumas's novel, scheduled to shoot in Spain over the following two months. The director was Richard Lester, who filmed the first two Beatles movies and many famous British comedies, along with *The Goon Show* radio program, which featured Peter Sellers. Faye had her agent negotiate an extra round-trip first-class ticket for me, thereby making it possible for us to be together during filming. I had never been to Spain, so the chance to spend time not only with Faye but also with Velázquez and Goya at the Prado was an offer I just couldn't refuse.

Faye had a large suite at one of Madrid's grand hotels, the Queen Isabella, where much of the cast was also in residence. Curiously, Faye was receiving many phone calls from Jack Nicholson regarding a new project, and she, in turn, made endless calls to her tenacious agent, Sue Mengers. Apparently not everyone involved in this mysterious project was as enthusiastic about Faye's participation as Nicholson was, but the calls kept coming at all hours.

For one week, the shooting location moved from Madrid to a small seacoast town, Dénia, in southern Spain. The hotel options were limited. When costar Raquel Welch secured the suite Faye had requested, I could feel tension brewing. We ended up in a run-down two-story stucco hotel with cracks on the outer walls exposing bent wire and weathered bricks. We had to walk through a little lobby where thin flea-bitten dogs lay about and old men, wearing Basque berets and dressed in black, sat at tables and played dominoes. As we entered, all eyes, even the dogs', turned toward us. A sense of foreboding filled the air as we were led upstairs by the owner to our room. It was small and painted acid yellow, with two old, sagging mattresses atop rusting bed frames on either side. Above one bed was taped a map of Spain; over the other hung an iron crucifix. In the back of the room were two narrow glass doors that opened onto a tiny balcony overlooking a rocky Mediterranean beach littered with driftwood. We could see black birds picking around the rocks and seaweed. To top it all off, the shower and bathroom were in the hall.

This dismal accommodation sent Faye into an unpleasant downward swing, a trait of hers that I would later come to know all too well.

I enjoyed being on set and witnessing the process of moviemaking. Filming was hard work, and any unexpected delays could make the atmosphere tense, since the stakes were so high and time costs money.

Christopher Lee was playing the role of Comte de Rochefort, and during one of the film's innumerable sword fights, he had been injured. An imposing figure known for portraying devilishly sinister characters, he was an engaging conversationalist. It was early afternoon, and as I was walking by the open door of his trailer, Lee invited me in. Sitting with him while he rested his sprained shoulder was the eccentric actor and comedian Spike Milligan, a star on *The Goon Show*. Both men were several glasses into a nearly empty bottle of Johnnie Walker. Lee was ranting that his injury was no fault of his, since he was trained as an expert swordsman, and recounted his many missions as a special forces officer in the Royal Air Force. "Why, I could outduel anyone on this set!" he loudly exclaimed in full theatrical voice to Milligan and me.

Suddenly we were interrupted by one of the director's assistants, who reported that a near disaster had occurred on set.

According to him, a sailing vessel carrying Charlton Heston, as the Cardinal, was to be greeted onshore by Faye and a group of her armored soldiers. It took the entire day to light the scene and practice securing the rowboats that carried the Cardinal from ship to shore.

The long, hot afternoon was surely sweltering for Faye, dressed in a heavy wig and layered gown with a tightly laced bodice. Richard Lester was worried about losing the light. Eventually, all cameras and lights were in place. The costumed actors hit their marks on the beach as the armored soldiers, with lances and flags, rowed small boats out to meet the ship. Just as Lester was about to shout "Action" — and while Lee, Milligan, and I were enjoying the bottle, oblivious to the drama taking place outside — there was a loud cracking noise coming from the ship. As if in slow motion, it began to sink. Total bedlam broke out. It was obvious that there wasn't much that could be done. Everyone watched, wide-eyed, as the actors and crew escaped to safety and the ship sank. Plans were made to try to raise it or find a replacement, but that meant a delay of several days and losses on an already tight budget.

Being marooned in our dreary hotel was not something either of us was looking forward to. Faye, fortunately, packed a large case filled with bottles of wine, gin, and cognac. When we arrived back at the hotel, we tried to order room service, but the menu was limited to paella.

We were starving. As soon as the food arrived, I poured us both wine, and we began to eat. I noticed that Faye was staring at me.

"What's wrong?"

"Peter! You eat like some escaped convict on the run. Hasn't anyone showed you the proper way to use your knife and fork?"

"But this is how I've always eaten."

"Well, mister, this is not the Bronx, and you're not on my uncle G.O.'s farm. It's high time someone showed you the proper way to use your knife and fork."

For the next hour, I observed then repeated her demonstration. First I learned the correct American style, followed by the English style, and finally the formal European style. I admired her for wanting to better me, but to this day, I still hold my knife and fork as if they were shovels.

Faye was becoming moodier the longer we stayed in this depressing place. Although I couldn't swim, I thought it would be adventurous to at least put my feet into the Mediterranean. Because I didn't have a bathing suit, Faye let me wear the only thing she had — a vintage knitted ladies' one-piece from the 1920s. Not wanting to accompany me, she lit a joint and watched from the balcony. I couldn't really blame her: I was a comical sight, with my pale, skinny body, biblical rocker beard, and sunglasses, wearing a woman's bathing suit, gingerly making my way across the rocky beach. Malnourished dogs prowled about, hoping I had food.

As I put each foot into the cold, shallow, murky water, I turned and waved to Faye on the balcony, and she gave an unenthusiastic wave back. I was around two feet from the shore when suddenly an incredible electric pain shot through my entire body. I fell into the water, and when I tried to stand, I realized something was wrong with my right foot. In agonizing pain, I yelled up to Faye, "I don't think I can move; I can't move!"

Wondering what was wrong, she shouted back, "I'll be right there!"

I thought I was going to faint as I saw Faye rushing toward the beach with two men from the lobby. "Ay, caramba! No! No!" They tried to explain to Faye that I must be carried back, for I had stepped on a sea urchin, which shot small sharp needles into the base of my right foot. "No bueno, no bueno — malo, malo!"

They lifted me from the water, carried me back to our room, and placed me on the bed. At the sight of my foot, Faye became worried. The sole had swollen and turned a shiny black-and-blue color. "Is there a doctor? We need to get him help!" She ran to the only phone, in the lobby, and called the production headquarters in Madrid, asking them to urgently notify the on-set doctor and have him come as quickly as possible.

By the time the doctor arrived, the pain was feverishly intense. I had to be rushed to Madrid, where there were several doctors waiting. The urchin's sharp spikes needed to be removed because the stingers can be poisonous and even fatal.

I felt terrible about the mayhem I was causing. Faye was understandably concerned about me but also relieved, because it gave us both an excuse to check out of that run-down hotel. The doctors numbed my foot and spent more than three hours removing the sharp needles.

The last movie scene I witnessed was a catfight between Faye, as Milady, and Raquel Welch, as Constance. In the script, Faye's character attempts to grab a piece of paper from Raquel's hand and pushes her. When the cameras rolled, Faye pushed her so hard that it stunned Raquel and everyone else on the set. This continued with each take, and with every push Faye became even more forceful. It was obvious to us all that this was no accident.

Finally, Raquel refused to do another take if Faye continued to push her with that level of ferocity. Yet on the final take, Faye did it again, and Raquel fell, spraining her ankle. Faye's aggression toward her seemed out of proportion to the loss of a hotel room. The reason did not come to light until many years later, when Faye married Terry O'Neill, Raquel's purported lover at the time of filming.

On one of my many days in Spain I happened to look at a *Vogue* magazine and noticed a striking fashion illustration by Antonio Lopez. I thought it, or something like it, would make a unique album cover. I showed Faye. She, coincidentally, knew Antonio, who lived in Paris. In this seemingly golden time in our relationship, we followed our whims wherever they took us. So when the filming was over, we flew off to Paris and stayed at a small hotel on the Left Bank, not far from Notre Dame

Cathedral. I was unaware that Antonio was such a highly respected art-ist in the fashion world. He shared a spacious apartment with his long-time lover, Juan Ramos, and a visiting guest, a very young and beautiful lady named Jerry Hall, who was just beginning her modeling career.

Jerry had a thick Texan accent. Neither she nor I spoke French, as everyone else did, a mutual awkwardness that connected us, much to the annoyance of Faye. One evening, Jerry and I were gazing out the window to the building across the street, where we could see an elderly man watching TV. This ordinary Parisian turned out to be Jean-Paul Sartre. Only in Paris could one see an incongruous sight such as a great philoso-pher in front of the television.

Antonio, using actual makeup, drew the eyes and lips of both Faye and Jerry on a large sketch pad. He worked quickly and extremely accurately. His renderings became the cover for the Geils album *Ladies Invited.*

Faye and I enjoyed Paris, visiting cafés and museums during the day and attending dinner parties at night. One afternoon we lunched with Jean-Paul Belmondo, who was even more striking in person than on-screen. Faye was fluent in French, but I didn't understand one word of their conversation. Still, I enjoyed watching these two mesmerizing movie stars. After lunch we headed to the Ritz for French 75s, but back at the hotel, late that evening, Faye went into one of her dark moods, the first since we had left Spain.

She took a bottle of cognac and locked herself in the bedroom. An hour passed. I could tell she had fallen asleep. Her moods worried me: they seemed to descend from nowhere, and chasing them with alcohol certainly didn't help. I decided it was probably best for me to leave her and Paris behind. The night clerk was fast asleep behind the small check-in desk when I woke him to find out how I might reserve a plane ticket and transportation to the airport. I fumbled, mimed, and spoke slowly, but he didn't understand me at all.

I went back upstairs and quietly opened the door, where I found Faye awake. I explained why I thought it best to leave, but she didn't want me to go. Instead, she suggested we walk along the Seine. She threw on her fur-lined beige trench coat over her nightgown, slipped on fire-engine-red Louis Vuitton high heels, and took me by the arm, saying, "Why are we in here when all of Paris is waiting out there?" It sounds corny now, but in that impetuous moment, it sounded so right.

We walked arm in arm while the sun rose slowly and the illumination from the streetlamps faded. Faye kicked off her shoes and wanted to dance. We began a slow foxtrot, swinging around and around, but as I dipped her, we almost ended up in the river. Laughing, we watched the sunrise reflected in the rippling water as the bells of Notre Dame began ringing for early morning mass. Faye took my hand and started running toward the church. "Oh, please — let's both go to mass!" Once inside the gray walls of the cavernous cathedral, with her scarf around her head, she seemed lost in some meditative prayer. The pews were full of faces illuminated by incense-filled shafts of sunlight, and it was then I noticed that Faye was barefoot. As the mass ended, we raced back along the river, hoping to find those elegant shoes, but like the morning sky, they had gone.

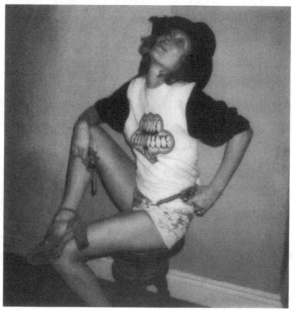

Shootin' high!

16

IT'S ONLY A MOVIE
Alfred Hitchcock

CARE FOR A drink? How about a nice single-malt scotch? Steve McQueen sent me a case of the stuff."

It was just two in the afternoon. "Well, are you having one?" I asked.

"Me? No. I got two big meetings back-to-back, but just make yourself comfortable. I can have Carlos bring anything you want."

This was the home of Freddie Fields, who at the time was one of the most powerful agents in Hollywood. His agency represented Faye and many other top stars and directors. We had met at various charity functions and later, memorably, at a dinner party at Connie Wald's house. Connie was the widow of producer Jerry Wald, who was rumored to be the inspiration for the unsympathetic, hard-bitten protagonist in Budd Schulberg's novel *What Makes Sammy Run?* In the early 1970s, intimate dinner parties were still very much in vogue among the old guard of the Hollywood elite.

Freddie spoke with a heavy New York accent and looked as if he had spent his entire day poolside. He dressed "LA casual" while radiating an aura of power. He wore distinctive turtlenecks under partially unbuttoned thin linen shirts, loose chinos, and smart deck shoes. I once remarked how much I liked his turtlenecks and inquired where he bought them. "They're an Italian cotton lisle–silk blend. Where you staying? I'll send you a box."

Turns out they came from Bijan, on Rodeo Drive, and back then each one cost several hundred dollars.

While Freddie was waiting for his two thirty meeting, his stunning and exotic ladyfriend joined him in the bar area. She was somebody I'd recognize years later as the star of *Dynasty*, Joan Collins. Freddie offered to call the studios and send over any film I might want to see in his private screening room during his meetings. I chose *Your Cheatin' Heart*, starring George Hamilton as Hank Williams.

Freddie was taken aback by my request. "You're kidding! You wanna pick *Your Cheatin' Heart*? Of all the movies you can choose from? Of all the movies in Hollywood's most extensive film libraries, you pick a fuckin' George Hamilton movie?"

Being a Hank Williams fan, I had always been curious about the film, which at that time was unavailable to the general public because of lawsuits involving Williams's estate. It was also rumored that Elvis Presley was first asked to star as the lead, but his manager, Colonel Tom Parker, had vetoed it because he couldn't obtain the publishing rights to Hank's songs.

Cocktail hour at Fields's grand château was a gathering of top Hollywood agents, stars, and extremely eager starlets. I was always searching for a way to improve the Geils band's contract with our label, Atlantic Records, and I thought recording a soundtrack might widen our exposure and enable us to negotiate a better deal. So I chose to stay behind after the band had finished a string of West Coast dates to try to secure such a deal. I asked Freddie if he knew of any directors or perhaps a film that might be in search of a soundtrack.

"I'll put some feelers out, kid, and let you know," he said, an unlit cigar and a drink in hand.

Two days later, one of his secretaries called, asking if I could meet with the film director and producer Roger Corman. I was excited at the prospect of meeting the man called the King of the B's and the King of the Drive-Ins. Corman was known for making low-budget horror, monster, and biker films geared toward the growing teenage market. He was also known for taking a chance on newcomers in the industry. He helped jump-start the careers of numerous actors and directors, including Francis Ford Coppola, Martin Scorsese, Peter Bogdanovich, Jack Nicholson, and Robert De Niro.

We were to meet at three in the afternoon at his office in West Hollywood, along Sunset Boulevard. Ideas for soundtracks to films like *The Wild Racers, Devil's Angels,* and *Attack of the Crab Monsters* were all racing through my head.

Mr. Corman had a modest but tasteful office on an upper floor of one of the few multistory high-rises on the Sunset Strip. An attractive and studious-looking secretary led me in. As I entered, he stood up to greet me. He was well groomed, with trimmed, graying hair, and he wore lightly tinted eyeglasses. Dressed in a fitted blue sport coat, an open-necked pink shirt, and gray slacks, he projected a smart, even somewhat European air.

"Thank you for coming," he said in a pleasant voice. "Freddie mentioned you were looking for a film that might need a soundtrack. Usually, it's an idea that would very much appeal to me. Unfortunately, I've stopped producing new works at the moment. I've recently only been involved in the distribution of foreign films, but if I do hear of something that might make sense, I'll surely let Freddie know."

Perhaps the meeting was just a favor to Freddie, because this was something Mr. Corman could have easily relayed by phone. But by taking the time to tell me in person, he revealed his natural curiosity about people and their ideas. We talked at length about Boston's many fine-art cinemas — specifically, the Brattle Theatre, in Cambridge, whose owner, Bryant Haliday — someone I'd known — was himself an actor and a producer of B films, including the 1960s works *Devil Doll* and *Curse of the Voodoo.* Along with the Brattle Theatre, Bryant owned the 55th

Street Playhouse, in New York, and had cofounded the prestigious Janus Films distribution company.

It was an honor to meet with Mr. Corman, someone who had spent his entire career free from the large studios and corporate entities encroaching upon the film world. Like Sam Phillips, the stand-alone force who first recorded a young Elvis, Howlin' Wolf, Johnny Cash, and Jerry Lee Lewis, Corman remained an independent maverick, and I found him to be intelligent, thoughtful, and a genuine gentleman.

I spent ten days hanging out in LA, hoping for some promising meetings. Fortunately, my good friend Earl McGrath, president of Rolling Stones Records, had a house in the city. Earl, one of the wittiest people I knew, never liked to be alone. He insisted that I attend his late afternoon cocktail gatherings, which always preceded the most memorable evenings. Dinner guests were an illustrious mix presided over by Earl's warm and engaging wife, Camilla. It wouldn't be unusual to find Joan Didion and her husband, John Gregory Dunne, painter David Hockney, actor Harrison Ford, author Christopher Isherwood, agent Swifty Lazar, and notable couple Anjelica Huston and Jack Nicholson among the guests who gathered there. However, in spite of my starry socializing, I still had no firm leads.

I was planning to fly back to Boston when one morning a call came from Freddie. "Peter, hold on to your hat. I just arranged a meeting for you with Alfred Hitchcock!"

My complete disbelief resulted in several seconds of dead air.

"Peter, are you there? I've gotten you a meeting with Hitchcock!"

I couldn't believe my ears. I had once been briefly introduced to Hitchcock in passing while dining at Chasen's with Faye. He had been keeping a low profile in Hollywood since the disappointments of his previous two films.

"What could possibly make him interested in me?" I asked.

Freddie explained, "He's working on a project that he hopes can attract a younger audience. Who knows? Your soundtrack idea might appeal to him. He can be so unpredictable. Whatever you do, though, don't be late. Hitch is a stickler for being on time." Freddie said the meeting would be at Hitchcock's home in Bel Air at two o'clock the following afternoon.

In my hotel room I sat dazed, visualizing his face stepping into the line-drawing caricature at the start of his television show. Flickering images from his many classic films ran through my mind. What I needed was a Valium and a good stiff drink. I canceled my plane reservation, sent out my only suit to be pressed overnight, and, since I didn't know how to drive, ordered a limo for early the next day. I passed on the stiff drink, but I did take the Valium.

In the morning I called the concierge and asked to have my pressed suit delivered to the room. "Mr. Wolf, your suit won't be ready until tomorrow."

"Tomorrow! It was due back today!"

The concierge responded in a dry, clipped voice — the kind you'd expect from a frustrated dealer of fine French porcelain — "I'll check, sir, but I don't believe you marked next-day delivery on your ticket."

I panicked. He was right; I didn't remember marking the slip. I swallowed my pride and asked, "Well, then, where can I buy a black suit? I'll need it early this afternoon."

He mentioned Giorgio's, on Rodeo Drive. Little did I know that it was one of the most expensive clothing stores in the country. For the cost of one suit I could've lived in Paris for a month. Instead I took a cab to a tuxedo-rental place and thought, *If Cary Grant can wear one, so can I.* Well, obviously, I'm no Cary Grant. As soon as I saw myself in the rental-store mirror, I was hit with a stronger anxiety attack than the one I had the day before. A tux was not for me.

I finally found a suit in a thrift shop. I was thoroughly exhausted by the time I returned to my hotel.

The limo came early, as ordered, and we headed out toward Bel Air, following Freddie's firm directive to not be late. We arrived near Mr.

Hitchcock's house, on Bellagio Road, a full hour before the appointed time. I asked the driver to pull over to the curb and wait. As the two o'clock NPR news came on the radio, we drove through the gates and up the path to Hitchcock's home.

It was a modest and tasteful two-story English country house that would have been the perfect setting for a classic Agatha Christie mystery. The house and garden stood in stark contrast to the grand estates that populated Beverly Hills and Bel Air. The limo driver let me out. Then the front door to the house opened wide, and rather than a butler or maid to greet me, there he stood, the master himself.

I was in awe, unprepared to meet this icon, yet I tried to appear as relaxed as possible. When I approached the doorway, he bent his head forward and greeted me with that recognizable and often imitated voice: "Good afternoon. Thank you for coming." He pronounced each word distinctly and extremely slowly, exactly as he did in his many movie trailers and on his popular television series.

We walked together through the vestibule, filled with freshly cut flowers. The walls were hung with important paintings in gilded frames, among which was a Rouault (one of my favorite artists). We entered a small, sunny sitting room carpeted with a light-blue-and-pink antique rug, with two windows that framed a view of an idyllic manicured garden. A couch and two chairs, upholstered in a delicate flowered pattern, furnished this genteel room. Centered on the polished cherrywood coffee table was an art deco vase holding a neatly arranged bouquet. Around it, magazines were carefully stacked in several piles.

He sat on one end of the couch, I on the other. "What can I get you to drink?" he asked.

I sensed that this was his way of checking to see if I was one of those hard-drinking, drugged-out, unreliable rock-and-rollers.

"Nothing — thank you, Mr. Hitchcock. I'm okay."

"Nothing? Not even a little nip?"

"Oh, no. Just plain tea with a dash of milk or cream would be fine." I hoped that such a distinguished Englishman would deem this proper.

"Tea, Mr. Wolf? Nothing to spike it up a bit?"

Now I was convinced he was testing me.

"Tea is fine, if it's not too much of a bother. Was that a Rouault that we passed in the hallway?" I asked, trying to start a conversation. "And is that a Klee over on that wall?"

"You seem to have an interest in painting."

"Yes. Before I got into music, I studied painting. And speaking of Klee, I studied with the son of Lyonel Feininger, who taught with Klee at the Bauhaus."

"What styles did you paint?" he asked.

"I guess the German expressionists are my biggest influences. My first painting, which I did at age eleven, was a copy of an Emil Nolde work. From there, I went on to Kirchner and Beckmann. I also have a great fondness for Soutine."

"Soutine? You love Soutine? Why, I own a Soutine!" he exclaimed.

"A Soutine! I'd love to see it."

"I'd like to show it to you, but perhaps some other time. It's in the next room, where I think my wife is resting. Are you sure you wouldn't like a drink or a light cocktail of sorts — perhaps an aperitif?" he asked again. When I politely declined his offer, he seemed disappointed.

Frowning, he looked down at his watch and said, "Pardon me." He walked across the room, picked up the phone receiver, and dialed. He waited a moment, then put the receiver to his chest. After a minute or so, he spoke several words into the phone, then mysteriously hung up. As he slowly walked back to the couch, he mentioned that he just had his heart checked. "Can you believe it? I call a number in Washington, DC, they listen to my heart, then they call my doctor in Los Angeles, and he sends me the findings. All quite amazing, what they can do these days."

A maid arrived with my tea. "How is it?" he inquired.

"Perfect," I replied. "Just the way I like it."

"You wouldn't like a little something else with it?" he asked, speaking more slowly than usual.

"Oh, no. The tea is just fine."

In reality, what I would have loved was a good stiff gin martini.

"Well, I'm making a film presently titled *Deceit*. It's going to have a cast of young actors."

I slowly sipped my tea, hoping he would ask if I had any interest in participating on a soundtrack.

"So much has changed over the years, especially with actors. I never had patience for Method acting. Now, take Charles Laughton. Though he worked long before the Method came along, Laughton would drive me insane. One day we were doing a scene in which he was walking across a floor. He would ask me what kind of shoes he should be wearing. Dryly, I replied, 'Ones that fit.' But no, that wasn't good enough for him. He needed to spend time walking in the shoes. At one point, he asked, 'What's my motivation for walking in this scene?' I became most impatient. I yelled, 'Charles! Like a chicken, to get to the other side! Now walk them shoes over here and let's get this damn scene finished!' Can you imagine? He needed to have an entire psychological motivation just for his damn shoes."

With a sideways glance, he asked, "You're not changing your mind about a little afternoon pick-me-up, are you? A glass of sherry, perhaps?"

I was craving a drink, but I stood fast. "No, sir. The tea is perfect."

"All actors are somewhat insecure," he continued. "And, of course, the women are even more so. Take Grace Kelly, whom I always enjoyed working with. She's aware of her beauty, aware of her talent, and, most important, aware of her limitations. We had a funny encounter while filming *To Catch a Thief*. We were on location in the South of France, about to do a ballroom scene with Cary Grant. Edith Head, who has been my costume designer, and a great one at that, designed a beautiful gold evening gown for Grace. As the technicians were setting up the lights for the scene, Edith brought Grace into my office to show me her gold dress. Now, how can I politely say this? Grace was known for not having too much up top, and that gold dress accentuated the issue, so I said to Edith, 'How about a little more in this area?' as I held my hands out in front of my chest. Ten minutes later, Edith returned with Grace, having put several layers of foam padding in her bra. I said, 'Grace, now there is hills in them thar gold!'"

Hitchcock laughed so loudly that it was as if he were hearing the story himself for the first time.

I'd finished my tea. Without saying anything, he mimed lifting a stemmed glass to his mouth. Again, I told him I was fine. He then abruptly got up from the couch, thanked me for visiting him, and added, "Let me walk you to the door." I thanked him for taking the time to meet with me and said I hoped I could come back, not just to enjoy his company but also to see his Soutine painting. "Yes. I'm sure that can be arranged."

Those were his last words to me; the driver already had the limo door open. We drove out of the gates and headed back to my hotel. Something didn't seem quite right, and I couldn't put my finger on exactly what it was. I didn't drink or smoke during the visit, which I presumed was appropriate behavior on my part. But still, something did not sit well.

As we approached Sunset Boulevard, we passed a landmark bar called the Cock'n Bull. It was famous for its clientele of old Hollywood stars, directors, newspapermen, and the hard-drinking Rat Pack. The staff made sure no celebrities were bothered by tourists or autograph seekers. All during my meeting with Mr. Hitchcock, I was craving a drink, and this was a good place to, shall we say, tie one on. That's exactly what I did — with bull shots. I heard that Humphrey Bogart ordered them back in the days when he and the original Rat Pack would frequent this place.

It was dark when I left the bar, feeling a bit tipsy and still somewhat disturbed about my meeting. Perhaps I should have been more aggressive. Everything seemed to be spinning as the limo driver took me back to my hotel.

The movie Hitchcock finally made was retitled *Family Plot*. It was to be his last film. For the lead role, he wanted Jack Nicholson, who, perhaps because of scheduling conflicts, turned him down, so he chose actor Bruce Dern. Karen Black costarred, and it was reported that she needed endless Method motivations before most of her scenes. The soundtrack was supplied by the popular and talented composer John Williams.

Years later, after Hitchcock's death, there were many biographies written about his life. I read several, and one detail caught my eye. Hitchcock's wife, who played an important role in his artistic decisions, strictly frowned upon his drinking alone at home in the afternoon. He could indulge, but only in the company of a guest.

So much for trying to impress the master with my fine, upstanding sobriety. But as he often enjoyed saying to his actors, "Why worry? It's only a movie."

17

THE DEEP END
Chinatown

IN 1974, THE Geils band and I had spent months touring before finally winding up in Wisconsin. Faye, on a brief hiatus prior to beginning her next project, joined us in Madison, where a blizzard was predicted for several days after her arrival. Our next gig was in Minneapolis, but with flights canceled, we were worried that we'd be snowed in. So we rented the only transportation available: a run-down old school bus, complete with a retired mailman as the driver.

The snow began with only a light powder as we set off on the four-and-a-half-hour journey. Soon the snow thickened, and the bus's heater broke. We slowed to around thirty miles an hour. After five hours, we were still only halfway to our destination. Our breath was visible as we shivered in the intense cold of the bus. Faye, however, seemed quite happy, saying, "It's like back in the days of Billie Holiday or Peggy Lee, traveling with the big bands." She had several bottles of Rémy Martin and a good supply of Bolivian marching powder, which she generously shared with several band members at the back of the bus in what turned out to be a freezing eight-hour ordeal.

Faye enjoyed life on the road, especially interacting with our ex-Marine truck drivers, the Mullin brothers, who were like older siblings to her. They would hang out together on the equipment cases during sound checks, and if there wasn't a drive the next day, you could be sure to find them with her in the hotel bar. Whenever Faye was recognized, they would act as her protective shield. Nobody was foolish enough to mess with the Mullin brothers.

After all the mysterious late-night calls in Spain, it finally came to light that Faye's next project would be *Chinatown*, directed by Roman Polanski and with a screenplay by Robert Towne. Jack Nicholson would costar. Jane Fonda was the producers' first choice for the role of Evelyn Mulwray, and Polanski had wanted Julie Christie, but Nicholson pushed for Faye. It created tension from the start. Faye's agent, Sue Mengers, a gruff, short, heavyset woman who spoke like a truck driver and was tough as nails, handled the deal. Sue and Faye had a volatile relationship for one main reason: Sue represented most of the top leading ladies, including Barbra Streisand, and Sue made sure Barbra got the first and best offers before any of her other clients did.

Faye headed out to Los Angeles while the band and I did one-night stands across Texas with ZZ Top. For some unknown reason, the group brought two large buffaloes with them, positioning one on each side of the stage during their performances. We enjoyed playing with the group, but the promoters always placed our dressing rooms near the pen where ZZ Top kept the buffaloes, and we couldn't avoid the intense odor of their never-ending shit piles.

Faye didn't sound happy when we talked on the phone. She wanted me to join her in Los Angeles as soon as I had a break, which I did, leaving the buffalo stench for Faye's midcentury-modern rental house, a gleaming glass box set high atop Bel Air. When I arrived, the housekeeper informed me that Faye would be late getting back from rehearsal.

I looked around. Even the ornate telephone seemed as if it were a prop from a 1930s French film.

Later that evening, the door opened, and Faye came in carrying scripts, books, and notepads, giving me a long kiss and letting everything fall to the floor. She sank into the couch, exhausted, saying, "I'm so glad you're finally here. Peter, darling, I need a drink, a large drink."

"What would you like?"

"Anything. Why not just bring the bottle?"

After a healthy slug of Rémy Martin, she let her head fall back against the couch, saying, "This movie is going to be a mountain of trouble — I can feel it already. Oh, God, I hope I don't have another Otto on my hands."

She was referring to the director Otto Preminger. He had once signed Faye to a five-picture deal. Otto was known to be extremely harsh and abusive, especially with actresses. After making one movie with him, *Hurry Sundown*, Faye unsuccessfully sued him, demanding that he release her from the contract, citing overt cruelty. She eventually had to buy herself out of the deal.

The next day she left early for a read-through with the cast and Polanski. When she returned that afternoon, she was in a fury.

"What's going on?" I asked.

"I knew it! It's like talking to a fucking brick wall. Now he wants me to be a bleached blonde! I can't fucking believe it."

I was about to say, "What's the big deal?" when she exploded.

"I'm not doing it! It's so fucking cliché. The noir blonde. Next he'll probably ask me to wear my hair to one side like Veronica Lake. I finally compromised and offered to wear a blond wig. That bastard said no, because he never liked Barbara Stanwyck's wig in *Double Indemnity*. That film was damn good, in my opinion. We should be so lucky. What about Mary Astor in *The Maltese Falcon* or Ava Gardner in *The Killers*? They didn't dye their hair, so why the hell should I?"

The phone rang. It was Sue Mengers. Faye carried it to her bedroom, anger revving up, before closing the door with a bang, saying, "Sue, I'm not touching my hair!"

Twenty minutes later, she emerged to announce: "Now Polanski wants to meet with me, tonight or tomorrow."

"Why not meet him?" I answered, not knowing how she might react. I tried reasoning with her. "It's like a fire on the verge of going wild. It might be good to try to put it out sooner rather than later."

"Would you go with me tonight? I don't want to be alone with him."

"Of course I'll go."

We sped off through hills and valleys in her white Mercedes convertible. I enjoyed watching Faye drive, cigarette dangling from the side of her mouth. Her concentration on the road was intense, as if she were aiming at a moving duck in a penny arcade game. We came to a densely forested area, tucked into which was a modernist wood-frame house. Roman greeted us at the door. Faye introduced me as he led us into a dark and rustic sitting room, with antlers, muskets, and Native American and African paraphernalia on the walls. Apparently Roman was leasing the house from actor George Montgomery, and the decor came with the rent.

Polanski was short, quite muscular, and fit, with brown hair that curled over his ears. He wore a tight gray T-shirt, beige pants, and sandals with white socks. The room was dimly lit except for a healthy fire ablaze in the stone fireplace at the far end of the room, creating long, dancing shadows on the walls. There were two leather couches and several Windsor chairs. He opened a bottle of fine French wine, explaining the vintage. Then he filled our glasses and toasted us, saying in his broken English, "To the film: may it be an artistic success, and thank you for coming tonight." He finished his glass and poured another before picking up a book that was open on the table. He read aloud in French, closing his eyes after every few lines.

Verse-nous ton poison pour qu'il nous réconforte!
Nous voulons, tant ce feu nous brûle le cerveau...

He paused, attempting to translate. "How would you say? Ah...
'Pour the poison'...ah, um...'once we burn our brains.'"
With his eyes closed, in deep concentration, he continued.

Plonger au fond du gouffre, Enfer ou Ciel, qu'importe?
Au fond de l'Inconnu pour trouver du nouveau!

He translated again. "Um...'Heaven or hell, anything will do. Deep
in the unknown of hell!' Such beauty. I never tire of these lines. What
genius."

I fully expected Vincent Price to appear from the long shadows.
Feeling the effect of the wine, I asked, "Whose lines?"

"Ah, of course. You don't speak French. Baudelaire...*Les Fleurs du
mal* — the flowers of evil."

Faye spoke to him in French, and just as they began a lengthy dialogue, a beautiful young woman appeared from the other room. Barefoot, she had thick light brown hair down to her shoulders and was
dressed in a diaphanous white nightgown that exposed her youthful,
delicate body. She, too, spoke French. I assumed it was Roman's daughter as she sat on the floor next to him. Roman got up to rearrange the
logs in the fireplace, causing the shadows to be even more vivid and
defined. I was thoroughly intrigued by him and the dramatic atmosphere he strove to create.

The young woman, transfixed, staring at Faye with doe-eyed admiration, got up, hugged Roman goodnight, and left. He then told us that the
girl, Nastassja, was the daughter of actor Klaus Kinski and was in Los
Angeles for tutoring as well as dancing and acting lessons while preparing
for her first film role. He added, "Klaus has not been much of a father."

As we drove back to Bel Air, I wasn't sure what had been accomplished, but I do remember talk of Faye possibly tinting her hair to
lighten its appearance for the camera.

In Hollywood, alongside grass and booze, cocaine had become

available at every gathering, dinner party, and script conference. In bars, clubs, and restaurants, there were continual trips to the bathroom. Often it was openly laid out as a display of connections and wealth. It seemed to run throughout the set of *Chinatown* like a dust storm in the Sierras. And as filming began, along with script changes, budget problems, and deadline concerns, the cocaine became ever more present.

Chinatown's set was far more intimate than that of *The Three Musketeers*. In contrast to Richard Lester, whose approach was humorous and relaxed, Polanski was serious and driven. One would assume Jack Nicholson would be the most nervous or demanding member of the team, since he had been responsible for picking so many of the key players, but Nicholson listened to Polanski and made suggestions that never seemed to cause a conflict between them.

Faye, on the other hand, asked many questions regarding her character's motivation. She would not hesitate to express her disagreement, and she was not comfortable with nor did she trust Roman. Perhaps it was because she knew she wasn't his choice for the part of Evelyn Mulwray. In every scene, just before the cameras rolled, Faye would call her makeup artist to apply Blistik to her lips. This became a running joke with the crew because they knew it drove Roman nuts.

At one point, just as he was ready to film Faye and Jack in an interior scene, he noticed a small piece of hair out of place on Faye's forehead. Her hairdresser was called to fix it. Yet the piece of hair returned, so Roman walked over and just yanked it out. The power struggle building up between them finally exploded after that, complete with headlines that screamed, DUNAWAY STORMS OFF CHINATOWN SET!

Walking off a set is serious. That night, the house on top of the hill in Bel Air was not a happy one. The phone kept ringing late into the night until a meeting was set for the following day with the studio brass, Faye, and Roman.

I had previously met Sue Mengers, and now I thought it might be constructive if I sat down with her to discuss how to keep the peace between Faye and Roman. Sue was delighted. "Honey, you're a doll. Meet me at the Palm at seven. If you get there before me, tell Orlando at the desk that you're meeting me."

Sue was around twenty-five minutes late. Still, she did a bit of table-hopping before finally joining me at her booth, declaring, "The traffic in this town is from hunger."

Sue was in her forties, with shoulder-length hair shaded silver and blond and two J-shaped curls framing either side of her round face. Her appearance was set off by huge square lightly tinted blue glasses that blended perfectly with her hair. She wore big strands of pearls and nail polish that matched her brightly colored floral caftan. I felt comfortable with her right away. Like me, she had grown up in the Bronx.

"See the putz over there? He's probably three times her age. She's not going to fuck 'im unless he gets her a part in Marty's new picture. I can tell you how that story's gonna end. You okay with white wine? Or a cocktail? Surf and turf, if that's your bag, is divine. For me tonight, a good rib eye and white wine is just fine."

"Sue, I'm trying to see if I can help keep the peace between Roman and Faye because I know how much time and energy you've invested in her career."

"Peter, listen, darling. I believe Faye is a great actress and one of the most beautiful women in this town, with a shitload of untapped talent. Every time I try to help her, she goes paranoid on me, as if I'm working for the other side. Look, Barbra ain't a day at the beach, but she at least listens. She won't fly into tirades unless she's got a justified reason. Faye — oy vey, I need a week in a rest home after I get off the phone with her. As long as she's my client I'll defend her, but sometimes she pushes people just too far, and I don't think she realizes it. This is a small town, and word flies around fast. You can have a couple of winners — and with one flop they forget about the winners and only remember the flop. Actresses don't have the longevity of actors. Look around: You don't see older women with younger men, do you?" Jokingly, she added, "You are over seventy-five, right? Listen, darling, I appreciate what you're trying to do for Faye, but she's like a mule, not an ass. A mule, if she don't wanna move, nothing's gonna move her, not you or me. Maybe Nicholson can reach her. He's good at that, because he's talented, and he's got the winning edge, and Faye certainly respects that. Does she know you're meeting with me?"

"No!" I was quick to say.

"I thought so. Oy vey, Faye," she responded as she cut through her rib eye, all the while casting her fishbowl eyes around the room. Toward the end of our meal, as she ordered a large strawberry shortcake with extra whipped cream on the side, we were joined by Robert De Niro and Dustin Hoffman.

"So, *bubbeleh*, how's it going with Evans?"

De Niro just shrugged. "It's okay."

Dustin told a story about a time when he was on a press junket and a reporter thought he was Al Pacino. Dustin, with a grin, said, "Wait until Pacino reads that interview. He's gonna shit in his pants!"

Sue and I laughed. De Niro, who was very quiet, attempted a smile. When I tried to grab the bill from Sue, she called me a schmuck. "Honey, let the agency pay."

I said, "Sue, you're my date tonight."

"Ha! You're like that putz over there with the young starlet. Don't think because you're paying you're gonna get me in bed. Ha!"

As I was walking her out to her car, she spotted Ryan O'Neal sitting with the musicians Stevie Winwood of Traffic and Glenn Frey of the Eagles. "You youngsters, let Peter hang out with you. I'm heading home to a pile of headaches."

I liked Sue. Faye hated her.

In the morning, Faye paced the floor, troubled by an upcoming scene in the script. She insisted that "only Jack will understand."

Faye took several phone calls from Nicholson, who was hoping to make the shoot on Monday go as smoothly as possible, and he invited her over to his house to discuss it further. Faye asked me to join her. After a sharp turn onto a private dirt road, we came to his secluded house overlooking a canyon. Nicholson was sitting on his couch, cocooned in a room hung with exquisite artwork. An amiable host, he chatted with us and with various other people who were hanging out there. Someone had placed an abundant mound of cocaine on the coffee table. As the evening wore on, the other guests seemed to drift away until it was just Jack, Faye, and me. They discussed Polanski and the best way to deal with his temperament. Jack invited Faye upstairs to work on the script, and Faye asked if I would mind waiting. I answered, "Of course not."

When a half hour became an hour, and then another, I called up the staircase — "Faye?" — but got no reply. I continued to wait in the living room.

Finally, as I saw the sun coming up, it occurred to me that what I thought might be happening was definitely happening. I called out her name again, louder and more forcefully, but still no response.

Beyond the sliding glass doors of the living room, the sun was now reflecting on Nicholson's pool. I felt I was being suckered, but I was stuck. I couldn't drive. I had no idea where I was. I searched around until I found an address label on a magazine so I could call a taxi. Soon a cab pulled up the driveway. I told the driver I would be out in five minutes.

I opened the sliding glass doors. Then I picked up the coffee table, laden with books and the large mountain of cocaine, walked over to the pool, and released it all into the water, watching it sink and settle on the bottom. For symmetry, I lowered a chair from the living room into the water, where it landed perfectly at one end of the table. Then I picked up another chair and lowered it at the opposite end. The white powder was dissolving, and a few books floated up to the surface. I felt certain that Nicholson, an art lover, would appreciate my homage to Duchamp.

I left LA, Faye, and *Chinatown* and boarded a flight home to Cambridge. I was conflicted and hurt but still in love with Dorothy Faye and contemplating whether our relationship was worth fighting for.

18

CAMBRIDGE UNBOUND
Robert Lowell and Bill Alfred

Poet Robert Lowell

IT FELT GOOD to return home to Cambridge, far away from the high-
stakes drama of moviemaking. As I wandered through the narrow
streets lined with small book and record shops, encountering friends
along the uneven red-brick sidewalks, I appreciated the comforts Cambridge offered that my recent stay in Hollywood didn't.

Back then, Cambridge was still a vibrant cultural outpost for writers, painters, and musicians. The combination of bohemia and academia
eased me into a calm state of mind.

My mood was considerably lifted when I discovered that one of my
all-time favorite musical groups, the Everly Brothers, was playing in
town. Seeing them on my home turf would be a tonic for my wounded
spirit.

In my childhood I had made a desperate but failed attempt to re-
create their angelic harmonies with my school friends when we formed a
doo-wop a cappella group called the Three Imps. It consisted of me and
two neighbors who lived in my building, with Richie Gold on clarinet.
It's still a mystery to me why we felt we needed a clarinet; we sure weren't

doing klezmer music. For many weeks we rehearsed the Everlys' hit "Bye Bye Love" before our debut as contestants in a Bronx Park talent show.

An hour before we were to perform, however, Richie's mother talked him into abandoning us and performing a clarinet solo as his entry in the contest. We surrounded Richie in the park's bathroom and shouted all sorts of threats, telling him what we would do if he didn't play with us. But there was no persuading Richie to go against his mother's wishes.

That day, too, I learned the hard truth of the old show-biz truism that one should never follow an act with animals or children, thanks to a pair of youngsters named Janet and Gary, ages four and five respectively, who brought the house down by tap-dancing while singing "With a knick-knack paddywhack give a dog a bone."

The night of the Everlys' concert I walked to the back of the venue toward the stage door. I knew the staff because I had played there many times. I spotted Johnny T., head of security, standing outside. "John, what time are the Everlys arriving?"

"They're already here. Just go on up and say hello — nobody's in the dressing room but the two of 'em."

I didn't climb but ran up the stairs to the second floor and down the long hall, following the sound of their familiar celestial voices. The dressing-room door was open, and there they were, Don and Phil, both strikingly handsome, with shining pompadours, wearing immaculate suits and playing their black Gibson 185s with stars on the fretboards. They noticed me standing by the door, but it didn't seem to bother them, so I discreetly slipped in and sat nestled in the corner. Their voices were beautiful, and it was enchanting to watch. For almost an hour — surprisingly — they sang nothing but songs by the Beatles, whom they had undeniably influenced. As soon as Don finished one, Phil would start another, never speaking, only singing, face-to-face. It was not a secret that the brothers had a somewhat fraught, combative relationship, so it seemed like they communicated purely through song. When they stopped playing, there followed a silence, and, like a church congregant, I quietly left. I hardly remembered the actual concert after the private recital I was so fortunate to witness.

Late the following afternoon, my phone rang. "Peter? William Alfred here. Am I interrupting anything?"

I would have recognized that voice anywhere. Its tone was soft and seemed to come from another era, one of manners and refinement. "No, Bill. It's great hearing your voice."

"Likewise, Peter. I'm having a bachelor's dinner at my house tomorrow — six thirty, cocktails at five. I'm serving lamb chops in an attempt not to overcook them, along with baked potatoes and spinach. Weren't we always made to feel spinach was the most important of all vegetables? I blame Popeye for that propaganda."

I understood him and agreed, saying, "But Bill, didn't we all grow up awaiting the Sunday funnies?"

Wistfully, Bill sighed. "I did love Krazy Kat. How sad that he seems to have vanished like some character from the age of Pericles. Now, if you can make it, you'll also get to taste my mother's secret lime ice recipe. I follow it as carefully as if it were a eucharistic prayer. So sorry for such short notice. I hope you're available."

"Bill, I'd be delighted to come."

"Good. Then see you tomorrow — and don't bring a thing. As my father would say, 'Button up tight when the cold winds blow!'"

I had met Professor Alfred before meeting Faye, but it was always in very formal circumstances, since many of my Harvard friends were also his adoring students. As soon as I met him, I understood why they were so enamored of him and his gentle ways.

The professor's house, appropriately for a classicist, was located on Athens Street. The neighborhood, slightly outside the confines of Harvard, was peacefully placed in the shadow of St. Paul's, the Catholic church where Bill attended mass every morning. The houses were close together, and the trees offered cool, welcoming shade in summer. In the early evening you could hear the sounds of dinner preparation from open kitchen windows. It was a mixture of blue-collar and middle-class homes sprinkled with residences of families from many generations past. Bill lived in a gray Victorian house with white trim, and although it was well worn and in need of a thorough makeover, it had an abundance of character, a prelude to what awaited one inside. An unpolished brass number 31 was centrally placed on the solid oak door, flanked by two narrow etched-glass windows allowing a hazy view of the inside stairs and small hallway.

In my ignorance, I was unaware that it was proper for dinner guests to bring something, like a bottle of wine or chocolates, not to simply arrive empty-handed with a large appetite. I was wearing what I considered my most formal outfit: all black, including tight jeans, a leather jacket, Capezio shoes, and a Freddie Fields–gifted turtleneck. With my ever-present Dunhill cigarette holder in my mouth, I knocked at five sharp, confirmed by the ringing of the bells of St. Paul's.

I heard a stirring from inside, then Bill opened the door wearing a suit and tie and a heavily stained long white chef's apron. "Come on in before the coppers get you! That is the greeting my father would say when we lived above a bar. May I take your jacket? Cal arrived early. Go right inside and introduce yourself while I keep a sharp eye on these chops...boy, oh, boy, lamb chops!"

Playwright and poet William Alfred

I stepped inside and handed Bill my jacket. Facing me was a long flight of stairs; to the right was the sitting room. The house had the warm aroma of furniture polish. The walls were covered with old wooden clocks of every shape and size. Bill rushed off to his chops, and I entered the sitting room, with its curtained bay windows that faced the street, allowing in rays of soft blue light that contrasted with the gentle yellow glow from the table lamps. There was a working marble fireplace and on its mantel, under a bell jar, a statue of Saint Francis. Bill was a devout Franciscan who had taken and lived by the vows of the order: prayer, chastity, and charity toward the poor.

On one side of the room were two soft easy chairs separated by a Victorian marble-topped cabinet that held his nightcaps — bottles of cognac and bourbon. On the other side of the room, an alabaster bust of Homer sat atop a table next to a long couch, upon which his other guest, Cal, was seated. There was something dramatic and intense in his bearing, stiff and deep in thought. It seemed as if, given the chance, he could absorb all the oxygen in the room. He looked like a man in a great rush who had forgotten exactly where he was rushing to. His salt-and-pepper hair was swept in several directions, and his glasses fit his handsome, angular face well. Head bowed, martini glass dangling precariously from his hand, he stared down at the patterns of the turquoise Persian rug.

Bill entered carrying two chilled thin crystal martini glasses, one for me and the other for himself. The martinis were made with Tanqueray, well shaken, and contained shards of chipped ice, a whisper of extra-dry vermouth, and, courtesy of advice from William Carlos Williams, a delicate slice of grapefruit rind.

Bill held his glass high and made a toast: "Here's to the company, absent friends, and confusion to the enemies — the son-of-a-bitch bastards, they know who they are! Forgive me, Lord!"

Cal didn't move, his eyes still absorbed in the patterns of the carpet. Smoke wafted in from the kitchen, and Bill quickly disappeared. I sat down at the far end of the couch. Several minutes passed during which neither Cal nor I spoke. Bill reentered, refilled everyone's glass, and, as he headed back to the kitchen, said, "Peter, have you introduced yourself to Cal?"

After a pause, I turned and said, "I'm Pete."

Cal didn't move. After a few moments, he finally spoke. "What is your surname?"

"Wolf," I replied.

"Are you German or Russian?"

"I guess a bit of both," I answered.

"What do you do?" he asked me, his eyes still focused on the rug.

"I play music," I replied.

"Do you play violin or cello?"

"No. I sing."

"What kind of music do you sing? Any opera?"

"No. I just pretty much do rock and blues-based stuff," I answered, watching his body give a sudden jerk. After another moment's pause, I asked, "What do you do?"

He swiftly turned, looking at me for the first time with a hard, fixed glare that gave off enough heat to melt his eyeglass frames.

As he was about to respond, Bill, fortunately, announced from the kitchen, "Gentlemen, dinner's on!"

I let Cal get up first and followed him into Bill's small kitchen. Bill took a shaker of martinis from his freezer and topped off our glasses, saying, "I can finally join the two of you for a formal cocktail." He then proceeded to uncork a bottle of Spanish red wine covered in a thin wire netting.

"So Cal," Bill remarked, "as I was telling you, I heard from Elizabeth and Harriet three days ago, and Elizabeth said the reading went very well."

Cal replied, "Yes, maybe so. I can endure Ginsberg in small doses, but he seems to enjoy readings as his own form of theatrics. The riffraff that come along to these dog and pony shows, and the thunderous stupidity of the questions you're asked — my God, is there still a functioning educational system in this country?"

At that moment, the clanging clocks throughout the house made their hourly presence known, and Cal almost jumped out of his chair.

"Good God, Bill! No wonder you're still single. Who the hell could put up with that racket, let alone try to get work done while worrying about the next hour's chimes? Holy Christ! One, maybe two somewhere around your house, but sixty? Are you mad?"

Cal at last seemed to have broken out of his stupor. He went on to say, "Just a wee bit of wine, Bill. You know, I shouldn't be drinking, but I don't have any classes until next week."

The chops were ready, and so were the baked potatoes, which weren't baked so much as cremated. Cal didn't seem to notice as he poured himself another glass and kindly filled mine before filling Bill's. It finally dawned on me. Cal, who was now explaining in minute detail the horrid state of most contemporary poetry, was the renowned eminent poet himself— Robert Lowell.

Ed Hood had first introduced me to the works of this extraordinary poet. It seems that Lowell had been given the name Cal, short for Caligula, in boarding school. It was common knowledge in the literary world that he suffered from deep bouts of what is now known as severe bipolar disorder. He had been subjected to the brutality of electric shock therapy and prescribed experimental medication that often left him exhausted, confused, and in a numbed, uncommunicative state.

As Lowell was talking to Bill, I studied him. He had something that few people possess: a charismatic face and captivating charm. I refilled my glass as these two friends trolled back and forth with opinions about which translation of Homer they preferred.

"I like Lattimore for the *Iliad* and Fagles for the *Odyssey*, but then there's also Fitzgerald," said Bill. They went through Coleridge, Roethke, Cummings, and Bishop. Though I wish I had paid closer attention to the discussion than I did to the wine, I tried to follow it all. They continued on to Chaucer, of whom Bill was a leading scholar, Dickens, Thackeray, and Hardy, until the conversation turned to the perennial question, Is there a work that can be defined as the great American novel?

Lowell debated the question. "The English have a wealth of great writers. Why does it need to be so categorically defined here in the States?"

Melville was mentioned before Lowell turned to me, asking, "What thoughts might our young gentleman have on the subject?"

I was caught off guard. "Ah...well...exactly what point of the issue would you like me to respond to?"

"Melville! Melville, of course!" Lowell replied, but I was lit, and Bill's kitchen was spinning.

"Well...ah...you mean the guy who wrote the one about the big white whale?" I was so inebriated that I couldn't remember the title *Moby-Dick*. It must have been because Bill was such a religious man that the good Lord then intervened on my behalf, saving me from further humiliation by instructing every clock in the house to again burst forth with chiming and gonging.

Laughing, Bill got up from the table, and Lowell put his hands over his ears. Bill then called us to join him in the sitting room while he reached for a bottle of Old Crow whiskey, setting out three glasses. I was reminded of Lowell's poem for his friend the poet Delmore Schwartz, written just a few blocks from the house where we were seated:

> We drank and eyed
> the chicken-hearted shadows of the world.
> Underseas fellows, nobly mad...

After that first night, I met Lowell several more times, always while dining at Bill's. He was friendly toward me, even recommending some recordings of Schubert lieder. At what was to become our final dinner together, we adjourned to the sitting room. The topic turned to how best to describe the all-American woman — and who that might be if there was one.

Lowell asked, "Is there such a thing as the quintessential Englishwoman or Frenchwoman? Why does one even need that archetype?" I might as well have been backstage shooting the breeze with rock-and-rollers. At the end of the day, we were all men in search of a muse.

I attended Lowell's funeral, at the Church of the Advent, tucked away in the lower part of Beacon Hill, not far from 91 Revere Street, where he grew up. "He has at last found peace" was the comment most heard from the attendees. I hoped he had, for with his fiery, hyperfocused mind, peace is what he deserved.

Years later I was having cocktails with Lowell's second wife, the writer and critic Elizabeth Hardwick. Her presence could envelop you, and her opinions were straightforward and honest almost to a fault, so abrupt that they could end friendships. I had a big crush on her, and I believe she knew it. Lowell was reported to have been returning to her the day he died. I told her about the Melville incident, being caught off guard by the great poet himself and saved by Bill's symphony of clocks. She paused, then laughed. With a mischievous gleam in her eye, she said, "Oh, those evenings at Bill's. You were saved from Cal by the ringing of bells. Now, honey, that's poetry!"

19

FUN FOR A WHILE
John Lennon and Harry Nilsson

THE RECORD PLANT studios were located in midtown Manhattan on several floors of a featureless office building. On any given day you might find David Bowie recording, Bob Marley mixing a live album, or Bruce Springsteen and his E Street Band camped out on the first floor in studio B. There, in the spring of 1974, the Geils band was mixing its fifth album, *Nightmares...and Other Tales from the Vinyl Jungle*, in studio A.

One evening as I strolled down the long, narrow hallway on my way to the bathroom, I noticed a blond, unshaved, scruffy-looking character sitting on a bench outside studio B. He was wearing an Irish walking cap. One hand held a bottle of cognac and the other an empty snifter. He looked like an aristocratic hobo as he sat chatting with a limo driver dressed in a black suit, a black tie, and a chauffeur's hat. As I approached, I could hear the scruffy fellow say to the driver, "Listen, if you take a quarter of your earnings each week and invest it in the stocks I mentioned, you'll have a comfortable padding of savings in five years. Now, wouldn't that be nice? Then maybe you can buy your own limo and go into business for yourself and not have to split your earnings with anyone."

As I walked by, he snidely commented in my direction, "Hey, who does this guy think he is — a Ringo Starr wannabe?"

In the bathroom I stood at the urinal, wondering *Who the hell was that schmuck?*

On my return to the studio, I thought I'd give him a little taste of the Bronx. I walked past him and said loudly, "Hey, buddy, I don't know about a Ringo wannabe, but I saw something that looked just like you floating in there, and I flushed it down the toilet."

In an instant he called after me, "Hey, that's pretty funny. I like a guy that can fire it back. Why don't you join me for a cheerful libation?"

He was a curious character with an obviously wry sense of humor. I found him surprisingly engaging, so I took him up on his offer. "I'm Harry," he said as he held out his hand for a shake.

"Pete," I said.

He continued, "I've been advising this dear fellow, who's been driving me around most of the week, on how to get himself some dividends and savings." The driver nodded in my direction.

Harry asked what brought me to the Record Plant, but before I could answer he got up and walked over to studio B's door. As he opened it, an explosion of loud music came spilling out. The driver and I sat staring in his direction. In a flash, Harry reappeared, carrying a carton of milk and an empty snifter.

"Let me make you a Harry special." He put down the glasses, poured in cognac, then added milk.

"Isn't this a brandy Alexander?" I asked.

"No! My man in black, that's like calling margarine butter. A brandy Alexander is a far more complicated mixture. A Harry special is a divine bit of simplicity. A good amount of Courvoisier VSOP cognac — don't settle for anything less — and a bit of vitamin D–enriched milk to add strength and vigor. Then pour the milk slowly down the side of the glass, so as not to crush the cognac, and voilà! You have the makings of a gift from the gods. I share this with you because I can tell you are a fellow *peregrinus*, or pilgrim traveler." He joyfully handed the glass to me, saying, "Cheers."

While we clinked our glasses together, he gave strict instructions. "No sipping, my man; just chug it down." I happily obliged, and he immediately refilled both our empty glasses.

The conversation turned to music. "You like the Drifters?" he asked.

"Like 'em? Hell, they're one of my favorites. As a matter of fact, I met one of their lead singers, Ben E. King, several times, and he's a real gent. 'Spanish Harlem,' 'Save the Last Dance for Me' — it don't get much better than that."

"Well, follow me. I'd like to play you something."

Harry got up and once again walked to studio B, holding the door for me. I entered the control room and in the dim lights saw the back of the engineer. He wore a cap similar to Harry's and was sitting in front of the recording console while moving the track mixers up and down. Tucked in the corner, by the tape machine, was Jimmy Iovine, who worked as an assistant engineer. I immediately recognized a sloweddown cover version of "Save the Last Dance for Me."

Harry refilled our glasses and filled the engineer's as he listened intently. When Harry started singing along with the track, I realized that the powerful and rough voice blasting from the studio belonged to this lovable bear of a man. Harry began singing a high harmony part to his own recorded voice. The man could definitely sing.

After a while he yelled into my ear, "Pete, let's let these guys do their thing." We left to rejoin the limo driver, who was still sitting outside the studio.

"Hey, Harry," I said in awe, "you're quite an amazing singer."

"Well, you gotta be when you're working with that guy inside."

It dawned on me that this fascinating character was Harry Nilsson. I was slow to realize it, since he neither toured nor did many TV appearances and had a rather reclusive public profile. Harry had several big hits in the late 1960s and early 1970s, including his recording of Fred Neil's song "Everybody's Talkin'," from the film *Midnight Cowboy*.

There are moments in life when you meet someone and have an instant connection, feeling as if you've known them for years. For me, this was one of them. Harry and I chatted like old friends.

A while later, the studio B door opened, and the engineer emerged. I almost fell off the bench when I realized it was John Lennon. As he walked toward us, he spoke in that utterly familiar Liverpool accent. "Harry, me ears need a bleedin' break. Let's head over to Downey's."

Harry introduced me to John as if I were a long-lost friend, and I was thrilled to be asked to join them. Downey's, a well-known restaurant and bar just around the corner, catered mostly to a theater crowd. On this Monday night it was fairly empty. John and Harry headed to the darkest far corner of the bar as I followed behind. The bartender had obviously served them many times before and asked if I'd be ordering the same.

Keeping up with Harry was one thing — he was a sharp, fast wit — but in the company of John, the conversation climbed to a higher altitude. There were no safety nets to catch you: either you stayed on the wire and contributed some clever responses or you dropped. If you wanted to remain with the company, you needed to be on point. John wasn't rude, but in order to hold his attention, you had to be like a master tennis player and return the volley.

A Record Plant assistant came to the bar, telling John, "Ringo's just called and was hoping to speak with you." Harry put the drinks on his tab, and we all headed back to the studio. Apparently John had promised to write a song for Ringo's new album. Once in the studio, he got his guitar and started noodling with a melody while Harry played drums. John seemed frustrated, so he moved on to the piano and asked the assistant engineer to record him singing "Goodnight Vienna." At the end of the song, John announced, "That version should do him." Watching John pull a veritable rabbit out of a hat was nothing less than magic.

Several evenings later, as I was leaving the studio, Harry was sitting on the hallway bench, drink in hand. "Ah, the man in black. 'Welcome, stranger, to the land of the forgotten men.' For a ten-pointer, what's the film?"

I answered without hesitation, "*My Man Godfrey.*"

"Right you are, Pete, and we have for you the grand prize: a set of American Tourister luggage filled with Palmolive products for the entire family to enjoy. How about joining me in a little Harry special?"

Things were moving slowly in Geils land because of technical difficulties on several tracks, so I gladly followed him into the studio. Jimmy was watching John's daredevil antics, attempting to walk across a row of swivel chairs lined up along the console.

Harry yelled, "John, it's Downey's time!" Once again I joined John and Harry around the corner, in the same spot at the bar, as three Harry specials were promptly placed in front of us.

John mentioned to Harry that Yoko might come to the studio later that night.

"Tanker up, tanker up, my boy!" said Harry, as he clinked his glass with John's and launched into a word-perfect recitation of Eddie Lawrence's comedy routine "The Old Philosopher." Eddie's comedy records were popular on the radio in the mid-1950s.

"'Well, lift your head up high and take a walk in the sun...'"

John quickly responded, word for word, with the next line of "The Old Philosopher" routine: "'You say you lost your job today...?'"

They continued to banter back and forth until in unison they loudly exclaimed, "'Hold your head up high, take a walk in the sun, and never, never, never give up that ship!'"

John and Harry also quoted extensively from *The Goon Show*, the influential classic British radio comedy. The hilarity of their banter was infectious.

Yoko did come to the studio that night, and she and John had a brief meeting in the outer office. When she left, John returned in a somewhat somber mood and began working on the playback for "Save the Last Dance for Me."

John mentioned that he'd invited some friends over, and later, after heavy joints were passed around, we moved into the studio, where Harry began banging away on the drums. John grabbed a guitar and started singing Gene Vincent's "Be-Bop-A-Lula." Into this chaos walked Paul Simon, Art Garfunkel, and an extremely shy Diane Keaton. When John noticed them in the control room, he immediately stopped playing and enthusiastically welcomed his invited guests.

One could tell John respected Paul. He began playing some of the tracks for him, placing him in the prime seat at the middle of the console. After one or two tracks, Paul was quiet, until "Save the Last Dance for Me," when John pushed the volume up almost full throttle. The music was blasting. Paul tried to lower it, but John kept raising it even louder. Paul shouted while holding his ears, "Goddamn it, John, it's so fuckin' loud you can't even hear the music!" Paul lowered it; John raised it again. The music presentation came to a halt. Another joint was passed around, and Harry grabbed paper cups for more Harry specials.

John discussed the need to finish an album of early rock-'n'-roll cover songs, and Paul mentioned that he and Art liked harmonizing to the Everly Brothers' "Bye Bye Love." John said he'd love to hear them sing it. They left the confines of the control room and moved into the brightly lit studio. We watched as Paul grabbed an acoustic guitar and they launched into the song. It seemed as if the session was becoming a Simon and Garfunkel mini concert.

Harry was having none of it, indignantly asking, "What the fuck are they doing?" After Paul and Art finished, Harry said, "Come on, John, let's get out there and show these guys how to rock it up." They moved to the studio, where Harry got on drums and John plugged in a guitar, and they started in on "Be-Bop-A-Lula." At this point, I think Paul realized the level of chaos that was quickly unfolding, and he, Art, and Diane Keaton left as Harry pounded away on drums and John tried to stop his amp from feeding back.

More musicians arrived and joined in. I drunkenly thought I might bring some order to the commotion by singing into an open mike. But instead of singing, I was mostly screaming off-key, uncharacteristically sharing a joint on top of all the alcohol. I was completely stoned and nervous alongside two of rock's most distinguished voices. Instead of bringing harmony to the situation, I made it even worse. Thankfully, everyone was flying so high that no one gave a damn — or even listened.

Hanging out, drinking Harry specials, and even making a bit of a fool of myself was perhaps like having too much of a good thing, but it was, as the song says, "Fun for a While."

20

FAITH, HOPE, AND CHARITY
Stormy Weather

THERE WAS A stretch of days when my phone would ring at around 5:00 a.m. Faye, three hours behind in LA, seemed troubled. She wanted to come to Boston in an attempt to repair whatever friction might exist between us after the *Chinatown* incident. This trip would also give her time for much-needed guidance with her mentor, Bill Alfred, on her new project, *The Towering Inferno*.

We met for dinner at Bill's house. It took "just one look" and Bill's superb martinis to get Faye and me beyond the drama of our last days together in LA. Bill presented us with silver necklaces depicting an anchor flanked by two fish. This ancient symbol of faith, hope, and charity has been worn since the sixteenth century by sailors seeking safe travels. Perhaps Bill, in his wisdom, knew the stormy waters that lay ahead for us.

Faye stayed at my apartment, and the separation seemed to have drawn us even closer. I was concerned about her, so I moved my schedule around in order to be with her in Los Angeles for some of the filming. She rented a house in Malibu. Although it was quite a distance from the filming location, on the 20th Century Fox lot, she felt that being on the beach, away from alcohol and drugs, would provide a calm, healing environment.

This was a much more relaxed and welcoming location to visit, a far cry from the tense and dark atmosphere on the set of Polanski's *Chinatown*.

The cast for *Inferno* included many well-established stars and Hollywood icons. I was star-struck by Fred Astaire, an idol to my father and Uncle Bernie. Astaire was reserved and extremely polite. He spoke of his love of songwriting and his friendships with Irving Berlin and Harold Arlen. He confided that although he loved almost all kinds of music, he did not like rock because "it didn't swing enough" for him. Surprisingly, he mentioned how much he enjoyed watching *Soul Train* and seeing the dancers create new steps, but he quickly added, "Doing something spontaneous is easy compared to the strict demands of learning a choreographed series of movements that need to be executed perfectly every time."

I was curious about how he kept up his stamina, spending day after day in front of the cameras, and he answered, "That's the easy part. The real challenge is getting through the grueling rehearsals. I only eat a light lunch, never dinner. People eat far more than they really need, and if I put on even a little weight, it affects my dancing."

Shelley Winters, who previously worked with producer Irwin Allen on *The Poseidon Adventure*, visited the set one afternoon. Shelley was engaging and spontaneous. I had previously met her in New York at a New Year's Eve party thrown by Lee Strasberg and his wife, Paula. As the clock struck midnight, everyone sang "Auld Lang Syne" while watching the fireworks burst over Central Park, bringing in the year 1973. Shelley, to the tune of Pete Seeger's "Where Have All the Flowers Gone," sang loudly, "Oh! Where have all my husbands gone?"

That night, Paula led me away for a private tour of the apartment, showing me an array of prized paintings and photographs. She whispered excitedly that she had "something very, very special" to share with me. As we headed down a long, narrow hallway, she stopped outside a door, opened it, and clicked on the light, showing me a bedroom that looked like it belonged to a teenager who had just rushed off for a date. The windows were covered with heavy curtains, and the double bed and dresser were festooned with clothes, some hanging out of the opened drawers and spilling onto the carpet. Bras, underwear, silk blouses, black turtlenecks, skirts, and nylons. The closets were stuffed with coats and dresses and shoes kicked off in all directions and splayed across the floor. I could not comprehend the chaos as Paula watched me. She leaned in, saying in a low whisper, as if someone in the room might be sleeping, "This is Marilyn's. She left it all to Lee in her will. It's so nice to know it's here, like she's still with us, safe and always so close." It struck me as eerie, almost like Christ's tomb, as if the Strasbergs were awaiting Marilyn's resurrection.

Because I didn't know how to drive, Faye, thoughtfully, had the studio provide me with a limo and driver while she was working. I enjoyed our life at the beach, though neither one of us ever ventured out or even touched the sand. During the day, the limo driver would pull up to the house and wait outside for me. It was a waste, for I usually stayed inside, either songwriting or talking on the phone, arranging the band's schedule. Happily, the driver was getting well paid by the studio.

One day I invited him to sit with me out on the back deck, facing the beach, where we ended up every afternoon thereafter. His name was Cornell, and he was straight outta Compton. With his thin mustache and handsome face, he was cool as cool could be. We immediately hit it off. Every hot, sun-filled afternoon, there we would sit. Like me, Cornell always dressed in black. Whereas I wore a three-piece suit, complete with watch fob, Cornell wore tight black riding britches, black riding boots, and a cap with an Afro comb sticking out from under it. He usually had a toothpick lodged in the side of his mouth and a thin, well-rolled joint pinched between his elegant fingers.

At one point a jogger who ran along the beach every afternoon like clockwork approached us and said, "For the last several weeks, I've seen you two hanging out here in the same suits, in the same spot, at the same time. Who the fuck are you guys?" It was Ryan O'Neal, who lived with his family several houses down and who had obviously forgotten that he and I had already met. He mentioned that Bob Dylan also had a house farther along the beach.

"He's a strange cat," Ryan said. "He's always playing with his kids on the beach, but one day my daughter told me, 'Bob said he loves to eat bugs,' and my daughter says he just grabs them straight out of the air, catches them in his hand, and eats 'em!"

Cornell said, "Shit, man, can't you see that dude is just having fun? He's messin' with them kids. He ain't eatin' no bugs."

We didn't spend every single night at the Malibu house; there was at least one occasion when it was too far from the set to commute back. It happened after a casual Hollywood gathering. You couldn't call it a dinner because there was no formal seating, just a serve-yourself buffet. The long table was adorned with platters of tossed salads, barbecued meats, and a vast assortment of exotically garnished vegetables. A self-service bar gleamed with Cuervo Gold tequila, vodka, scotch, wine, and Mexican beers floating in large ice buckets. The staff was sent home early while joints and cocaine were passed among guests as if they were just simple hors d'oeuvres.

In the spacious living room, the four couches, armchairs, and over-size floor cushions were occupied with an array of recognizable faces, including Dennis Hopper, Carrie Fisher, Robin Williams, Penny Marshall, Michael Douglas, Michael Caine, and Timothy Leary.

Faye and I were late arrivals. She eased into a conversation with Michael Caine, and I spotted Harry Dean Stanton, Hoyt Axton (whose mother cowrote "Heartbreak Hotel"), and Kris Kristofferson in a corner playing guitars, so naturally I gravitated toward them. By 2:00 a.m., the guests who had to be on their respective sets at six that morning began leaving. Faye and I decided to spend the few remaining hours before dawn in her dressing room. It was located on the 20th Century lot, only a fifteen-minute ride away, so she'd be there and ready for her morning call.

The studio guard checked us in. The lot was dark, empty, and eerily quiet. Driving past the Old West saloon, a pirate ship, and a medieval castle, we eventually arrived at the only block with streetlamps and several office buildings, one of which housed Faye's dressing room. It consisted of two areas: a back room with a long couch upon which Faye immediately passed out, and a front sitting room with two easy chairs where people could discuss the details of the day's shoot.

It was around four thirty in the morning, and I wasn't tired. I took out a bunch of "Greetings from Hollywood!" postcards that I had previously bought at the airport. I wrote out twelve of them to friends and family, addressed and stamped them, and, peering out into the street, noticed a mailbox on a corner around a block away. I wandered over, alone in this empty place, and mailed my cards. When I sat back down in the front room's easy chair, I fell right asleep.

It wasn't long before I was awakened by the assistant director yelling, "Faye, darling! Time to rise and shine, honey! Big day today — you're in the crowded-elevator scene where you get stuck between floors. Won't that be fun?" Faye wasn't moving, so the assistant director got on his walkie-talkie: "Bring a bowl of ice, pronto!"

In came her hairdresser followed by her makeup man. Then an assistant rushed in, placing a large bowl of ice on her makeup table. I could hear Faye saying, "Holy shit. It can't be six yet, can it?"

"No, my love. Early call today. You and the boyfriend had a late night reading *War and Peace*, right? Let's get your pretty face into that ice!"

After several minutes, the door swung open, and in walked Paul Newman, Steve McQueen, and O. J. Simpson, each carrying a can of Coors beer. They breezed past me into Faye's back room, where I could hear Paul Newman laugh and say, "Honey, you should have partied with us. We had a civilized night of mischief, and it would have been far more fun with you!" There was gossip and banter before they discussed the day's upcoming scenes. As the three were leaving, Newman tipped his cowboy hat to me and said, "Here, kid," handing me his beer. "You can probably use this more than me." A polite nod from McQueen and O.J., and they were gone.

Beer was the last thing I wanted. I could hear the rustling from the other room as they were getting Faye's hair and makeup ready. Through the window, I watched as several flatbed trucks pulled up onto the street. A group of workers jumped out and to my astonishment began loading the streetlamps onto the truck. Then, in disbelief, I watched as the mailbox, the very one in which I had placed all my postcards, was hoisted up and dumped onto the truck. The entire street turned out to be just another movie set.

In this town, as in life, I thought, what you see isn't always what you get. As my postcards said, "Greetings from Hollywood!"

Throughout our time in Malibu, Faye was committed to keeping herself sober. We were quite happy. The afternoon before I was to leave, Faye wanted to walk on the beach. Arm in arm, we made our way toward the shoreline.

"Peter, I'm afraid about you going tomorrow."

"Afraid?" I asked. "Why?"

"I'm afraid something will come between us. You might lose interest. Hearts do change, Peter, and I don't want to lose you. I love you very much."

I loved Faye, but her next words left me reeling: "Let's get married."

Faced with the enormity of this prospect, I blurted out, "Faye, you don't want to marry me. I don't have a pot to piss in. I don't know what's going to happen with the band. You should be with someone who can really provide for you. I can't do that now."

"Peter, I don't care about anyone else. I believe in you." She looked at me with passionate intensity, and her belief in me transcended my doubts and fears. I said yes.

Faye began arranging the wedding almost immediately. With so many calls to make — to my family, the band, friends, and my manager —

and a quick trip back East, I had no time to be nervous. Faye asked her hairdresser to be the bridesmaid, and one of her assistants, T.M., became my best man. The night before our wedding, Faye entered the living room carrying a suitcase.

"Where are you going?" I asked.

"Peter, I can't sleep here on the night before our wedding. I'm still a small-town southern girl at heart, and it's just not proper. I've arranged a car to pick up T.M., then swing by to get you, and I'll see you at city hall, high noon." A long kiss followed, and she said, "Peter, don't leave me waiting at the altar."

I chose to wear my yellow suit in homage to Jerry Lee Lewis, who had worn a yellow suit the first time I saw him in person, at the Alan Freed Cavalcade of Stars. I might have been marrying a movie star, but I was still a rock-and-roller, and that would never change.

The next morning, I had the jitters. T.M., my best man, arrived early. Seeing the shape I was in, he thought it might help settle my nerves to stop en route for a beer at a local bar. It was cool, dark, and empty as we sat together. I asked T.M., "Were you nervous when you got married?"

He paused and took a long slug from the bottle. "No, not the first time. Maybe a bit the second, but it wouldn't be normal if you weren't a little nervous."

"T.M., if you don't mind me asking, what happened to your first marriage?"

T.M. took another slug. "You see, Pete, my second wife is an angel, God bless her. If I didn't meet her, Lord knows what would have happened to me, but you play the cards you're dealt. My first wife, well, let's just say she had some mental problems. She shot our kids then killed herself."

I almost choked on my beer midswallow; this certainly wasn't the answer I expected. I felt awful for T.M., and his terrible tragedy snapped me out of my reverie.

T.M. and I arrived early at the Beverly Hills municipal courthouse and were ushered into the private chambers of a certain Judge Wolf.

Faye's hairdresser arrived, but no Faye. Standing next to me, holding a bouquet of flowers tied with a pink ribbon, was a woman I didn't recognize. The judge entered carrying several books, sat behind his desk, and said, "I thought because two people in the arts are joining together, I would like to start this ceremony by reading a work of the playwright George Bernard Shaw, a Tennyson poem, and a Shakespeare sonnet." It was then that I finally realized the woman standing right beside me was Faye. Her hair was set in waves, piled high atop her head, with tendrils of ringlets hanging down the side of her face, and her fine features were disguised in heavy makeup and false eyelashes. Wearing a flouncy chiffon dress, she really seemed like a small-town southern girl waiting for her beau at the altar. Judge Wolf elegantly read his chosen pieces with conviction, along with the ceremonial text, making us man and wife.

There was a kiss. Everyone applauded. Before we left the chamber, Faye's hairdresser brushed out her hair, and I was surprised to find a flurry of photographers awaiting us. Stopping, with her arm tucked inside mine, Faye happily obliged, giving them all an opportunity for the perfect shot. We darted into a waiting limousine and sped down Sunset Boulevard. Another wave of photographers greeted our arrival at the Scandia restaurant. I had never heard of this lush place, but it was apparently an extremely chichi spot where everyone from Sinatra's Rat Pack to the new Hollywood elite wined and dined. Joining us were Faye's hairdresser and T.M., along with two strangers to me — Hollywood's most powerful PR agents, Henry Rogers and Warren Cowan, responsible for alerting the press to our nuptials.

The celebration began with champagne toasts followed by martinis as the waiters hovered around the table. The drinks then came by the trayful. All that was missing was Bette Davis reciting her famous *All About Eve* line, "Fasten your seat belts. It's going to be a bumpy night." When the time came to get the bride home, T.M. and I led Faye out through a side door, safely away from the paparazzi, and into the waiting limo. We headed down Sunset toward Malibu. This was the first time she and I were alone (aside from the driver) as man and wife. Once settled in the back seat, she passed out.

It was a quiet ride, and dusk had settled in before we finally arrived at the Malibu house. Faye was out cold, and I had forgotten to take the house key when I left. The door and gate had automatically locked. I searched Faye's handbag and found no key, so I climbed over the fence and made my way to the back deck, where, luckily, a window was slightly open. I ripped the screen and crawled through, making my way to the front of the house. The driver took Faye's feet, and I lifted her by the shoulders, then we carried her inside, gently placing her on the couch. I felt indebted to the driver, for it was clear that he understood the delicacy of the situation, and he quietly left.

The scene seemed suddenly to turn from color to black and white, straight out of a low-grade noir, with long shadows and a femme fatale stretched out cold across the couch, wearing a chiffon dress and only one high-heeled shoe. The reality finally hit me: our future might lie in the vacuum of this scene. My energy drained, and with the waves of the Pacific crashing onto the beach, I collapsed into an overstuffed chair, staring transfixed and spellbound at the woman who was now my wife.

For the next five years, Bill Alfred's gift of the necklaces that sailors used to help navigate stormy waters — faith, hope, and charity — would seem ever more prophetic.

21

NO WINE BEFORE ITS TIME
The Great Exchange

Wꜰᴇɴ ꜰᴀʏᴇ ᴀɴᴅ I arrived back in New York after our wedding, there were stacks of telegrams, cards, dinner invitations, and gifts aplenty waiting for us.

I was on the phone attending to band business while Faye was off being fitted for a *Vogue* photo shoot. The doorman buzzed to let me know that a delivery of two wooden cases had arrived and was being sent up to the apartment.

The card attached to the cases read:

> *Peter and Faye, congratulations!*
> *May these bottles bring you much joy.*
> *A selection of our personal favorites for two of our personal favorites.*
> *Ahmet, Nesuhi, and everyone at Atlantic Records*

The gift, sent to us by the president of my record company, was from Sherry-Lehmann, New York's most distinguished wine store. One crate of white, one crate of red. Each bottle had been personally chosen by Ahmet Ertegun and his brother, Nesuhi, both authorities on the world's greatest wines.

My experience with wine was rather limited. In the band, some drank Boone's Farm; some drank Ripple; some drank Thunderbird. For special occasions, we had André cold duck, Mateus rosé, Blue Nun, and one of my favorites, Almaden Mountain Chablis. I later came to discover the finer tastes of Bolla valpolicella and Soave Bolla, neither costing more than six bucks a bottle. How could you go wrong?

Using a screwdriver, I opened one of the wooden crates. The bottles were carefully rolled in fine tissue, then packed in straw. I tore open the tissue, revealing the labels: Château Lafite Rothschild, Petrus, Château Lynch Bages. Underneath the name of each vineyard were the words *premier cru*, whatever that meant. The same with the other crate: Le Montrachet, Domaine de la Romanée-Conti. All so carefully placed inside.

I looked at these unfamiliar and exotic bottles and called Sherry-Lehmann. "Is the manager there? This is Pete Wolf. You just sent over two crates of wine."

"Of course, Mr. Wolf. I'm the manager. I hope they arrived okay and are to your liking."

"Well, I was wondering: Is it possible to exchange these?"

A pause. "Why, of course, Mr. Wolf. I know Mr. Ertegun called me directly when he placed your order, but if there is something that doesn't meet your expectations, we'd be more than happy to make an exchange."

"What if I wanted to exchange all the reds for Bolla valpolicella and all the whites for Bolla soave?"

A very long pause, then: "Mr. Wolf, you jest of course."

"Well, no. Can you do that?"

"Let me see if I'm understanding you clearly. You want to return all the bottles that Mr. Ertegun personally selected for you and your wife and exchange every one of these fine bottles for ... Bolla?"

"Yeah, that's right."

Extremely long pause. "Mr. Wolf, if you're actually serious about doing this — I mean, actually serious — I will have to go into my inventory and calculate how that would translate as a complete exchange. Are you sure this is what you want?"

"Yeah."

"Very well. I'll get back to you as soon as I possibly can."

"Okay, and thanks very much."

Several hours passed before the return call came. "Mr. Wolf, we have calculated the exchange, and since we do not stock Bolla wines, we have ordered the wine you requested from another distributor and will collect the two cases that Mr. Ertegun purchased for you when we deliver them."

"That sounds fine — thanks."

"I must tell you, Mr. Wolf, after thirty-seven years as a sommelier and wine merchant, I have never had a request quite like yours."

It was a nice compliment, and even I was rather impressed with myself. And why not? I had just turned two cases of wine into well over fifty cases, which I later had stacked in the back service hallway. I couldn't wait to show Faye.

22

DINNER AT EIGHT
George Cukor and Peter Sellers

I AWAKENED ONE PARIS morning to find Faye in the other room, dressed and packing. "What's going on?" I asked.

"I didn't want to wake you until I had to, but I thought it would be good to leave for London today."

"London? Why London?"

"Well, mister, besides being a great city, there's some press and business I need to attend to there. We're staying at the Savoy in the Charlie Chaplin suite. It overlooks the Thames, and it's quite beautiful. I've arranged dinner with George Cukor."

"*The* George Cukor?"

"Why, yes, silly. There's a project he's developing, and nobody can direct a woman as well as George Cukor."

I knew exactly what she meant. His films, including *Gaslight, The Women,* and *My Fair Lady,* captured the sharp wit and intelligence of his leading ladies. He directed Marilyn Monroe in her final, unfinished film, *Something's Got to Give,* and elicited from her a sweetness and maturity that, by all accounts, would have made it one of her most memorable achievements.

We entered the grand spectacle of the Savoy's lobby and were greeted like royalty by the manager, assistant manager, and our own personal butler.

"Let's have a proper cocktail," Faye announced. Although it was a bit early, I wasn't one to argue. Several drinks later, we were in the elevator being guided to the Charlie Chaplin suite, with a view of the Thames so stunning it was easy to see why Monet once set up his easel on the balcony.

Faye showered, rolled her hair in curlers, and slipped into a long terry-cloth robe. With a cigarette in one hand and a glass of champagne in the other, she asked me to help her choose the right dress for dinner. The phone rang, and I heard her say, "Why, of course. Indeed you're right — that would be far more relaxing. Say, about seven? Or should it be — pardon the pun — dinner at eight?" Putting the phone down, she explained that Cukor preferred to eat in our suite, where it was much quieter, rather than in the Savoy Grill, though Faye had been really looking forward to dining in the restaurant.

Exactly at eight, the bell rang. I answered it, and there, in a trim gray suit, blue silk tie, and blue silk hankie neatly folded in his vest pocket, stood a small balding man with inquisitive eyes framed by smart, well-fitting glasses. With a wide, pleasant smile, he extended his hand and said, "I'm George." He was formal in a relaxed way, with an energetic grace, a vast intelligence, a sharp sense of humor, and a wonderful ease with storytelling. I took to him right away.

The butler arrived with menus and drinks, though Faye thought a second bottle of champagne was in order. Mr. Cukor instead asked for a Dubonnet, explaining, "I hardly drink these days, but if I do, I find that a Dubonnet on the rocks with a splash of soda water and a slice of fresh orange does the trick."

Drinks were served under the efficient and discriminating eye of the butler, who watched the staff as they soundlessly set our table with linens and fine bone china. A parade of carts was wheeled into the room, awaiting the butler's inspection of each covered dish before the staff was allowed to place them, ever so gently, on the table. Mr. Cukor was smiling as he observed the pageantry. He seemed to notice every detail, which wasn't surprising, since many of his films helped define the term "the proper service."

Mr. Cukor became nostalgic after his second Dubonnet. He mentioned the many times he'd been in this very suite, visiting Katharine Hepburn, Vivien Leigh, Sir Alec Guinness, and Judy Garland, of whom he said, "I did so admire her and felt she was victimized too often in life. I still feel angry that they cut key scenes from *A Star Is Born*—scenes containing important character development. That decision, I believe, robbed Judy of her Oscar. I felt dreadful when she lost."

He went on to say, "What I find interesting is, I worked with so many of the greatest actresses Hollywood ever produced—Garbo, Harlow, Joan Crawford—and which actress do I get the most questions about? Monroe. I never even completed that last film with her. I find it so strange, this constant fixation. True, she certainly was a real star, but she kept deteriorating as our work together progressed. It was difficult to witness. We shot around her, trying everything to help. Sad, very sad. She had such presence on camera; that fact can't be denied. Viewing the daily rushes, I couldn't believe the transformation. She had to be aware of the magic she was creating—you can't fake something like that."

After dinner, Mr. Cukor thanked us for a charming evening and left the suite. Faye wanted to go downstairs to the hotel's American Bar for some proper martinis. Upon entering, we bumped into Peter Sellers. He and Faye were already acquainted. The three of us adjourned to a table until last call. Peter invited us back to his house, where he had an extensive record collection. He was generous with his rare aged cognacs and very strong hash. As the rising sun was putting an end to the evening, Faye asked Peter if he'd reenact his three characters from *Dr. Strangelove*: Captain Mandrake, President Muffley, and Dr. Strangelove. Without hesitation, he launched perfectly into all three, line by line. As we were getting ready to call a taxi, Peter offered to drive us back to the hotel. We were all several sheets to the wind, and Faye and I thought a taxi was the wiser choice, but Peter insisted on driving. We zoomed off in his convertible sports car, zipping through winding country lanes.

I was crouched in the tiny back seat when Peter turned to ask if I wanted to see his imitation of an American driver. Before I could answer, he swerved into the right lane. Faye and I pleaded with him to get back in the proper lane, but Peter was enjoying his prank too much. Then a lorry came around the bend, straight toward us. At the last minute, Peter, hysterically laughing, turned the wheel into the correct lane. We instantly sobered up and were wide awake as he veered into the main entrance of the Savoy. Faye tried to talk him out of driving home, but Peter, back in character as Dr. Strangelove, stood up in his car and yelled, "Ze führer is awaiting my quick return!," then roared off, singing, "See what the boys in the back room will have."

23

ROCK-'N'-ROLL CIRCUS
The Rolling Stones

Jamming with Mick

B ACK IN THE summer of 1964, the Rolling Stones arrived in New York City to play Carnegie Hall on the final date of their first American tour. I was working at a record store called the Classical Music Shop, which specialized in rare opera recordings and was located just two blocks away from the Americana hotel, where the Stones were staying. From the store window I watched in envious wonderment as a mob of screaming girls gathered outside the hotel's entrance. The air was thick with the heavy vapor of teenage desire, excitable shrieks mingling with the sounds of the city. I knew all about Beatlemania, but this was the first time I witnessed, up close, the real impact of the British Invasion.

The Classical Music Shop was for longhairs, a term once used for classical-music buffs. Rock-and-rollers never entered the place, but suddenly, peering into the store's window, were three faces I instantly recognized: those of Charlie Watts, Brian Jones, and Ian Stewart, the Stones' sometime roadie and piano player. Brian, the most flamboyant of the three, approached the counter where I stood. He asked me for directions to the famous jazz club Birdland and wanted to know where they might find a store that sold rhythm-and-blues records. Attempting to look cool and nonchalant, I recommended some shops and suggested they check out the clubs in Greenwich Village. If my boss hadn't been a close friend of my father, I would have quit my job on the spot and run away to join their rock-'n'-roll circus. Little did I know then that my very wish would one day be answered.

The first time I realized we were somehow on the Stones' radar was in 1971, when the Geils band performed in New York at the Fillmore East. I was surprised to notice Mick Jagger standing at the side of the stage, intensely watching the band.

When we played our first Stones show, in 1975, my rock-'n'-roll dream came true at last. We performed for a crowd of fifty-one thousand fans at the Liberty Bowl, in Memphis, on a scorching hot July Fourth weekend. Opening the afternoon were blues pioneer Furry Lewis, followed by Charlie Daniels, the Meters, then the Geils band. The previous week, Mick had the novel idea that the Stones should make an extravagant entrance atop elephants to begin their set. The promoters managed to locate some pachyderms from a nearby Ringling Brothers circus. The day of the show, the trainers practiced having the elephants walk across the stage, but the boards couldn't support their weight. This dangerous idea was abandoned, but with no time to clean up the mess left behind, we had to navigate our way to the stage through mounds of elephant dung. Even that could not diminish the thrill of sharing a bill with the Stones.

Elephants aside, the Stones wrote the book on how a successful tour should be run, from VIP access to top-notch catering and well-stocked dressing rooms. Their abundant generosity ensured that even the supporting acts lacked for nothing. Their tours were expertly organized by staff and crews, most of whom had been with the band for decades, which speaks volumes for the Stones' loyalty.

I was awed by Mick's extreme discipline, something I had never witnessed before in the rock-'n'-roll world. Every day, after a morning coffee or tea, he would work out and prepare for each performance just as an athlete would train for a marathon.

To celebrate the final night of the tour, in Jacksonville, Florida, the Stones' security staff blocked off an entire hotel floor, creating an open-door nonstop party atmosphere.

Faye and I checked into our room, several floors below. We were in the midst of unpacking when there was a loud pounding on the door.

I rushed to open it only to see a haggard-looking Earl McGrath, president of Rolling Stones Records, with his shirt half tucked into his pants, his jacket wrinkled, his tie hanging loose around an open collar, and a nearly empty bottle of vodka tucked snugly under his arm. He yelled, "What the hell are you both doing? You should be in the lobby or you'll miss the plane to Jacksonville!"

"But Earl," I yelled back, "we're *in* Jacksonville!" Obviously the party was already in full swing.

At 4:00 a.m., after having joined the festivities upstairs, where Keith's music had blared so loud you could hear it through every open door, Faye and I returned to our room. She was exhausted, but I was just getting my second wind and wanted to check out what was happening on the beach, where band and crew members had been gathering as the night progressed. The hotel was beautifully situated on its own stretch of private shoreline. "Peter, please be careful. You know you can't swim," Faye said as I headed out the door.

The beach party was in high gear, with bonfires, limbos, luaus, and skinny-dipping. I walked along the sand with concert promoter Bill Graham, then spontaneously jumped, fully clothed, into the shallow waters for a dip. From Keith's open balcony door many floors up, I heard the sounds of a jam session. Soaking wet, I ventured upstairs and found Keith and Ronnie Wood playing, their sound amplified by a couple of tiny Fender amps, while Charlie Watts drummed along on the coffee table. I was still wet from the beach, so Keith gave me a white Moroccan tunic to change into. The Atlantic Ocean provided the perfect backdrop to the music, and I sat on the floor inside a large open closet — out of the way, but I could still hear every note.

Hours later, Faye awoke to find I was still gone. She called Earl's room to see if I was there, and he told her he last saw me on the beach. She then called Mick, who also said he last saw me on the beach. She called Keith's room, but since no one answered she went upstairs to see if I was there. Ronnie told her that I had been, but quite a while ago. Faye was worried and went looking for Bill Graham to ask for his help in finding me. Bill mentioned that the last time he'd seen me, I was walking along the beach and then went swimming in the shallows.

"Bill, he can't swim and he was drinking. What if he went too far and got pulled out by an undertow?"

Bill snapped into action, calling hotel security. After half an hour of searching, they called the police and finally the Coast Guard. The beach was crowded with staff, police, and crew members, and the water was full of Coast Guard boats, searching up and down the coastline.

Keith and Ronnie were watching the search from a balcony when suddenly they heard a voice behind them ask, "Hey, what's going on?"

They jumped in surprise to see me emerging from the closet. "Wolfie, everybody's looking all over for you. Faye's in hysterics: she thinks you drowned."

I had apparently fallen not into the ocean but into a deep sleep on the floor of Keith's closet. It just so happened, earlier on, that Keith's son, Marlon, had come to the room to see his dad and had closed the closet door, not seeing me asleep inside.

When the drama was over and the search called off, Earl hugged me, saying, "My little Huckleberry Finn, too bad you're not gay, 'cause what a way to come out of the closet."

We were invited on several other Stones tours throughout the States and across Europe. In 1981 we were honored to be billed as "special guests of the Rolling Stones." Also on the bill were George Thorogood and a new artist on his first major stadium tour: Prince. Though Prince was still mostly unknown at the time, both Mick and I were enthusiastic fans. I had previously seen Prince supporting his album *Dirty Mind,* and when we played his hometown, Minneapolis, he attended some of our shows, after which he and I often chatted.

We kicked off the tour at the LA Coliseum in front of ninety-four thousand die-hard Stones fans. That first night, Bill Graham, the promoter, announced to the crowd, "Please welcome to the stage a new artist from Minneapolis, Minnesota...Prince!" Prince came out with his band, wearing calf-high Cuban-heeled boots and a long trench coat. Since almost no one in the audience knew who he was, he received only polite applause.

He started by singing a midtempo funk tune, "Jack U Off," and the crowd watched, bewildered, as he spun around the microphone, letting his trench coat fall open to reveal his bare chest and tight black bikini underwear. The crowd began booing while Mick and I watched from the side of the stage. By the third number, it only got worse; bottles and debris were hurled at the stage. Prince hurriedly left, followed by his band, as the crowd cheered. Prince was so distraught that he flew back to Minnesota that night.

Late night with Keith

I was present when Mick called Prince to persuade him to return for the next LA show, two days later. Surprisingly, Prince did return, but word had spread about this unusual opening act, for as soon as Prince's name was announced, before he even started to play, the booing began, followed by bottles, chicken parts, beer cans, all scattering across the stage. Prince had enough and ran off, canceling his participation in the rest of the tour.

At the start of the European leg of the tour, in 1982, we stayed at the Carlton Tower, in London. It was there that Keith, Ronnie Wood, Bobby Keys (Keith's closest friend, whom he met during the Stones' first tour of the States), and I put together a doo-wop group, the Carltones. We would crowd into the bathroom, giving us plenty of echo for blending our voices, and take advantage of every opportunity to try out our repertoire. Our rehearsals would often turn into such drunken affairs that we'd make alley cats sound like Pavarotti. Ronnie sometimes taped these sessions, which we'd critique into the wee hours, none of us realizing just how out of tune we sounded. We decided to premiere our act in Budapest, where Bill Graham was throwing a surprise birthday party for Jerry Hall. Our long-awaited Carltones debut ended after just one dissonant number, probably because we were either too drunk or not drunk enough.

In Lyon, I sat drinking wine in the hotel lounge, where I was joined by Charlie Watts and Ian "Stu" Stewart, about both of whom there are not enough positive words to say. Ian, an exceptional boogie-woogie piano player and an authority on many barrelhouse-blues piano styles, was with the band from the very beginning as a crew member and part-time keyboardist.

After the three of us had gone through several bottles, the bar manager, an amateur drummer and enormous fan of Charlie, sent over some exquisitely rare bottles from the cellar that were hard to resist. When one rarity was finished, another appeared. Ian and Charlie were discussing which Montreux Jazz Festival was the most memorable when I asked Charlie, a jazz enthusiast with a deep historical knowledge of all forms of the genre, "Who is your all-time favorite jazz drummer?"

"Well, Peter, that's a difficult question to answer, since there are so many great players I admire, but I guess if I was putting together a combo I'd most likely pick Philly Joe Jones."

"Jo Jones?"

"No," Charlie said. "Philly Joe Jones."

By then I was too trashed to remember that there were, indeed, two great jazz drummers—Jo Jones, who played with Count Basie, and Philly Joe Jones, who played with Miles Davis. I said, "You'd pick Jo Jones over someone like Art Blakey? Art Blakey towers over this fuckin' Jones guy. Charlie, that's probably the most ignorant answer I've ever heard, especially coming from a drummer of your caliber. Man, I thought you had taste."

Charlie, admired by everyone for both his rare talent and his gentlemanly elegance, had the courtesy to delicately move aside my wineglass before leaning over the table and popping me square in the jaw. I spun around like a top and went down, then slowly climbed back up to the bar stool. Without missing a beat, the conversation resumed as if nothing out of the ordinary had happened, the three of us shifting gears to talk about piano players, tenor saxophonists, and our favorite recordings. Several more bottles were sent to sample until we all somehow returned safely to our hotel rooms, where, fully clothed, I passed out on the bed.

The next afternoon there was a gentle knock on my door. I opened it, and there, dressed in an impeccably tailored three-piece suit and tie, was Charlie Watts. "Peter, Stu said he believes I owe you an apology for my behavior last night."

"Charlie, if anybody deserves an apology, it's you. I believe I ran off at the mouth, and you just let me know it."

Charlie seemed quite relieved that there was no issue between us, and through the years that remained evident.

* * *

In any hotel, if you got off the elevator on Keith's floor and made it past the security guard, you had only to follow the sound of Jerry Lee Lewis's pumping piano to know where Keith's room was. When the door opened, you entered a souk of dim lights and lampshades covered with silk scarves like those you might find in the labyrinthine passageways of Marrakech. Through clouds of cigarette, grass, and hash smoke would come the lingering scent of Guerlain's Habit Rouge.

Keith welcomed all, and his sofas were often filled with his traveling entourage, usually including saxophonist Bobby Keys and Keith's father, Bert, puffing away on a pipe over a high-stakes game of dominoes. Keith was a most attentive host, escorting you to a small kitchenette laden with bottles. He always liked to prepare your first round, after which you were on your own. Keith's wit was as sharp as the blade he carried, and he had an enigmatic charisma as potent offstage as on. He never failed to make me feel welcome.

After hearing so much about the famed French Riviera, I found Nice disappointing. The beach was just a strip of pebbles surrounded by grand hotels, bars, and casinos in which I'd never find a five-dollar blackjack table. The Geils band did one concert there, but we had a week off before our next show, in Ireland. I joined Mick at the Riviera's hottest disco, thronged with the moneyed elite and royal families and guarded by heavy security — a place where you had to know somebody and be preapproved before you could even get in the door. Mick and I were escorted to a private VIP room peopled with the same crowd you'd encounter at Studio 54: Liza Minnelli, Ryan O'Neal, Alana Stewart, and Halston.

I said to Mick, "This is somewhat lame: you go across the ocean and see the same faces you always see. I'd rather be spending our days off in Ireland." Our next tour date happened to be right outside of Dublin.

Mick was game. "Peter, I lived in Ireland. I love the place, so why don't you and I fly there tomorrow, and I can have Jerry meet us?"

Traveling with Mick was an experience. He made certain that everything was well organized, with nothing left to chance. An ever-present stir of excitement hovered around him, and when people recognized him, which was almost all the time, I enjoyed observing not only how well he handled the attention but also how he chose his speech inflections — from Cockney to posh depending upon the situation.

When we walked into the lobby at the Shelbourne hotel, in Dublin, we found the entire staff, led by the manager, standing at attention, awaiting Mick's arrival.

"Welcome to the Shelbourne, Mr. Jagger. I'm the manager, and we are honored to have you as our guest. All the requests you made have been arranged. Here, sir, is my card and personal number if by chance you need something and I'm off the premises."

On the journey over I'd told Mick that my one wish was to finally have a real pint of Guinness on its home turf. Everyone in the know agrees that Guinness never tastes as good as it does in Ireland. Before checking into our rooms, Mick asked the hotel manager, "Where is the bar? Since we left France, my friend here has been longing for a well-pulled pint of Guinness."

"Sorry, sir. If you were twenty minutes earlier, we could have accommodated you. There is, however, a minibar in your room for your pleasure."

Mick gave him a disappointed look. "Certainly something can be arranged for my friend here. I would enjoy a pint, too."

"Well, sir, the laws are strict regarding pub hours, but if you go to your rooms and come back downstairs in twenty minutes, then discreetly slip into this unmarked door, which opens to the pub, I'll try to arrange things."

Mick gave me a wink, knowing that my first Irish Guinness would soon be at hand.

Twenty minutes later, we followed the manager's instructions and slipped in the side door of the pub. There, standing behind the bar, was a uniformed bartender awaiting our order.

At last a beautiful, treacle-toned pint, topped with perfectly creamy white foam, was placed in front of me. I relished my first sip of that heavenly brew; it was far better than I could have hoped. We sat enjoying our pints while Mick planned the next day's activities — deciding whom to visit, where to have lunch, and what to do for dinner.

This was the first of several free days we had before the upcoming Stones concert at Slane Castle. It would turn out to be the largest music event ever held in Ireland. Ticket demand was so high you'd have thought the pope himself was appearing. It seemed fitting that the Chieftains, the world-renowned traditional Irish folk band, would be one of the opening acts.

The following morning, bright and early, Mick was ready to begin. For me, an insomniac, it was a struggle. Mick took the wheel of our rented car, his bodyguard beside him, while I sat in the back seat. Mick was a fast but safe driver, hugging the narrow turns as we headed into the countryside, as postcard-perfect, bucolic, and green as a scene from the great John Ford film *The Quiet Man*.

Mick was trying to find a place he had once lived. We knocked at the

With Mick Jagger, Keith Richards, and Ronnie Wood

door of a modest-looking house, seeking directions. A middle-aged woman answered, and she immediately recognized Mick. "Oh, my dear Lord, it's you! I can't believe Mick Jagger is standing at my door!" After giving him directions, she asked, "Can you wait a moment, please, so I can get my camera?" Mick waited patiently, then his bodyguard took their picture. "God bless you! My husband and I will see you at Slane's; we've got our tickets. This is unbelievable."

Everywhere we stopped, whether for petrol or a pint at a quiet country pub, everyone recognized Mick. It seemed as if the entire country would be attending the concert. "Welcome to Ireland, Mick!" was a common response. The farther into the countryside we traveled, the friendlier and more respectful people were. "We love you, Mick; we love the Rolling Stones" was the sentiment we most often heard during our travels.

Weeks before, during our concert in Nice, there had been horrific bombings in London's Hyde Park and Regent's Park for which the IRA later claimed responsibility. Meanwhile, the rest of the Stones, in Cannes, were worried that the IRA might attempt to sabotage the upcoming concert, particularly since the band was British. In Ireland, Mick received one panicked phone call after another about possibly canceling the show — first from Charlie, then from Keith, then from Ronnie. Mick was trying to reassure them by describing how friendly everyone had been to him. There had not been even the slightest hint of hostility.

Still, Mick realized there might be some validity to their concerns, so he called Garech Browne, who managed and recorded the Chieftains and was very well versed in the who's who of politics in Ireland. A member of the Guinness family, his beloved brother Tara had died in a car crash and been immortalized in the Beatles' classic "A Day in the Life."

We joined Garech for lunch in a semiprivate booth at the hotel. Not long after we were seated, a gray-haired gentleman in his late seventies, wearing a brown Irish tweed jacket and brown corduroy pants, slowly approached our table, leaning on his walking stick. Garech introduced the man, who had a long beard, as a professor and historian of the poetry and politics of Ireland. I presumed he was somehow involved with the IRA.

Garech mentioned the concert and the band's concerns about possible interference. "Well," the scholar replied, "there are people I know who do have great influence over our patriot brothers, and I could try to contact these agents, but if a healthy financial contribution were discreetly presented, this would help guarantee that there would be no interference at the event."

I thought this might be a good time for me to excuse myself and use the loo while further details were discussed. When I returned to the table, there were handshakes all around. The eminent scholar bade everyone adieu, then slowly departed. Mick seemed pleased by the outcome of the meeting and couldn't wait to report it to the band.

The next day, Jerry Hall, who had just arrived from London, accompanied Mick and me to Slane Castle, where we dined and spent the night before the concert. I had never been in a real castle: the closest I'd come was buying hamburgers at a White Castle back in the Bronx. The staff showed us to our rooms so we could shower and dress before dinner. I had no formal clothing, so Mick kindly lent me one of his spare tuxedos, even showing me how to properly adjust my tie and vest.

Dinner was served at a long table elegantly set for eighteen guests. The conversation was a bit too dry for my taste. After cigars, cognac, and port, I was glad when everyone retired to their rooms. That evening I learned that castles, although impressive, are not very comfortable — Slane was drafty and noisy throughout the long night, with sounds akin to the ghost of Jacob Marley dragging a ball and chain across a cold stone floor. I tossed and turned on a sagging mattress; it made me rethink the maxim "A man's home is his castle."

The concert was a success for all involved. Afterward, Garech, Mick, and I joined the Chieftains in their dressing room. At one point the wily old professor of poetry and Irish politics sauntered in, walking stick in hand, and sat down between Mick and Garech. After pouring himself a generous glass of whiskey, he tipped his head back and quickly emptied it. "You see, gentlemen? I told you there'd be no problem. The generous donation was most welcome, but I neglected to mention at our lunch that our patriot brothers would never cause harm anywhere near a place where Irish lads and lassies are enjoying themselves." With a roguish wink and a tip of his cap, he left, and the Stones' circus kept rolling on.

With Chuck Berry and Keith Richards

24

REDUCE, REDUCE, REDUCE
Julia Child

Harvard square, in Cambridge, was like the Left Bank of post-war Paris. Small privately owned shops mixed with cafés, clubs, and artists' studios; it was home to street musicians, painters, intellectuals, writers, and celebrities. You could see Elizabeth Bishop, Robert Lowell, Kurt Vonnegut, Al Capp, John Berryman, Edwin Land (inventor of the Polaroid camera), and Jorge Luis Borges if you kept your eyes open. It was also not unusual to see a very tall Julia Child and her husband, Paul, strolling together on the Cambridge streets.

In the early days of Julia's television show *The French Chef*, many of my friends were dedicated fans — in particular Ed Hood. He often gathered a group together at his apartment to drink cocktails, smoke grass, and get stoned before watching her show. Ed considered Julia "the bee's knees" and would insist on silence as we watched her putter about in her kitchen, flopping around the meat and poultry. Once, when Andy Warhol was a guest at Ed's (although I never saw Andy drink or smoke grass), he, too, found watching her a riveting experience. If by chance

Julia dropped the whole chicken, which did happen several times, we would break out in hysterics.

The names and locations of the stores where she bought her produce, meat, fish, and wine were common knowledge among loyal fans of her show. I often bought my fish at the Fishmonger, where she shopped. It was owned by Dorothy Borden, a young, energetic woman who ensured that either she or her staff went to the pier every morning to purchase the daily catch. They also made fresh fish soups, chowders, appetizers, crab cakes, and dips.

I was shopping there one afternoon when Dorothy asked if I was free the following night. Her date had canceled, and she wanted me to be her guest at a dinner party she was attending. I always had a pleasant rapport with Dorothy, so I gladly accepted her invitation. As I was leaving the shop and just about out the door, she said, "Let's meet here at five, so we won't be late to Julia's at five thirty."

"Julia's? Julia Child's?" I said in surprise.

"Yes. She's inviting all the top Boston chefs for a wine tasting and dinner. Robert Mondavi is the guest of honor, so it should be quite the evening."

I couldn't wait to tell Ed Hood and his Julia Child Stoner Club. Perhaps I would even get to see her kitchen, which was reported to be duplicated down to every detail, including pots and pans, on the set of her television show.

I met Dorothy as planned, and we drove the short distance to Julia's home, on Irving Street. Upon our arrival, many of Boston's leading chefs were already mingling around the plates of hors d'oeuvres served on Ritz crackers. Empty wineglasses were lined up on one side of the table. The house was tastefully simple and comfortable but could have used a touch of refurbishing. Julia appeared from the kitchen in her apron with her guests of honor, Robert Mondavi and his son. She thanked all the chefs for attending and further informed everyone that Mr. Mondavi was going to give a short speech about the special wine he was presenting for this gathering. The hors d'oeuvres were almost gone. All that remained were small bowls of Planters salted peanuts and Pepperidge Farm cheddar goldfish.

Everyone stood in the small sitting room outside the dining area, trying to get a peek at her famous kitchen. Mondavi's son began his welcoming speech. "You have all been invited here today to be part of the first group to taste what my father has spent years perfecting. It is the merging of two historic wine houses, the Rothschilds and the Mondavis, creating for the first time in Napa Valley a special blend. This singular vision we are calling Opus One. I have already opened the bottles to breathe, and they are ready to be poured. I hope everyone will enjoy this long-awaited labor of love."

The guests gathered by the glasses while several young ladies carefully poured the wines. Soon, Swiss cheese on Ritz crackers were placed on the table along with small bottles of mineral water.

All the while, I noticed an older man sitting in a chair, quite apart from the gathering. Dorothy mentioned that he was Julia's beloved husband, Paul, who had dementia. The room was filled with chatter and exclamations about the wine: "Oh, how lovely and so very well balanced"; "So smooth and elegant"; "Delightfully round and long on the palate." Finally, Mrs. Child announced, "Dinner is now ready to be served."

We headed into the dining room, where a long French country–style table was laid with baskets of sliced baguettes. From one side of the table you could see most of the kitchen through the open doorway, which helped diminish its mystique. Out came bowls of clam chowder while the assorted chefs seated around the table chatted about their restaurants, remodeling issues, and staffing problems. "Julia, this soup is amazing!" said the chef with the longest pedigree, and the others expressed their agreement. Following the chowder, we were served individual bowls of coleslaw. The dinner guests waited patiently for the next course. As the last bowls of chowder and coleslaw were cleared, Mrs. Child loudly announced, "Thank you all for coming. Would anyone like coffee, decaffeinated or caffeinated? We have both. Unfortunately, we don't have much of a formal dessert, but there are some Pepperidge Farm cookies and maple ice cream for those with a sweet tooth."

You could sense the bafflement and surprise among the guests around the table. Dorothy whispered in my ear, "She sent someone over this morning to buy all the chowder and the coleslaw at my shop."

The guests, taking the hint, extended their gratitude for the invitation, for a most enjoyable dinner, and, of course, for the opportunity to taste such extraordinary wine.

As they headed out to their cars you could hear them talking among themselves. "Where should we go for dinner? How about Chinatown?"

25

FIVE O'CLOCK ANGEL
Tennessee Williams

IN 1973, I was seated in the corner of a crowded greenroom at the Dorothy Chandler Pavilion, in Los Angeles, awaiting a performance honoring the twenty-fifth anniversary of *A Streetcar Named Desire*. In the starring roles of Blanche DuBois and Stanley Kowalski would be Faye Dunaway and Jon Voight.

In the hubbub, a guest knocked against me, spilling the contents of my wineglass all over my trousers. As I blotted it with a handkerchief, an unmistakable voice leaned down to say, "Well, you see, even while sitting all alone, the world can be such an unpredictable place." I looked up into the grinning Cheshire-cat face of the evening's guest of honor, Tennessee Williams.

Suddenly, the lights in the greenroom began flashing, signaling that it would soon be time for the performance to begin.

When I found my seat, I was surprised to see Tennessee, with his entourage, seated next to me. We exchanged introductions before the house lights faded. He broke out in loud laughter during the card game scene, when one of the characters tells a joke to the other players at the table. He was thoroughly enjoying the humor of his own words, and people seated around us began expressing their annoyance, unaware that the laughter was coming from the playwright himself.

Sitting beside him, I couldn't help but think back to my younger self, who at the age of fourteen became obsessed with Williams's works. Perhaps it was the initial impact of seeing Marlon Brando play Stanley Kowalski on-screen, but in any case, thanks to the Bronx public library, I was able to read all his plays from cover to cover. I can't say I understood most of what I read; it took years before that happened. As I got older, the plays became clearer to me and far more meaningful. Such was my devotion to his work that I continually played the Caedmon recording *Tennessee Williams: Selections from His Writings Read by the Author*, on which he read poems, scenes from *The Glass Menagerie*, and one of my favorites, the short story "The Yellow Bird," which I could recite from memory. His collection of poems *In the Winter of Cities* traveled with me everywhere.

"The Yellow Bird" was also one of Faye's favorites, and she was considering making it into a film. Tennessee was enthused about this project, and we ended up spending many memorable evenings with him and his agent, Bill Barnes. We would often meet in New York at Tennessee's suite in the Hotel Elysée or the hotel's illustrious Monkey Bar. The nights usually ended at Faye's apartment for numerous nightcaps.

Tennessee had a distinctly full, deep, bellowing laugh that rang out when he reacted to an absurd or witty comment, often one that came from his own mouth. His mind worked continuously, with the precision of a Cartier wristwatch, all the interlocking gears in constant motion.

One evening, I brought out my copy of *Winter of Cities* and asked Tennessee if he would consider reading three of my favorite poems: "Life Story," "The Beanstalk Country," and "Gold Tooth Blues." Fortunately, I had my cassette recorder with me, and Tennessee graciously let me tape his reading.

In 1975, Tennessee came to Boston to see a performance of one of his later works, *The Red Devil Battery Sign*, a dark play that takes place in a

Dallas hotel cocktail lounge soon after JFK's assassination. The rehearsals and rewrites took place in New York, and by the time the play finally premiered, in Boston, there was already talk in the theater world that it was yet another Williams play in trouble. Faye and I met Tennessee at his suite in Boston's Ritz-Carlton, where a small entourage gathered, including Maria St. Just, who would later control the rights to Tennessee's work after his death.

Tennessee was quiet, not unfriendly but preoccupied and far more self-absorbed than he had been during any of my previous encounters with him. As he finished his wine, he said, "It was in this very city after many long sleepless nights that I reworked *Battle of Angels.* A strange feeling to be back in this same hotel." St. Just tried unsuccessfully to lighten Tennessee's mood.

Tennessee wanted to arrive at the theater before the start of the play. As we entered through the stage door, he and St. Just were ushered into a meeting while Faye and I waited in an empty dressing room. Tennessee reappeared, now in a better mood, and we followed him as he stopped by each actor's dressing room. When we got to the last one, he opened the door to find Anthony Quinn doing stomach crunches on a slant board. Tennessee sarcastically said, "Tony, nice to see you're keeping in such fine shape."

Quinn, not stopping his crunches, snapped back, "Tennessee, why the hell do you have me appear in this play without my shirt? I think you're doing it just to torture me!" They both laughed as Faye stuck her head in for a quick hello, since Quinn was the star of one of her first films, *The Happening.* "Faye? Oh, no — he brought you here to further humiliate me?"

The Red Devil Battery Sign weaves in and out of hallucinatory dialogue. Quinn played the role of King Del Rey, an over-the-hill mariachi musician suffering from a brain tumor, and Claire Bloom played the Woman Downtown, a victim of shock treatments administered by the right-wing Red Devil Battery Company.

After the performance, we adjourned to the Athens Olympia, a theater-district restaurant that was home to the city's finest martinis and discreet high-backed leather booths. Quinn was seated with one party, and Bloom sat with another. Strangely, Tennessee didn't go over and greet either of the actors. I later found out that the producer of the play, David Merrick, was thinking of possibly replacing Claire Bloom with Faye. Sadly for all involved, the play ran less than two weeks before its final performance, dashing Tennessee's hopes for a Broadway opening.

Years later, following my divorce from Faye, I met up with Tennessee for cocktails — which he called his five o'clock angels — at the Pier House hotel, in Key West. When I arrived, he was seated at a table on the outer deck, overlooking the ocean. He was with his sleeping pug, curled up near his feet, and a man in his midtwenties whom he introduced as his employee. Sensing something was wrong, he asked what brought me to Key West, and I glumly mentioned that my marriage to Faye was over.

He called to the waiter for another glass, filled it with wine, and handed it to me.

I could see his sad but penetrating eyes through his sunglasses. He had recently written in the *New York Times*, "No one is more acutely aware than I that I am widely regarded as the ghost of a writer, a ghost still visible." How humiliating for an artist of his stature to publicly write those words. He had survived a life filled with deep disappointments, despair, love, and heartache and had used his genius to turn his pain into some of our greatest works of dramatic art.

He looked at me and said, "Peter, the heart survives, but it's the deep scars that will remain, like a lover's initials carved on the trunk of an old maple tree." The three of us sat quietly, staring out at the vast Atlantic Ocean.

26

KISS AND SAY GOODBYE
Exeunt

IN THE AUTUMN of 1979, it had been a month since I'd last seen Faye. She had left our home in Boston without any reason other than needing space. For many months prior, I could feel her drifting away, but my efforts to get closer had been met with a stone wall. Faye longed to have a baby, but her emotional instability and her increasing alcohol and drug use further compounded the volatility of our relationship. I feared we were not in an environment conducive to raising a child. This widened the gulf between us. We had reached an impasse, but we agreed that putting a brief pause on our careers to focus our energy on saving our marriage was the priority. We were planning to begin therapy together in Boston, but as the time for that approached, Faye remained in New York, not wanting to commit.

I came to New York to visit my father, who had been rushed to the hospital, gravely ill.

I called Faye from a pay phone in the hospital lobby, hoping for words more comforting and caring than "Oh, Peter, I'm so sorry to hear about your father. I'd certainly come meet you, but I'm in the midst of a new project and so many business meetings. Let's chat later — if not tonight, tomorrow." I was shaken up after my grim hospital visit, seeing my father so frail, so I stopped off at a nearby bar.

After knocking back quite a few, I cabbed over to our apartment, at 300 Central Park West. As I approached the entrance, Billy, the doorman, said, "Mr. Wolf, I feel so strange having to say this to you, but we have strict orders from your wife not to let you enter the building." I knew Billy; we always chatted together. He was a big music fan. I could see it was an uncomfortable situation for him. He added, "You didn't hear this from me, but if you went around the building, through the service entrance, there might not be anyone on duty tonight."

I pretended not to hear Billy; he knew me well enough to know I'd keep it under my hat. I entered the back of the building and took the service elevator up to Faye's floor. The rear door of the apartment was locked, so I walked around to the front. From inside I could hear Al Green on the stereo and intimate laughter and conversation between Faye and a man. It did not sound like a business meeting. I took out my key to open the door, shocked to discover that she had changed the lock.

My heart was pounding, and a rush of adrenaline overtook me as I hurled my body full force at the heavy, thick wooden door. Unbelievably, it came crashing open, hanging by one hinge. I entered to see Faye and photographer Terry O'Neill both frozen, staring in disbelief. I was in shock myself: I couldn't quite believe what I just did or understand how I did it.

Terry ran into the bedroom as Faye screamed, "Mister, what in the hell do you think you're doing? I can have you arrested!"

Not backing down, I shouted, "Faye, I'm still your husband, and I've got every damn right to be standing here."

Faye, switching gears, tried to calm me with an Oscar-worthy performance. "Peter, you've got every right to be here, and I know how upset you must be. How is your father? Is he okay?"

In the state I was in, just this one crumb of concern was enough to soften me.

"Peter, please. Sit down and let's talk," she said as she led me over to the sofa. "We're both so confused and sort of lost. Why don't we set a time and meet tomorrow? Then we can see your father together. I'd really like that. Did you eat anything today? Do you want something? Please, let's sit down. Oh, Peter, we've been through so much. We'll get through all this — we always do."

I had felt estranged from her for so long that I lapped up her words like a hungry stray, forgetting all about Terry in the bedroom. This was the soothing voice of Dorothy Faye, the woman I loved, the woman I married.

"If you don't want any food, let me open a bottle of champagne, and let's drink to your father getting well." She came back with a tray carrying two crystal flutes and a bottle of Cristal. She filled our glasses and made a toast: "To your father — may he come home soon." We drank, and Faye said she was getting hors d'oeuvres from the kitchen.

There was an intercom system in the apartment, and each phone had five buttons. The first two were outside lines, and the other three were intercoms between rooms. I saw one of the intercom buttons light up on the phone beside me. I quietly lifted the receiver and heard her say, "Don't worry, darling. I'll be getting rid of him shortly. Just give me a little more time. Stay put and keep quiet, and everything will be okay."

By the time Faye returned with cheese and crackers, I was beside myself. I smashed my champagne glass to the floor, where it shattered across the living room. I yelled out to Terry, "Come on outta there! If you don't, I swear you're gonna learn what the fucking Bronx code is."

What that meant I didn't know, but it felt good yelling it. Terry, however, remained locked behind the bedroom door.

Faye shouted at me to leave. "Get out. I'm calling the police!"

I spotted several silver Halliburton camera cases. I calmly opened them one by one. Each was filled with photo gear — cameras and lenses of all sizes. I picked up a long lens and shouted toward the bedroom, "Terry, come out or I'm going to start smashing up your shit!"

There was no reply. The bedroom door remained locked. I threw the lens, and it exploded when it hit the slate floor. Faye, horrified, screamed for me to stop. Next came a Nikon with a telescopic lens. Then, one by one, the finely organized trays of glass lens filters. Yet when I spotted the Leica, as wild as I was, I just couldn't summon the anger to smash that holy relic. It remained the lone survivor of my fury.

I knew I had to leave quickly. I charged out the smashed front door, which was still hanging by one hinge, and headed toward the service elevator. But I decided it was wiser to take the stairs. I sped down the twenty-one flights faster than a marathon runner and was back on the street in no time. I heard sirens and saw the flashing blue lights of police cars, shocked that she had really called the cops.

The morning after

My repeated attempts at a reconciliation were continually thwarted. A divorce followed, highlighted by a major disagreement over who was the rightful owner of our cherished copy of Otis Redding's record *Otis Blue*.

Months later, as I walked down Madison Avenue, I spotted Faye with Terry. They passed me by, so engrossed with each other that they didn't even notice me. Although their marriage did not last, through this union Faye adopted a baby, fulfilling her dream of becoming a mother. With the passing of time, we rekindled a friendship.

Faye seemed hopeful about the possibility of a second chance, and she suggested a reconciliation between us, but that was a road I would not go down again.

When I hear Hank Williams sing "I Can't Help It If I'm Still in Love with You," I am right back on that New York City sidewalk, an invisible observer of the woman I once loved.

It's so easy for the mind to forget the wrongs when the heart still wants what once felt so right.

Long Way Back Again

"I FEEL THAT GYPSY WIND"

27

ONE MORE ROUND
Ahmet Ertegun and Bhaskar Menon

WHEN THE GEILS band first signed with Atlantic Records, in 1968, we had had no lawyer and no manager. But we were desperate to be recording artists, especially on the historic Atlantic label. The company knew how much we wanted a record deal, so it presented us with an antiquated contract and royalty rate circa 1952. We were committed to the label for six years or until we fulfilled all our contractual obligations, whichever came first. The deal required us to make two albums a year, and the costs of recording, manufacturing, advertising, and promotion were all charged back to the band. If we were lucky, we might receive a small royalty, but we hardly ever did. To add insult to injury, the label took half our song-publishing earnings. We were naive then, but as time passed, we came to learn just how exploitative this contract really was.

Ahmet Ertegun, along with his brother, Nesuhi, headed the label. Later they added another partner, Jerry Wexler, who was responsible for signing us to the company. Ahmet and Jerry eventually had a falling-out regarding the direction of the label. The disagreement became so heated that Wexler left the company. This was a development that pleased Ahmet but put many of the artists Wexler signed, the Geils band included, in a kind of limbo. Fortunately, by 1978, we were nearing the end of our disastrous contract with Atlantic.

During our early years at the label, I spent a great deal of time in New York, traveling back and forth from Boston, since I represented the band in all its business dealings. The label's offices were located in a nondescript building on West 60th Street and Broadway and occupied the entire second floor. The atmosphere was always lively: interaction among the staff and recording artists created a real family environment. On one side of the floor were the executive offices, and on the other side was a hallway that led to the famed Atlantic recording studios.

On my first day there, I rode up in the elevator with Ben E. King, singer-songwriter Brook Benton, and King Curtis, the beloved and brilliant saxophonist, who ran all the studio affairs.

I always made it a point to check out the sessions that might be happening in the studios, and I got lucky several times, catching Aretha Franklin on one day and Rahsaan Roland Kirk on another. (Kirk was the first person I interviewed when I was a late-night disc jockey on Boston radio.)

In 1973, the Geils band was performing several shows in LA when I found out that Ahmet was in town, staying in a private bungalow at the Beverly Hills Hotel. The next afternoon, I called his room. The phone was answered by his close friend Earl McGrath, then head of publicity for the label. I knew Earl from the New York offices, and many times he and I would end the day at a local watering hole. Earl, pleased to hear from me, said, "Ahmet has stepped out, but you should definitely come over at five, and we'll all have drinks." Earl later confided that Ahmet had actually been in the bathroom, and upon hearing I'd be stopping by, he became terribly annoyed, not only because he didn't know me well but also because he rightly assumed I was visiting with a business grievance.

I had often seen Ahmet walking the hallways at the Atlantic offices in New York, usually smoking a small, thin cigar. With this in mind, I went to an exclusive tobacconist in Beverly Hills and bought their most expensive box of small, thin cigars, which neither I nor the band could afford. When I arrived, Earl answered the bungalow door and told me Ahmet was on a phone call to London. I was thankful that Earl was there because I knew he understood my nervousness. "Hey, man, have a drink and relax. Ahmet is glad you offered to stop by — we got vodka, red wine, white wine…"

At that moment, Ahmet appeared. He was a tidy man, balding, with an immaculately trimmed goatee. His clothing, from his eyeglasses to his velvet Gucci loafers, exuded wealth. He had a princely air, having been born into a distinguished Turkish family. Educated in the finest boarding schools and universities in Europe, he spoke and read five languages fluently. His father was the Turkish ambassador to the United States, and he and his brother, Nesuhi, grew up in Washington, DC. As teenagers, they became obsessed with jazz and the music of New Orleans. They held dance parties at the Turkish embassy, hiring their favorite musicians for entertainment — artists such as a young Duke Ellington, Cab Calloway, and Louis Armstrong. In the late 1940s, with money borrowed from their dentist, they started Atlantic Records, which quickly became one of the most distinguished independent record labels of its time.

I handed Ahmet the box of cigars, which he graciously received. He asked if I'd care to join him and Earl for a drink. I, of course, accepted. Earl, already several glasses in, asked, "So what do you need to see Ahmet about?"

"Well, Ahmet, we're playing out here, and we'd love it if you and Earl would come and see the band perform tomorrow." (We were headlining a bill at the Santa Monica Civic Auditorium with Little Feat opening.)

Earl knew from our New York bar chats that we were being grossly underpaid. So, pouring his third vodka and soda, he blurted out, "What's your royalty rate?"

You could tell from Ahmet's face that he had been caught by surprise. He gave Earl a cold, hard stare, which Earl, stirring a drink with his finger, pretended not to notice.

"Maybe several points per album with no advances," I nervously replied.

"What? Holy shit — and that's supposed to be split six ways?" said Earl.

Ahmet, not about to get trapped, intoned, "Well, perhaps Earl and I could come and check out the band."

Just then, Ahmet was saved by a knock at the door. He rushed to open it. Standing there was a small, sturdy man, well dressed, in a smart suit with a shirt open at the neck. He looked to be Latino. Ahmet introduced him to me as Edson. Earl poured more drinks, then Ahmet mentioned that he and Earl had a quick meeting to attend and invited Edson and me to either stay in the suite or go to the hotel bar. He suggested we all meet at eight that evening at Mr Chow's restaurant, adding, with a saturnine gleam, "Don't forget — Mr Chow's. We're gonna have lots of fun — trust me, baby!"

When they had gone, Edson asked, "Do you wanna stay here or grab a drink at the bar? The bar might have some pretty ladies to look at."

"Sounds like the right move to me," I said as I finished the tall glass of vodka Earl had poured.

In the Polo Lounge, Edson and I, accompanied by several burly men who, I assumed, formed his entourage, sat at the bar and ordered some drinks. There were indeed attractive ladies there, all in the company of much older men. Edson said, "Some very pretty scenery around here. How do we get them away from their uncles?"

The busboy was staring intently at Edson and rushed over to the other busboys at the end of the bar. Soon thereafter, a bunch of faces peered out from the kitchen door, staring at us. The look they gave us made me think they had spotted a bank robber with a million-dollar bounty on his head. Edson didn't seem to notice.

He told me he thought this place was too stiff and maybe we should try another bar. As our entourage walked toward the valet parking station, every hotel worker stopped and stared. When the valet took the ticket, he stood, open-mouthed, as if he were in the presence of one of the twelve apostles. The car quickly arrived, attended to by ten valets, who surrounded us and spoke in what sounded like Spanish. As we slowly pulled out to leave, it seemed as if the entire staff had gathered by the driveway, all waving and shouting.

Approaching the Sunset Strip, I asked my new drinking buddy, "Say, what's going on? Seems like a lot of people recognize you. What do you do?"

"I play football."

Not being a sports fan, I wasn't surprised that I didn't know him. But I thought, *Okay, we're both a little drunk, and he's pulling my leg; he seems too small to be a football player.*

We stopped off at two other nightspots. At the second, a statuesque blonde sidled up to Edson, and she was soon joined by several of her lady friends, all equally stunning. It was almost time to meet Ahmet, but the swarm of admirers made our exit difficult. The crowd followed us outside as Edson's entourage helped get us safely into his car.

When we arrived at Mr Chow's, we found Ahmet seated at a long table with some very recognizable celebrities. Earl had saved a seat for me next to him and poured me a full goblet of wine. I asked him, "Who is this Edson guy? Is he really a football player?"

Earl, with cigarette and drink in hand, said, "What Muhammad Ali is to boxing, he is to football. Hands down, he is the greatest soccer player in the world. Ahmet calls him by his first name, Edson, but the world knows him as Pelé."

Later, the party moved to the home of actor Dennis Hopper. As the sun was rising, Pelé, with a car full of partygoers, offered me a ride back to my hotel. Ahmet and Earl did come to see us play the next night, but in all the following years I spent with Ahmet, the question of royalties never came up again.

Once we were back in New York, Earl invited me to join him and

Ahmet on many of their late-night sorties through the city. A typical evening would begin with a dinner party hosted at either Ahmet's East Side brownstone or an extravagant restaurant such as La Côte Basque or La Grenouille or, for less formal dining, at Mr Chow's or Mortimer's. Often we would make a quick stop at the Carlyle hotel for yet more cocktails and a performance by the society staple Bobby Short (who was also an Atlantic artist), singing from the Cole Porter songbook. Then over to the bar at Buddy's Place, owned by the legendary jazz drummer Buddy Rich. Performing with him one night was jazz vocalist Joe Williams. When we entered, Joe, coincidentally, was singing the song "Chains of Love," written by Doc Pomus but credited to none other than Ahmet himself.

At some point in the evening, we would join Ahmet's wife, Mica, at her table in Reno Sweeney, a nightclub frequented by high-fashion and high-society figures. Seated with us might be Diana Vreeland, Lee Radziwill, Diane von Furstenberg, Barry Diller, and the ever-bulging heft of Jerry Zipkin: when he smiled, something he did quite often, you could almost play on his teeth like a piano. I once asked him what he did. He gave me an extra-large grin and said, "Do? *Do?* Darling, I'm rich!"

I was often amused by snippets of chatter from around the table: "Oh, how I hate it when a man wears his sport jacket draped over his shoulders — it looks so tacky." "My Lord, who did her face? She looks like she's walking in a wind tunnel. She should have seen my guy for her eyes — he's the best in the world."

We would sometimes return uptown to the 67th Street apartment of Jane and Jann Wenner, owners of *Rolling Stone*, where we imbibed further cocktails, although some would partake in more illicit pick-me-ups. Jane and I had gone to high school together, and I would often visit Jann in his elegant and opulent office at the magazine. Jann was always generous in offering me his counsel regarding the inner workings of the music industry. I considered Jane and Jann good friends whom I looked forward to seeing whenever I was in New York.

Sometimes we headed downtown to the Lower East Side cold-water loft of Earl McGrath's longtime friend Larry Rivers, the so-called godfather of pop art, who loved to throw parties and honk on his sax to a crowd of both highbrow and lowbrow fellow midnight travelers.

The night always ended at Earl's cavernous midtown apartment. Earl was one of the wittiest men I've ever known. He could walk into any venue, whether an elegant dining room or a cheap sawdust-on-the-floor bar, and in no time become the center of attention. Joining our gatherings were assorted roaming strays who always latched on to our group during the evening's safari. Earl's apartment was well stocked with liquor and whatever else one might desire. His art collection was fit for a museum, and all his acquisitions were given to him by his artist friends: David Hockney, Cy Twombly, sculptor Robert Graham, Brice Marden, and the omnipresent Andy Warhol.

This period of roaming the city ended several years later, when Studio 54 exploded onto the scene and absorbed celebrity nightlife like a black hole enveloping an entire universe.

On one occasion I was Ahmet's guest at a charity fundraiser. Record executives were big on charity events. They would donate the company's money — which they had at their disposal because they owned the lion's share of profits from their artists' recordings, so if the truth be known, it was really the artists' money — to various causes large and small. At that point, the Geils band had finally made its last contractual recording for Atlantic Records, and I was still managing all its business affairs. I often found it difficult to reconcile the friendship-business aspect of Ahmet's and my relationship, so with drink in hand, I approached him.

"We're friends, Ahmet, but could I have your ear for a business-related question?" I paused for effect, then continued. "The band would love to maintain its relationship with Atlantic. We just finished our last recording. What do you suggest is the best way to proceed to keep us on the label?"

I was under the impression he would say, "Why don't you have your lawyer call our lawyers? Let's work something out."

Instead he did something very cunning. He replied, "Listen, baby, why don't you go out and speak with other record companies and see how much they're willing to offer you? I don't want to present a deal that might be unfair to the band."

At first I thought that was very kind of Ahmet, but in hindsight, I realized he was being a strategic chess player and banking on the fact that our albums had achieved only minor sales and we had no major hit singles. Who would want to sign us to a deal worth very much?

That almost turned out to be true.

It fell to me to meet with various label presidents and A and R staff. My first step was to hire a lawyer. Music lawyers back then were becoming celebrities in their own right. I met with almost every lawyer I'd heard about, and many of them said they'd do a deal, but it would be costly. One lawyer, who worked for Paul Simon and Bruce Springsteen, said he'd help us, but it would cost the band fifty thousand dollars. This colossal sum was unrealistic, considering that we were severely in debt.

I met with every industry bigwig of the time — lawyers who worked with David Geffen, Bob Dylan, Joni Mitchell. None was interested. My mood was pessimistic, but during a stretch in Los Angeles, I happened to run into a lawyer named Abe Somer, whom I'd once met at a party. We arranged a meeting at his office.

Abe was several years older than I, of medium height, and very thin, with slicked-back hair and a hooked nose. Along with my troubles, I brought a sandwich to his office. When I finished my tale, Abe was stunned. He said, "You guys have worked for so long and put out so many records — I can't believe that you're coming to see me with your lunch in a brown paper bag, telling me you're in the red. You have no money, and you didn't really make a cent off Atlantic Records. This is crazy!" He added, "Look, I'll help you, and I won't charge you. I'll get you a deal, and once we get a deal, whatever you think is fair to pay me, you pay me."

This was an offer I couldn't refuse. Abe was one of the top lawyers in the music industry. He worked with the Beach Boys, the Mamas and the Papas, the Doors, Harry Nilsson, and George Harrison. Most important to me, he had just negotiated a very handsome deal for the Rolling Stones, who were also leaving Atlantic Records.

Abe gave me a list of label presidents with whom I should meet. He believed that an in-person one-on-one between an artist and a top executive would be more meaningful than a call from a lawyer. I later realized that this was his way of having me do all the legwork. First up was Walter Yetnikoff, president and CEO of Columbia Records. A meeting was set up in New York, and as I entered his office, he said, "Peter, it's funny you walked in here. The Geils band is one of the bands I want to sign. You and Bonnie Raitt are two amazing artists from New England. I'd love to sign you both."

"Great, Walter," I replied. "Why don't you have your guy call my guy?"

But time went on, and no phone call was made. Abe said, "He's just shucking and jiving. I don't think he's interested, so let's move on."

I exhausted the list: Joe Smith at Elektra, Mo Ostin at Warner Bros., Jerry Moss at A&M. Executives at United Artists and RCA. I even went to smaller labels such as Casablanca Records. They had a few big artists, including Kiss and Donna Summer, alongside some other disco artists who were selling like hotcakes. I called the president of the company, Neil Bogart, who seemed happy to hear from me.

Casablanca was located in Los Angeles. Still not knowing how to drive, I took a taxi. It's always strange taking a taxi in LA, since most industry people have their own car or a driver. I walked into the lobby, where several security guards were posted. In those days, this was not a common occurrence. One guy wanted to pat me down for weapons, which I thought was even stranger. Upstairs, the motif was the Sahara desert. The office was resplendent with plastic palm trees, murals of camel caravans, and actual sand dunes. In this oasis, I was escorted by teams of glossy disco-style secretaries, each one exotically attired, before finally being presented to Neil Bogart. I could smell the pungent aroma of marijuana in the air.

Neil sat behind a wide desk. Several other people were lurking in the room. "Man, we are big fans; love that you came over to see us," he said.

"Thank you, Neil. We have no more albums with Atlantic, and we're looking to find a new home."

He said, "Let's do something. It'll be great." Then he continued, "Listen, why don't you guys make a demo recording and let me hear what you sound like?"

I said in surprise, "A demo?"

"Yeah. All the new bands we sign send us demos."

I replied, incredulously, "Neil, we have ten albums out on Atlantic. I can send you the catalog — that's our demo."

I realized that these guys were so stoned, so lost in their own success, that nothing regarding Geils was ever going to happen with them.

Leaving Casablanca's tawdry offices, I was despondent. After visiting every major label and several minor ones in New York and LA, I had nothing to show for it. Finding a pay phone on the corner, I called Abe and groaned into the receiver, "Weeks are now turning into months. There's nothing out there, Abe."

He suggested we meet for dinner at the Palm, the epicenter of the entertainment industry in LA. Like many of the popular restaurants in the city, it had "power tables" where only people of great importance were seated. Abe certainly was one of them. Once there, he tried to keep my spirits up, but I was past the point of believing anything would ever happen. I was certain that unless our final Atlantic album, *Monkey Island*, sold magically well, it would probably be the end of the Geils band's recording career.

As we sat contemplating this dim future over a couple of large, cold martinis, a fellow with greased-back hair and a mustache, in his thirties, wearing blue jeans and a silver satin bomber jacket emblazoned with CAPITOL RECORDS on the back, approached our booth and asked, "Are you Peter Wolf of the Geils band?"

I nodded, and he responded, "Wow, man, I'm such a huge, huge fan!"

I thanked him, and he continued. "I'm Jim Mazza; I'm from Detroit. I've seen you guys about ten times. You're one of the greatest front men in rock, and the Geils band is the most hard-driving band in America."

That, coupled with the gin, made me even more depressed. I thanked him for his kind words and introduced him to Abe. Jim said, "Yeah, you know, it's so funny. I just got out of a meeting with Bhaskar Menon."

Abe quickly piped up. "Did you say Bhaskar Menon?"

"Yeah. We're starting a new record label, and Bhaskar is having me run it for the company. It's going to be a small boutique label, and I always dreamed about signing a band like Geils."

I looked at Abe, and Abe looked at me. Our eyes locked in delight, both of us thinking: *Could this be the moment that Lady Luck has finally smiled upon us?* Abe asked Jim to sit down and tell him all about the new label, prefacing the conversation with, "Well, you know, before coming here tonight, we just got out of a big meeting with Columbia Records. I'm representing the Stones on their new deal, and they are also extremely interested in signing Peter Wolf and the Geils band."

Jim, surprised, said, "I thought you guys were on Atlantic."

Abe leaned in and quietly said, "Well, Jim, just between us, we're looking for a new home."

Jim responded excitedly, "Wait a second! Are you telling me there's a possibility that we could sign the Geils band?"

Abe replied, cautiously, "Yeah, if you're ready to make a good enough offer."

Jim jumped at the bait. "Gentlemen, please don't leave this table. Can you wait and let me call Mr. Menon?"

Abe explained that things were moving fast, but if he could do it quickly, we'd wait. Jim rushed off to the phone booth as Abe and I sat looking at each other.

"Abe, we don't have a deal with Col — "

He cut me off. "Pete, let me handle this. Keep your mouth shut and don't say a word."

I asked Abe who this Bhaskar guy was, and Abe replied, "Maybe one of the most powerful men in the record industry. He oversees EMI Records worldwide. He even makes Ahmet and Atlantic seem like small potatoes." EMI Records, which owned Capitol, was such a long shot that Abe never even considered approaching them.

Jim hurried back to our booth and asked if we wouldn't mind waiting twenty minutes, adding that Mr. Menon was on his way. Abe's eyes opened as wide as the six zeros that make up a million, assuring him that we would wait. Abe ordered a very expensive bottle of wine and made pleasant small talk with Jim. Not wanting to betray my nervousness, I quietly sat staring at the olive afloat in my half-finished martini.

A half hour later, in walked an extremely distinguished gentleman in his midforties He was of medium build, his hair neatly trimmed, and he was finely dressed in what looked like a hand-tailored Savile Row suit. Like Ahmet, he carried a royal air of great elegance and wealth. With a polished, clipped Indian accent, he introduced himself. Abe asked him to please join us, so he slid into the booth next to me.

"It's with such great honor and pleasure to meet you both. Few things would get me out of bed at this time of night, but my very good man here, Mr. Mazza, tells me one of the great rock groups is looking for a new home. Such opportunities of this high importance do not happen frequently."

Abe continued his cat-and-mouse game. "Well, we're just about to sign a deal with Columbia Records, and as a matter of fact, I'm meeting with them tomorrow."

Bhaskar interjected, "No, no, Mr. Somer. My esteemed friend here, Mr. Mazza, has just mentioned that fact of information to me on the phone, but you are like a wish come true for this young man, and hopefully it will be a dream come true for all of us at EMI Records worldwide. We want to discuss the possibility of signing the band. We also might be able to offer you something that can possibly put Columbia Records in the rearview mirror."

Abe looked at me as if to check that we were both hearing the same thing. He sat back and let Jim continue his sales pitch about EMI Records. Bhaskar ordered a martini, and my nerves were so tightly wound that I ordered a fresh one, too. Jim and Abe were already working out deal points as Bhaskar and I sipped our cocktails.

That second martini turned into a third. Bhaskar said to me, "You know, my dear friend, why don't we let these gentlemen hash out all these monotonous details while we go off and get to know each other without the intrusion of business chatter?" We proceeded outside and waited for the valet, who rushed to get Bhaskar's car. It was a brand-new top-of-the-line Porsche convertible. We took off down Santa Monica Boulevard to the Beverly Hills Hotel's Polo Lounge, where we indulged in several more cocktails. We then adjourned to the Four Seasons Hotel bar, where we continued our conversation and consumption.

Bhaskar suggested we head back to the Palm to see how business was developing. When we arrived, the valets jostled with one another, each hoping to get behind the wheel and drive this glorious new Porsche. We returned to the booth, where Jim and Abe were still deep in their discussion of deal points and international releases. Little did any of us realize the importance of that evening. Our first EMI album would go on to nearly outsell everything we ever recorded for Atlantic *combined*, while our third EMI album became the number-one-selling record not only in America but also throughout the world in the year it was released.

Abe suggested to Jim that they continue their discussion in the morning. They departed while Bhaskar and I remained behind for one final round of martinis. He discussed his early childhood in India and described his move to London, where he swept the floors of the very studio in which the Beatles recorded, adding, "After being just a sweeper, I slowly made my way up the corporate ladder to become the worldwide CEO of the company."

I happened to find out later that Bhaskar was far from a floor sweeper: he was in fact from one of the most prominent families in India and had been educated in England at Christ Church, Oxford. He first became the head of EMI in India, then was transferred to London, where he continued his steady ascent and did, in fact, become the company's worldwide CEO. I guess if Abe could tell tales about Columbia Records wanting to sign us, it was fair game for Bhaskar to spin his own tales about his lowly entry into EMI.

The lights came up at the Palm, signaling closing time. Last call was announced, so we doubled up our final order. Bhaskar asked if I needed a ride. I lied, not wanting to inconvenience him or be seen ordering a taxi, saying, "Oh, no, Bhaskar. I have a car." We continued to chat outside the restaurant as the valet drove up with Bhaskar's car, mistakenly leaving the driver's-side door open. We continued our talk, oblivious to the fact that the car was there—until we heard an almighty crash. Another valet had driven a Mercedes right into the open door on the driver's side of the Porsche, ripping it off.

Bhaskar, not missing a beat, turned and saw the door lying on the pavement, then called the valet, who came rushing over. Bhaskar asked him, "Which gentleman runs the valet service?" The manager appeared, full of flustered apologies. Bhaskar said calmly, "No, no, no, there's no need to apologize. Why don't you just buy the car from me right now and save us all a lot of headaches?"

The manager looked bewildered by Bhaskar's suggestion, then stuttered, "I'm only an employee of the valet service, and I could never afford a car that expensive, sir."

Bhaskar was quite understanding and proceeded to get into his doorless car, offering, "Well, we will figure it out in the morning." We all stood there, nervously worrying that without the door, he could easily fall out. I asked the valet, "Do you have some way we can secure him? The seat belt has been torn out."

One of the attendants came running back with rope, and we proceeded to tie Bhaskar to his seat. In our martini haze, he and I thought this was a brilliant plan, and we both laughed hysterically while he was being encircled with ropes. Once tightly secured with double and triple knots, Bhaskar, with debonair charm, bade me farewell. "My dear Mr. Wolf, this has been such a memorable evening, an honor and pleasure. You're a true gentleman, having the thoughtfulness of making sure I'm secure and safe. I'm beholden to you. Are you sure I can't give you a lift to your hotel?"

"Oh, no, sir. It's okay."

He smiled and said, "Well, I certainly hope we speak again soon," and off he roared down Santa Monica Boulevard. I stood on the sidewalk along with the valets, watching as he stopped for the first red light and then for the second. His blinker came on as he slowly turned a corner. *Oh, good,* I thought. *He seems okay, and he's definitely tied in tight.* I asked the valet who was carrying off Bhaskar's door to call a taxi, and I headed back to my hotel.

The next morning, I was awakened not only by a loud pounding on the door but also by an aggressive pounding inside my head. I staggered over slowly, the room spinning, as I opened the door and saw a bellman standing there with a large white box, beautifully wrapped in blue ribbon. I took the mysterious box, inside of which was a bottle of Louis Roederer Cristal Rosé champagne and a handwritten note.

My dear friend,

Thank you so much for a thoroughly entertaining evening. I will make sure Mr. Mazza and Mr. Somer finish their work so we may have the honor of you and your extraordinary band on our new label.

With my best,
Bhaskar

P.S. After about ten minutes of honking my horn nonstop, I eventually woke up my wife, and after several attempts, she was finally able to cut me loose.

Sir, you tie a very good knot!

28

KNOWS TO NOSE
Pinkpop Festival

A FTER TEN YEARS, the Geils band was finally headlining arenas. It was the summer of 1980, and we were about to embark on a tour of the Midwest, when I received a phone call from our booking agent, Frank Barsalona. He was excited about a great opportunity for us. A popular up-and-coming rock group, Van Halen, was scheduled to headline the prestigious Pinkpop Festival in the Netherlands. I was friendly with their lead guitar virtuoso, Eddie Van Halen, and I was pleased that his namesake band was shooting up the charts. This festival was the perfect venue for them: Eddie and his brother Alex's Dutch heritage and the fact that this was to be their first-ever performance in Holland was exciting for native fans and press alike. However, their lead singer, David Lee Roth, had apparently broken his nose and needed surgery, forcing them to cancel their performance.

Our agent was thrilled that the promoters suggested us as the replacement headliner for the festival. Pinkpop took place every year and involved around ten groups, an eclectic and unpredictable lineup.

This diversity made it an important event to play and an even more important event to headline.

I traveled on ahead of the band, stopping off to do advance press in London, where I was informed upon arrival that Van Halen would be able to play the festival after all. According to their manager, Roth's father was in the medical field and was able to get David back on his feet pretty fast. There was, however, a new twist: Van Halen didn't want to headline but instead wanted to play in the slot just before us. At this point in their career, it was a known fact that their strategy was to play the underdog in an attempt to steal the thunder away from any band that played after them. They were confident in their ability to undermine the headliner, thereby hoping to gain a greater following.

I wasn't worried. We were a damn good live band and could hold our own. Working our way up, we'd opened for many great artists: the Stones, the Who, the Faces, Janis Joplin, and B.B. King, to name but a few. When Geils headlined, we tried to be supportive of the opening acts, knowing that if they connected with our audience, one day they, too, might be headliners. This proved to be the case with U2, Tom Petty, Billy Joel, Bonnie Raitt, Iggy Pop, and the Eagles, among others.

London has always been one of my favorite cities, and I was glad to make a stop there en route to Amsterdam, not only to meet the press and our European record companies but also to patronize English pubs. In particular, I have an addiction to sweet and tasty English bitters. A well-pulled fresh pint is, in my opinion, pretty hard to beat.

While I was in London, the record company supplied me with a car and driver. Eager to make the most of this trip, I called some musician friends and arranged to hook up with Nick Lowe, my old friend from his days as a member of the group Brinsley Schwarz. He was working in his studio with Elvis Costello, whom I had met on his first tour of the States.

After a couple of meet and greets with the record folk to plan the press junket, I jumped in my car, off to visit Nick. As we headed toward his studio, I told the driver how much I loved English bitters. He acknowledged this with, "Sir, I don't think you'll find any tonight. The pubs are set to close pretty soon — in around fifteen minutes."

"Fifteen minutes!" I replied. "Pull over to the first pub you come to!"

"Sir, I don't advise stopping anywhere in Camden. There's been a lot of trouble here lately, and these pubs can get pretty rough at night."

"Listen, I gotta have some bitters. Please, just pull over. There's one up ahead!"

"But sir, I don't think it's a wise idea."

"My friend, I'm from New York City — the Bronx, to be exact. Trust me: wherever we are, it ain't gonna be as rough as the Bronx."

"If you insist, sir." He pulled over to a pub on the corner, and I jumped out, hoping to at least catch last call.

The pub was totally empty except for three stocky men in their early thirties standing at the bar. This flat-capped trio wore faded denim work trousers, and their shirtsleeves were rolled high onto muscular tattooed arms. I was dressed from head to toe in black: leather pants, Cuban-heeled boots, turtleneck, leather jacket, all topped with a cool black-felt Borsalino fedora and Ray-Ban sunglasses. They sized me up as I approached the bar. The bartender continued chatting with them. Only when I called out to him did he begrudgingly make his way over. I asked for four pints of bitters.

"Four pints? You know we're closing up in ten minutes."

"Yeah, I know. Just pour me four good pints, and I'll be on my way."

The man nearest to me asked, in a thick Cockney accent, "Where you from, mate?"

"The States."

"From the States, you say now. What you doing 'round here?"

"I'm working."

"Working where?"

"Just working."

As the pints were being poured and delivered one by one, I guzzled them down as fast as I could. I reached into my pocket to find a mess of crumpled ten-pound notes all mixed up with a bunch of dollar bills. Some fell to the floor, and I bent down to grab them.

"Where you rushing to?"

"I'm meeting up with some friends."

"Friends? What friends do you have 'round here?"

"I don't know if they're from around here. My driver is taking me."

As soon as I heard those words come out of my mouth, I knew it was a blunder, but the bitters had gone right to my head.

"Driver! You got a driver?"

Two pints were left, so I wanted to pay up and finish as quickly as possible.

"So you got a driver and you're working here in Camden?" His tone told me it was best to hurry up and leave. I paid the bartender and, not knowing how long a drive we had, thought it would be wise to take a leak.

"Where's the bathroom?"

"What, you havin' a bath, luv? It's in the back, down a flight of stairs. You can't miss it. If you do, you'll smell it!" answered the bartender, and the men guffawed.

I headed down the dimly lit concrete stairs. At the urinal, I realized the large quantity of liquids I had consumed meant that a quick whiz was out of the question. At the sound of heavy footsteps behind me, I turned to see two of the men from the bar standing there.

A swift punch was thrown at my nose, followed by a landing shot to my jaw, and down I went. The other man gave me some good hard kicks in the ribs with the heel of his heavy work boot, saying, "Get back to your driver and stay the fuck out of Camden, you fucking wanker!" They ran out. I must have been in shock, because I staggered to my feet, zipped my pants, and rushed up the stairs to chase after them. I asked the bartender, "Where the hell did they go?"

"Go? I don't know what you're talking about."

I careened onto the street. My driver was waiting in front, but I could see them up ahead, walking fast and turning the next corner, a block and a half away. There was a bobby standing on that corner, and I ran to him, explained that I was attacked in a pub, and pointed to the three men, who were still in sight. The bobby and I gave chase while he took out his whistle, blowing it several times as it echoed off the wet and narrow cobblestone street.

We were running for at least two blocks, the bobby furiously blowing his whistle, when suddenly a group of men jumped from two unmarked vans. Some chased the men from the pub, and three of them ran to tackle me. I was pinned to the ground by a hard shoe to my back. Unaware until that moment of the severity of my injuries, I saw blood trickling and pooling in the cracks of the street. The pain was stabbing at my head and chest. I could hear the conversation between the bobby and the men from the van. They were, apparently, undercover detectives who had been waiting all night following a tip about a large shipment of heroin to be delivered to a nearby terraced apartment.

The head detective told the bobby that at the sound of his whistle they had assumed he was chasing all four of us. It was then suggested that the best option was to take everyone down to the station. Fortunately, they put the three men in one van and me in another. When we arrived, I was put in a cell — more like a cage — in an alley behind the police station. Soon after, the three men from the pub were thrown into the adjoining cell. They clapped their eyes on me, trying to grab me between the bars, telling me what they would do when they got their hands on me — "You're a dead man!" — and hurling other similarly eloquent threats.

I was menaced and spat upon in that alley for what seemed like forever until at last a detective unlocked my cage and walked me to a small windowless room. There was a single light hanging from the ceiling, a small metal table, an ashtray stacked high with cigarette butts, and a bunch of heavy wooden chairs where two detectives, pasty-faced, sweaty, and balding, were sitting, waiting for me.

"Could you tell us what happened?"

"I need to see a doctor!"

"You won't be seeing anybody until you tell us what happened."

I shouted, "I'm an American, and I want to see a doctor! I've got blood pouring out of my face, and my ribs are killing me. I need to see a doctor now!"

"Sonny, we're in charge here, and you won't see any doctors until you answer our questions."

The room seemed to slowly begin spinning as the pain intensified. I almost slid from the chair, but one of the detectives caught me just in time and said to the other, "Best get Chief McLaughlin."

Several minutes passed before a quiet, soft-spoken man entered the room. He told the detectives, "I'll handle this from here on in." Through my one remaining good eye, I saw that the chief appeared to be in his early sixties, with hair slightly gray and neatly combed. He wore a brown Harris Tweed three-piece suit with a wide striped tie. Delicate round frameless glasses covered what seemed like sad and compassionate eyes. He could easily have been a chaplain.

"Young man, you're awfully hurt. We don't have a doctor here, but we do have a nurse, and I'll have him come look at you right away. It would be a great help to me, though, if you could tell me in your own words what happened to you tonight."

I tried to recount everything, from leaving the hotel and stopping at the pub to the encounter in the men's room and the detectives throwing me to the ground.

"We're sorry about that, son, but our detectives thought you were all together and running from our officer. Ah, here's the nurse."

The nurse examined my skull, and when he touched my nose, I almost hit the ceiling. Another bolt of pain shot through me as he felt my rib cage.

"He might have a broken nose and possibly a rib or two, and that's a pretty deep cut under his right eye. I can try to stitch it."

"No!" I shouted. "I want a hospital! I need to go to a fucking hospital, now!"

"Easy, son," the chief said. "We need to have you sign some statements first."

"Listen, I ain't signing nothing!"

"You need to help us, then we'll be happy to help you," the chief said softly.

"The only way you can help me is to get me to the hospital. I got a whole day of interviews tomorrow with about ten newspapers and magazines, and let's see how they react to London's finest not allowing me to get proper medical help!"

"Interviews? What do you mean, interviews?"

"Two days from now I'm supposed to perform in Holland!"

"Are you a performer?"

"Yeah. I'm in the J. Geils Band."

"The J. Geils Band? Sorry, son — never heard of them. But listen, laddie. The men who roughed you up tonight are a pretty dangerous lot, so be glad you're still breathing. We've been trying to snag that bunch for a long time now, and finally, we caught them red-handed. It would be a great help to us if you sign a statement saying that they attacked you, unprovoked, in the pub, then we can lock them up for quite a while. Now, wouldn't you like that?"

"Listen, I'd like to help. But get me to a hospital now, and I can sign whatever the hell you need later."

The next thing I remember is being on a gurney, and I could make out that several people were standing over me. One said, "Take it easy and don't try to move. You're in pretty rough shape. Cracked rib...the nose is swollen but maybe not broken...can't be sure. Looks like you got a pretty nice shiner on your right eye, and we'll stitch the cut under your left. It's going to take a bit longer because we're making small stitches very close to each other, so it won't leave much of a scar. Your driver is in the waiting room, and you should be out of here shortly. They told us you're in a band. What's the name of your group?"

"The J. Geils Band."

"Sorry — never heard of 'em."

I don't remember the drive back to the hotel, but thank God the people at the hospital gave me a nice supply of painkillers. In my delirium, I must have asked for Quaaludes, because they supplied me with a small bottle of the English version, Mandrax. Also, the driver must have informed the record company what had happened, because there was a message tucked under my hotel-room door that read, "All interviews will be canceled until further notice."

Several hours later, I awoke from a deep sleep to the sound of knocking on the door. It was two people from the record company with a doctor. He gave me a once-over and a strong shot of some sort of painkiller followed by toast, jam, and tea. Afterward, I wasn't feeling as bad as I had expected.

When I finally looked in the mirror, I saw a black-and-blue shiner as big as a doughnut. My entire face was puffy, and I had black stitches under my left eye.

I stretched out on the bed, woozy from the doctor's injection, drifting in and out of sleep.

I can't remember how I left London. I do remember waking up on a plane headed to Amsterdam. The doctor's shot was wearing off. At the airport I was met by a promoter and his assistant who had been forewarned about my misadventures. I was walking with a limp. When I removed my sunglasses, the promoter flinched. Nervously, he asked, "Peter, are you sure you're able to perform?"

I assured him, "If there's a doctor who can give me a shot of something for the pain, I should be okay. Whatever happens, we're not going to cancel."

The night before the show, I had a hard time sleeping, so in the morning I headed down to the concert site early. When I arrived, bands were going through sound checks. I spotted our road crew on the far side of the stage and joined them. Everyone knew what had happened, and it was a comfort to be among friends again. UB40 ran through a few songs, followed by the Jam. The sound check was wrapping up as four Mercedes limousines slowly pulled to the front of the stage area. Out jumped the favorite sons of the Netherlands, Van Halen. The band charged up the ramp, milling about, chatting with their crew, eagerly watched by the ever-present press. Surprisingly, their lead singer, David Lee Roth, had only a small Band-Aid across his nose. The promoter, who was standing next to him on the stage as he was jumping around, threw me a puzzled look. He asked David how he was feeling, to which he replied, "Oh, great, man! Can't wait to get onstage tonight and rip up the place!"

David and the promoter walked toward me.

With all the enthusiasm of a used car salesman, David said, "Hey, man, great to see you, and thanks for stepping in when I broke my nose."

"No problem," I replied.

The promoter, as perplexed as I was, said, "Peter, take off your sunglasses."

David's eyes bulged in horror. "Holy shit, man! What the hell happened to you?" I had obvious battle wounds, while Roth was picture-perfect. We silently sized each other up. David and I were lead singers, each to varying degrees demanding, difficult, obsessive, paranoid, neurotic, and competitive.

Ironically, both he and I would end up being kicked out of our bands, but for very different reasons. Now there we stood, nose to bruised nose, trying to decide who was the wiser strategist.

The Geils band arrived from Boston later that afternoon. With my ever-increasing intensity of pain, I don't remember doing the sound check. But an hour before showtime, the promoter came backstage with one of the leading sports doctors in the country. His specialty was treating injured soccer players. After examining me carefully, he gave me three shots: one by the ribs, one near my cheek, and one in the arm.

By the time we were ready to hit the stage, I felt a euphoric glow coursing through my body. It seemed like I was floating. I was moving without any pain. In fact, my legs were zipping around the stage with unusual ferocity.

The stage was high, with a ten-foot chain-link fence between us and the audience. Toward the end of our set, I wanted to feel more connected with the crowd. I lowered myself from the edge of the stage, then dropped to the ground, jumped onto the chain-link fence, and climbed over it. The audience, clambering up the other side, took hold of my striped shirt and pulled me into the crowd. Security guards tried in vain to pull me back but, still flying high from the shots, I was enjoying every moment of it. When I finally did make it back, my sunglasses were gone and my clothes were shredded, but we ripped through song after song. Several powerful encores later, we walked offstage while the crowd yelled for more.

That night in the hotel bar, the crew and I indulged in pints of Belgium's finest. My medication gradually began to lose its effect. A crew member walked me back to my room, where I passed out cold. I surrendered to the reality of a long, painful night.

The following afternoon, we gathered in the lobby, awaiting the airport van. The promoters came to bid us farewell, carrying bundles of newspapers and big smiles on their faces. They translated the headlines for us. Our performance was well praised in the press, but they weren't as kind to Van Halen.

Four Mercedes limos pulled up to the front of the hotel for Van Halen. Their crew came out of the elevator with Eddie Van Halen, who walked up to me and asked how I was feeling. He told me to call him the next time I was in LA: "There's always room for you at the house." Then David Lee Roth walked by, festooned with a bevy of Dutch maidens, enjoying every moment, with no Band-Aid to mar his perfect California tan.

As I climbed into our van, the promoter's assistant came running up to tell me that his office had just received a phone call from Chief McLaughlin of the Camden police, wondering when I might be coming back to make a statement.

I liked the chief; he had treated me with compassion and understanding. But somehow I didn't think I'd be returning to Camden for a long, long time.

29

EVERYBODY IS A STAR
Sly Stone

I WAS WALKING PAST the entrance to a subterranean club, Jonathan Swift's, on a freezing-cold night in 1982. A handwritten sign taped to the door read: SLY STONE TONIGHT. ONE SHOW, 8:00 P.M.

Astonished, I could not believe what I was reading and went downstairs to inquire. The place was empty, with chairs stacked on tables and only one bartender setting up. I asked him if what the sign said was true. "Is Sly Stone playing here tonight?"

"Yeah," he replied.

I pressed him further. "I mean, *the* Woodstock Sly Stone? The 'I Want to Take You Higher' Sly Stone?"

"Yeah, that's what they tell me," the bartender said.

Could this strange, surreal occurrence, like something out of a lost episode of *The Twilight Zone*, really be happening?

I hung around the neighborhood for several hours until the eight o'clock showtime. The snow began to fall, and my thoughts returned to a very different place and time, when the Geils band was starting out and Sly was at his musical peak.

* * *

For our second album, *The Morning After*, released in 1971, our new producer, Bill Szymczyk (yes, a tongue twister, pronounced "sim-sick"), thought it best for us to record as far away from the Atlantic brass as possible. So we made our first trip to LA. Destination: Record Plant West. Having at last arrived in the city of dreams, we knew the pressure was on.

As we worked in the studio every afternoon, we couldn't help but notice a large white Winnebago that was always parked right next to the front entrance. We had no idea what it was doing there.

Bill engineered and produced our sessions. He was a stickler for finding the best placement for microphones and instruments, and he meticulously rearranged the equipment depending on what was needed for each individual song. One afternoon, he suggested that our harmonica player move his amp to another part of the studio. He did so, and in the process he unplugged an extension cord from a wall socket.

Several minutes later, an enormous hairy block of a man stormed into our studio, yelling, "Who the fuck pulled the plug on Sly's trailer?"

We were stunned. Who was this dangerous grizzly bear? With his greased-back hair, unbuttoned shirt, and massive neck hung with long gold chains, he had "wiseguy" written all over him.

"Yeah, Sly's fucking trailer," he shouted even louder. "When I come back, if that fucking plug ain't put back, there's gonna be some real fuckin' trouble around here!"

When he left, nobody moved or said a word until the studio's assistant engineer explained that the extension cord that had just been unplugged was supplying the electricity to the Winnebago parked out front. That is how we discovered that Sly Stone had been camped out and living in that white Winnebago for weeks. Not only was he living there, he also had a twenty-four-hour hold on a studio down the hall from the one where we were working.

I would often hang outside the studio building to check out the poetry of the California streets — the unobtainable women, the sleek cars, and the sunshine. On one such day, during a break in recording, the door of the ever-present Winnebago slowly opened to reveal the man who almost single-handedly, alongside James Brown, created the musical genre known as funk — Sly Stone himself.

He was much shorter than he appeared onstage, with his trademark Afro, skintight white pants, calf-high jewel-studded boots, and glittering French-ruffled shirt, unbuttoned to reveal a medallion on a gold chain and a necklace from which hung a large Star of David pendant. His face was almost fully covered by oversize blue wraparound sunglasses, giving him the look of a mysterious masked bandit. He was heading right in my direction and suddenly stopped three feet from me. He lowered those enormous shades and instructed in a low, gravelly voice, "If you see Bobby, tell him I'm inside." He then dance-stepped his way toward the door and disappeared into the studio. I had no idea who Bobby was.

I was a big fan of Sly, having seen him and his band perform several times in Boston and New York. They would come onstage already playing and dancing, bobbing and weaving around one another. Their choreographed dance moves, along with heavily syncopated musical parts, created a joyful and soulful experience. No two shows were ever the same. Sly was street. No filter, just pure street.

I owned one of the first portable cassette tape recorders long before they became a common item. I had recorded more than thirty mix tapes of my favorite songs, and it was a great luxury to be able to travel with the music I loved. One night, after a session, I was sitting alone on an amp in the studio, listening to "Harlem Shuffle," recorded by Bob & Earl. Suddenly I felt warm breath on the back of my neck. I turned, and there, standing right over my shoulder, was Sly Stone. In his slow, familiar growl, he said, "Man, I sure do love that song. Damn, that's a good one."

When the next song came on, Brenton Wood's "Gimme Little Sign," he said, with more enthusiasm, "Oh, man, that's another great one." While he listened, he commented on everything: "Check out the bass line"; "Nice guitar lick"; "Love that bridge."

I couldn't help but notice how intensely he listened.

"Man, where'd you get all that great shit?" he asked. Sly was once a disc jockey in San Francisco, and I was about to mention that I, too, had been an all-night DJ, but I sensed he wouldn't want to hear about that, or really anything else, because he was listening so deeply. When my cassette ended, he slowly danced himself out of the studio, as if the music were still playing.

Sly appeared again the next day, standing right outside our studio door. We were rehearsing a number, and during the break the band went to the control room while I remained in the studio. Sly strolled up to me, and in that slow, low, cooler-than-cool voice he said, "Man, I love the sound that harmonica player gets through his amplifier. What's he got in that thing?"

I replied, "Nothing, really. It's just an ordinary Fender Twin Reverb. You could buy one anywhere."

He sauntered over and closely inspected the amp, especially the back of it.

"Man, you ain't shitting me, are you? Come on, what's inside that thing?"

I repeated, "Nothing. It's just a regular Twin."

He stepped back, lowered his blue sunglasses, gave me a long stare, and said, "Man, I think you're shitting me." Then, again with a cool dance strut, he slowly bopped out of the room and strolled down the long hall to the studio where he was mixing a new song for his forthcoming album.

The following day, when we returned to the studio, the harmonica amp was missing. We alerted the management, the maintenance department, and everyone else who worked in the building. We were told categorically that no one had entered the studio. The amplifier had mysteriously disappeared while all the other instruments and equip-ment were left untouched. Now, I'm no Philip Marlowe, but I was pretty certain what had happened to that amp, and I was not about to pursue my hunch.

Coming and going through the door of Sly's Winnebago was an A-list of artists I could only ever dream of meeting, from Billy Preston to Stevie Wonder to one of my favorites, Bobby Womack. Bobby's "Lookin' for a Love" would become one of the first important showstoppers in the Geils band repertoire.

As our final studio days drew to a close, we recorded a jam track entitled "It Ain't What You Do (It's How You Do It!)." I had exhausted my vocal cords with a long scream that I mistakenly thought would be an appropriate addition to the song. Before recording the next take, I headed down the hall to use the men's room. As I opened the door, I was startled to see three men dressed in business suits sitting in a cor-ner on the tiled floor. Seated cross-legged in the opposite corner was Sly, decked out in his signature tight pants, ruffled shirt, and wrap-around sunglasses. I was so taken by surprise that I quickly turned to leave. Sly said, "No, man, you come on in. Do your thing." This was an awkward situation. I used the urinal, and it became obvious that the three suited men were from Sly's record company. I had heard about record executives traveling to meet with their artists, but I'm sure that having a marketing meeting on a bathroom floor wasn't their idea of a good time.

As the execs were leaving, Sly came up behind me.

"Hey, what you doing, man?"

As he went to use the next urinal, I said, trying to be funny, "Hey, what you doing?"

He laughed and said, "Yeah, you gotta do what you gotta do."

Just as I was about to leave, I thought I'd try to engage him in some sort of conversation. Being such a fan, I knew that early in his career he had produced several recordings for other artists. I mentioned how much I liked those records, especially the ones he produced for Bobby Freeman and the Beau Brummels.

"You really like that stuff? Man, let me tell you, that stuff was shit! I just did all that shit for the money, dig? See, some things you do for the music, and there's some things you do just for the money. That's the game you always got to spin, understand?"

I nodded. Trying to keep the dialogue going, I said the first thing that popped into my head, which was the title of the jam we were working on in the studio. I blurted out, "It ain't what you do, it's how you do it."

As I was opening the door to leave, Sly said, "Hold it, man. I don't think I buy that shit. What do you mean, It ain't what you do, it's how you do it?"

I replied, "Well, it's like those early projects we just talked about. Some were for the music, and some were for the money. So it ain't what you do, it's how you do it."

He lowered his sunglasses till we were both staring at each other eye to eye. To paraphrase a lyric from a classic Wynonie Harris song, his eyes looked like cherries swimming in buttermilk.

He stepped between me and the door and in that low, slow voice said, "Now, listen, man. Imagine you're driving down a road and you're whistling and enjoying the sunny day, just looking at the beautiful blue sky, and you notice a paper bag lying out there on the road. You drive over that bag, but it happens to be filled with babies, and you just keep whistling, driving your merry way down the highway. So you see, it ain't what you do, it's how you do it."

I was stunned by his response and foolishly tried to reason with him. "Well, listen, Sly, it's one thing if you're driving down the road and you just see a brown paper bag out there and you drive over it. It's another thing if you're driving down the road and you see a brown paper bag that you know is filled with babies, and yet you still drive over it. See? It's two different things. So it ain't what you do, it's how you do it."

I thought I did a pretty good job with my response, but he had a puzzled look on his face.

"I don't care how you fuckin' wanna put it, man. That bag was on the road, and that bag was filled with babies, and now them little babies are dead! And you could've been the motherfucker who drove over that bag and killed all them babies!"

At that point, he unhooked a bullwhip that was fastened to his belt and began swinging. The force of it cracked against the bathroom floor.

I felt this was the appropriate time to make a quick exit. I opened the door and rushed down the hallway, but Sly followed close behind me, yelling, "You killed them fuckin' babies! You killed them fuckin' babies!," all the while snapping his whip. He was closing in fast when I reached the studio door, swung it open, and slammed it shut behind me. I could hear him laughing as he kept cracking the bullwhip against the door.

The next day, a persistent, hypnotic electric drumbeat was blasting from the open door of Sly's studio. I was nervous when I saw him approach me in the hallway, but he just nodded. "Hey, man," he said, and I nodded back, relieved that the dead-baby chase was forgotten.

Later that day, I was outside having a smoke when he came out of his Winnebago, walked up to me with a big smile, and asked, "Is there any way you could make me a copy of that cassette you were playing the other day?"

I was honored he wanted a copy. I duly made it and went to his studio. The door was open, and Sly noticed me standing in the hallway listening to the drumbeat of the electronic Rhythm Maestro while he and his engineer were turning up the faders for each individual instrument.

The engineer brought up on the faders several voices with various guitar parts and what I assumed was the lead vocal. Sly sang along with the track, bobbing up and down in his chair, as if he were performing onstage. The mix began to take shape. It was raw and primitive, different from anything he had previously recorded. The track, "Family Affair," became his next runaway hit single. That recording, with its bare, haunting vocal performance, still resonates with me and moves me every time I hear it.

Returning home from a tour of the Midwest, I found a certified letter waiting for me from Stephen Paley, who worked closely with Sly at his record company, Epic. I knew Stephen from early on, when he photographed the covers for the first two Geils albums. Once, during a shoot, I told him about my encounter with Sly. He always joked that he wanted to arrange a luncheon with me and Sly at which he would serve us baby-size sandwiches in brown paper bags inside the men's room at Epic Records.

The certified letter contained an elaborate gold-embossed wedding invitation to "a golden affair," celebrating the marriage of Kathy Silva and Sylvester Stone, due to take place at Madison Square Garden on June 5, 1974. All guests were asked to wear gold. (This event was possibly outdone only by Hank Williams, who in 1952 had not one but two sold-out wedding ceremonies at the Municipal Auditorium in New Orleans when he married his second wife, Billie Jean Eshlimar.)

Most people in the music industry assumed Sly's wedding was only a publicity stunt and doubted he would even show up. I was out on tour and unable to attend, but by all accounts the ceremony turned out to be quite the event. Halston designed the bride and groom's clothing, and afterward, there was a private A-list party on the Starlight Roof of the Waldorf-Astoria hotel.

Later that summer, for one week, Sly was the cohost on *The Mike Douglas Show*. It was during guest Muhammad Ali's interview that one could sense the beginning of Sly's downfall. Ali said, "I'm here to talk about the discrimination, hypocrisy, and prejudice that Black folks are facing in America."

Sly kept interrupting the Champ, telling him, "Lighten up! We're just here to entertain."

Although Ali was a fan of Sly, he was enraged that Sly appeared so obviously stoned on national television. The ensuing argument and Sly's incomprehension made it difficult to watch. As the years passed, Sly's odd and unpredictable behavior increased as his record sales decreased.

So there I was, just past a decade after my first encounter with Sly, heading toward the small club where he would be performing. There was no tour bus and no line of ticket holders. I went down the stairs and discovered, in the dim light, that the room was only one-third full. I waited alongside the smattering of equally curious onlookers. There were instruments onstage, and at 9:00 p.m., three young musicians came out. Each tuned his instrument, and the guitarist announced, "Ladies and gentlemen, please welcome to the stage the legendary, the amazing...Sly Stone!"

The stage, however, remained empty. As the band played on, the guitarist looked toward stage right, and again announced, "Please welcome to the stage the amazing Sly Stone!"

Once more the emptiness remained, until suddenly Sly finally appeared, and our collective doubt was washed away. He was wearing what seemed to be the same outfit he wore for his mesmerizing performance at Woodstock so long ago: the same rhinestone jumpsuit, wide-brimmed rhinestone hat, and sky-blue wraparound sunglasses.

Pacing the stage like a bewildered tiger trapped in an underground cage, Sly did not acknowledge the audience until he moved behind his electric keyboard. He let the band jam for a while, then moved to center stage, arms outstretched, as if he were nailed to an imaginary cross, and bent his head back, looking up. The audience followed his stare, finding nothing but a bare ceiling. Once more behind his keyboard, with the microphone close to his mouth, he sang "Everybody Is a Star" in that unmistakable low, rough, gravelly voice. He seemed deep inside the music, and his mood changed. He worked through "Everyday People," holding true to the melody, then sang "Family Affair" with so much emotion that he might have even transcended his own recorded version. The audience was spellbound as he ended the song with moans reminiscent of fellow Texan Blind Willie Johnson's chilling recording of "Dark Was the Night, Cold Was the Ground."

Suddenly, leaping away from his keyboard, Sly yelled to the band, "Hit it, fellas!" He raised his hands and shouted to the audience, "I want to take you higher," to which all assembled returned the shout "Higher!" over and over, until he disappeared offstage as quickly as he'd entered.

I could almost hear the questioning audience wondering, Is that it? A handful of songs. Maybe twenty minutes. The band continued to play until the guitarist thanked everyone for coming and the house lights came on. There was a gentle round of polite applause followed by hushed whispers, like those one might hear at the wake of a distant relative. The audience members donned their coats and headed quietly toward the exit.

Witnessing Sly's performance had an immediately profound effect on me. I sat there reflecting on the future of my own career. After almost seventeen years, the Geils band had finally achieved the success we had worked so hard for, but I could already feel tensions building within the band. Success is relative, but once you've obtained a certain degree of it, few things can prove to be more maddening than trying to prevent it from slipping away. I didn't know it then, but soon I'd be facing cataclysmic changes of my own — the end of the Geils band and the beginning of a new career as a solo artist.

I suddenly realized that only the bartender was left, collecting the empties. I contemplated, for a moment, going backstage, but instead I put on my coat and hat and headed for the door, climbing the stairs into the cold, snowy night.

How far a drop can it possibly be when you fall from the public eye? It was a long walk home.

30

FRATRICIDE
The Rise and Fall of a Full House:
The J. Geils Band

J. Geils billboard, Sunset Boulevard, 1975

WHEN BRUCE SPRINGSTEEN was inducting the band U2 into the Rock & Roll Hall of Fame, he said, "Bands get formed by accident, but they don't survive by accident. It takes will, intent, a sense of shared purpose." His statement offered insight and straightforward clarity, and it applied only too well to the beginning and end of the J. Geils Band.

My first band, the Hallucinations, came to a premature end when several members decided to pursue careers as fine artists. I, on the other hand, set painting aside and focused all my energy on music. I needed a new band and began searching for a group I would feel musically compatible with.

In a small coffeehouse, I came across a band that called itself the J. Geils Blues Band, named after the guitar player, John Geils. I was particularly struck by the musicianship of John and Dick Salwitz, the harmonica player. I introduced myself, and we hit it off, agreeing to get together and jam. After several sessions, it was clear that something clicked. I suggested bringing on board the Hallucinations drummer, Stephen Jo Bladd, to join their bassist, Danny Klein, in filling out the rhythm section. That is how the J. Geils Band was formed. Lastly, to round out our sound, we added a keyboard player, Seth Justman.

Tom Petty once told me, "There's no such thing as democracy in a band." Usually one or two key players will take the lead. Together they form an artistic bond and partnership, one that shares musical tastes, ambitions, and vision. It is most often they who make the major decisions for the rest of the group. This pattern repeats itself throughout rock music history, from Lennon and McCartney and Jagger and Richards to Henley and Frey. In the Geils band, the bond between me and Seth formed the key-player dynamic. Our writing partnership and vision for the band would eventually send us on an upward trajectory.

John, Dick, and Danny were involved with a local manager who insisted we could only perform under the name the J. Geils Band. I was so happy to have found a group to play with that the band name seemed incidental. However, as we became more popular, many people mistakenly assumed that I, the lead singer, was J. Geils, a confusion that would follow me into my solo career.

It wasn't long before I realized that the band's manager was not able to help the group go the distance. When his contract finally ran out, I took over the managerial duties and secured us a booking at the Boston Tea Party, where the Hallucinations regularly played. Fortuitously, on the night of the Geils band's first important show, a notable promotion man from Atlantic Records, Mario Medious (the Big M), was at the club promoting Dr. John, the gifted New Orleans artist. After our set, as I entered the dressing room, the Big M asked, "Hey, who was them brothers out there playing all that blues stuff?"

I told him, "It wasn't brothers — just us."

"You shitting me?" the Big M said. "Listen, I come from Chicago, and believe me, I know my blues shit! What label you guys on?"

"We're not signed to any label," I told him.

"You gotta be shitting me! Damn, I'll call one of the owners of Atlantic Records, Jerry Wexler, right now. He's my boss, and I'll get that mamma jamma to sign your asses to the label. I'm the Big M. I get shit done!"

And he did. Jerry Wexler called a good friend of mine in Boston, Jon Landau, and asked if he knew about us. When Jon gave him a positive report, three days later, Jon and I were in Wexler's office. After barely any negotiation, Wexler pulled a contract out of his desk drawer. With no lawyer representing us, with no understanding that the terms of the contract were archaic and unfavorable compared to other group contracts of that time, we ended the meeting fulfilling a dream: the J. Geils Band became Atlantic recording artists.

Now we urgently needed a lawyer and a booking agent. I searched for advice in a book called *This Business of Music: A Practical Guide to the Music Industry for Publishers, Writers, Record Companies, Producers, Artists, Agents,* considered the standard text in its time. I noticed that the coauthor, Bill Krasilovsky, was based in New York. I located his number and called him up. He turned out to be a true ethical gentleman, and he became our lawyer. My friend Fred Lewis, whom I met during my nights as a disc jockey, was promoting blues and R and B records. He jumped on board to help me coordinate things. Still, we needed an agent.

The most exclusive booking agency was Premier Talent. I called the owner, Frank Barsalona, one of the most respected people in the music industry. After many conversations, he booked us, sight unseen, into Bill Graham's famed Fillmore East, in New York, as the opening act for Black Sabbath. Several encores followed, and the J. Geils Band was on its way.

A decade later, after we finally fulfilled our obligations to Atlantic and serendipitously landed a recording contract with EMI America, our record sales grew. After seventeen years as a band, playing continual one-nighters to a fiercely dedicated fan base, we finally were not only out of debt but also number one on the charts, selling out arenas from coast to coast.

Bands that have a long history are not unlike a family: growing, adapting, and changing over time, sometimes for better, sometimes for worse. If cracks appear between the two key players, like a marriage breaking apart, the whole family unit can become divided.

Success, if it does come to a band, often comes with its own special price. Rewards may abound, but resentments left to fester below the surface can explode when you least expect it. As novelist Graham Greene wrote, "Success is more dangerous than failure, the ripples break over a wider coastline."

For the Geils band, success took its bite with razor-sharp teeth, causing a divide between me and my bandmates. They chose to change course and follow a captain whose blind compass would soon have them smashed hard against the rocks.

And then it happened…the writing partnership between Seth and me suddenly fell apart. He chose instead to collaborate in songwriting with his brother, leaving me to seek out a new writing partner. His choice to end it was further compounded by a disagreement over which musical direction the band should take.

I wanted to remain "roots"-oriented. The other members wanted a heavier synth-pop sound. I brought in songs that were rejected by the band as being "a step backward." The group had several meetings without me and planned what I can only describe as a coup d'etat. I was asked to attend a meeting—and it turned out to be my last. As the other members of the group sat quietly, Seth, my longtime collaborator, said his final words to me: "Peter, I really think it'll be best for all of us if you go your way and we go ours." So there it was: Et tu, Brute. Blindsided, I walked out of that meeting in shock. It was one of the coldest days of my life.

Lawyers immediately flew into Boston trying to find a solution, but the band held firm without me. The president of the record company, EMI, and then the head of our booking agency flew to Boston, explaining to the band the dire consequences of their decision, but to no avail. Seth became the new lead singer — the front man, songwriter, and producer for the new J. Geils Band.

Frank Barsalona, our agent, took me out for dinner after his final meeting with the other band members. In disbelief, he said, "After all these years, the band finally made it. It's really quite unbelievable. I've dealt with the craziest of the crazies; the drugs, the girlfriends, the managers — nothing even comes close to this. Nothing as stupid, as senseless, and as wasteful in what these guys are insisting on doing. So, Peter, let's start thinking about your solo career."

Petrified, I just sat there, my food untouched.

Shortly after the split, I went on to release an album called *Lights Out*, which rose to the top ten on the *Billboard* charts. All the songs on that album were the very songs the band had rejected. The J. Geils Band then released *You're Gettin' Even While I'm Gettin' Odd*. As a result of poor sales, the band was dropped from the record company, and the "new" J. Geils Band came to an ignominious end.

The abrupt loss of camaraderie and musical brotherhood was a betrayal whose psychological impact on me was severe. I stayed away from live performance for almost ten years — until Bruce Springsteen, who was appearing at the Boston Garden, asked me backstage if I'd like to join him during an encore. Nervously, I confided to him that it had been a decade since I'd been on stage. The news seemed to take him by surprise. But he replied, "Pete, better be ready, because tonight, I'm calling you up there."

That evening, I regained the confidence to overcome the crippling anxiety the breakup had caused.

Years later, in an effort to satisfy the unwavering loyalty of our fans — and, in some sense, in a misguided attempt to overlook the past — I agreed to take part in the Geils band's ill-advised reunion concerts. Time had not papered over the cracks and only further exposed the band's deep fractures, futile grudges, and petty jealousies.

Bruce's Rock & Roll Hall of Fame speech indeed spoke the truth, for in the end, what got me back out there was will and intent, with one additional necessity, friendship. I may have been burned in the past, but I rediscovered a fire within me that nobody would ever put out again.

Long Line

"DESIRE HAS NO REST"

31

PINK 'EM
Don Covay

T HE TELEPHONE RANG in my hotel room. "Mr. Wolf, there's a
Mr. Covay downstairs who claims he's a guest of yours." It was the
way the caller said "who claims" that made me immediately head down
to the lobby.

This was the exclusive Carlyle hotel, the last of the grand white-glove
five-star establishments left in the city. For at least six months I had been
occasionally living in a small suite where the weekly bill was next to
nothing at the discretion of the Carlyle's owner, Peter Sharp.

As I stood waiting for the elevator, I thought back to the time when I
first met Don, in 1970, right after the recording of the first Geils album
in New York. Our producers had worked with many of Atlantic's important soul artists and asked me whom I would like to meet. Without hesitation, I replied, "Don Covay." They were bemused by my choice. "Peter,
you could meet Wilson Pickett, Joe Tex, Ben E. King — even Aretha —
and instead of all these great artists you pick Don Covay?"

I could understand their bafflement. Don was basically known as a songwriter, but his first two albums for Atlantic were pure classics that had made a deep impression on me. His voice didn't have the polish of many of his contemporaries, but he projected a depth of personality. The images in his lyrics had charm and character and possessed a real street sensibility. They made me believe that his songs came right from his own life experiences.

The producers set up a meeting with Don and the Geils band in a room at the Americana hotel. When I met Don that evening, he certainly didn't disappoint. He was as I imagined — even a whole lot more.

I asked if it would be possible to take a picture with him and, surprisingly, he said no. I was somewhat taken aback, but he explained, "No pictures in the hotel room. You see, someone could take that very photo, block you out of it, and add a woman to it. Maybe she might be naked or something and try to cause lotsa problems, so no photos in the hotel room!" This paranoia could have come right out of one of Don's songs. It became the band's inside joke before we gave press interviews: "No photos in the hotel room!"

With Don Covay

When I was living at the Carlyle, in the summer of 1983, I was at loose ends, looking for a new songwriting partner after my longtime collaborator ended our working relationship. Don's wife had recently passed, and it was hitting him hard. At the suggestion of Atlantic's promotion man, the Big M, I had called Don to see if he wanted to get together and collaborate on some new songs. This would be a boost for me as well as for Don, whose grief over the loss of his wife had turned him into a virtual recluse.

Upon entering the lobby, I saw Don at the front desk. He was hard to miss, wearing a light brown suede leisure suit with lacing down the sides of the pants, a brown leather vest, a Day-Glo red shirt, shiny blue snakeskin boots, mirrored sunglasses, and a large-brimmed white cowboy hat. He was chatting to several expensively dressed Italian ladies who were checking into the hotel, surrounded by several assistant managers and a cluster of bellmen piloting carts stacked with their Louis Vuitton luggage.

"Been to Italy several times," I overheard Don saying to one of the ladies. "Yeah, one time I performed at the Sanremo Festival — you ever hear of that? Man, it was wild. All them Italians not speaking a word of English, and yet they still understood all the songs."

As I approached Don, he yelled out my name, then gave me a tight bear hug that lifted me off the floor. He proudly introduced me to the ladies, as if they should know exactly who I was.

I suggested we grab a cab and head across town to a friend's home studio to do some songwriting. "We don't need a cab," he replied. "I got my chauffeur waiting for us outside." Don kissed each of the ladies' hands and wished them a pleasant stay.

The waiting car was a run-down black 1960s Cadillac Coupe de Ville. The rear fender was tied on, and one of the brake lights was missing. Don's driver, Clarence, jumped out to open the back door for us. In the driver's seat, it seemed Clarence was having trouble getting the car to start, but then it finally jerked forward. Not missing a beat, Don began philosophizing about the art of songwriting.

He was in the middle of explaining how he wrote and recorded "I Don't Know What You've Got But It's Got Me" for Little Richard, with Jimi Hendrix on guitar, when a loud noise erupted from the front of the car. Don casually mentioned that his other, newer car was "in the shop" and questioned Clarence as to why it wasn't ready yet. Clarence didn't reply as he focused on the rush-hour cabs weaving in and out of traffic.

A slight smell of oil began to fill the car as Don kept talking. "Little Richard called me Pretty Boy, and coming from Richard, that was quite a compliment, man. He taught me so much about the business. He, Chuck, Fats, Bo, Jackie Wilson — they all got screwed outta the money they rightfully earned. Richard could tell ya stories about some of the things that went on, and are still going on, that you wouldn't believe!"

Black smoke began billowing out from under the hood. Don took no notice, continuing, "Sam Cooke was not only one of the greatest singers and songwriters, he was an inspiring businessman who wanted to do things the way he envisioned, and damn, he was succeeding until he was shot!"

By now the smoke was so thick that I didn't know if Clarence could see the road in front of him. Another loud bang came from the motor as the vehicle jerked to a sudden and abrupt halt. Clarence quickly jumped out and tried to open the hood while cars honked behind us. Don, unfazed, continued the conversation. I suggested to Don that it might be best if we tried to grab a cab — so we did, leaving poor Clarence stranded during rush hour in the middle of Madison Avenue while large clouds of black smoke poured out from the open hood.

Eventually we climbed the stairs to the third-floor studio owned by my friend Peter Bliss, a talented songwriter and musician. It was one of the hottest days of summer, and the place had no air-conditioning. Don carried on, recounting his many adventures with the unpredictable Wilson Pickett and his brotherly love for Solomon Burke and Aretha Franklin, for whom he had written the number one hit "Chain of Fools." He grabbed a guitar and began singing it until he started uncontrollably laughing.

With Little Richard, 1965

"Pete, this is the shit I learnt from Little Richard. I gotta tell ya! I had just written a number one song for Aretha. So I called up one of the heads of her record company, Jerry Wexler, and told him, 'Jerry, I'm at the Americana hotel, and I got a song for Aretha that's gonna be a bigger smash than "Chain of Fools."' Jerry gets so excited he asks me to sing it right there on the phone, but I tell him, 'Jerry, it's still just in my head. I need to get all the parts down. I need a good reel-to-reel tape machine and an electric piano and an amp to record it before I forget it.' I can tell Jerry was really excited. He says he's going to call Manny's music shop and have them quickly send me the stuff I need.

"Now, as soon as it arrives, I call Jerry back and tell him I need a bass. I got a kickin' bass line that I can't lose, so he sends up a brand-new Fender Precision bass. I wait a while to call him again and tell him it's almost finished and even better than I first thought, but I just need a Les Paul guitar to put on the final touches. Well, now I have a room full of top-notch brand-new equipment, and you know what I did with it, Peter? You know what I did? Ha! I sold it all! Sold it all for really good

money! I knew I wasn't going to get paid all the royalties I earned on that
record, so at least I could get some satisfaction in giving him a taste of his
own medicine. Ha! Richard sure got a good laugh out of me getting away
with that. Now, there's an idea for a song…Baby, I'm gonna give ya a
taste of your own medicine…See, now if I write that one and it becomes
a hit, then I'll get 'em back twice! Yeah, man, I tell ya, they sure do treat
ya different when you're makin' 'em what they really want the most—
m-o-n-e-y! Have mercy!"

We kicked around some ideas and agreed we wanted something up-
tempo, with a danceable beat. I told Don of an incident when the Geils
band was playing in Berlin. We found an after-hours club located in the
basement of a fancy well-known restaurant. Alone, on the dark, empty
dance floor, was a girl so intriguing that I got up and joined her. We
danced till the club was about to close. The music stopped, the lights
went out, but still we held each other close, dancing.

Don jumped up from the couch. "Man, that's it! Dancing in the dark.
I can see the whole thing playing out in my head…You're both in a disco,
and ya wanna keep on dancing even though they might be wanting to
close the joint. Maybe she's there with another guy and you don't know it
and things get kinda messy…Gimme that guitar. Let's write it and call
it 'Dancing in the Dark.'"

Don was all about the story, and slowly it came together. Somewhere
along the way, one of us came up with what Don called an insurance
hook—the song lyric "Lights out, blast blast blast." Don exclaimed,
"Man! That's how we'll start it. Let them DJs know right away we mean
business. Damn—being in a club and ya hear that, it's like, dance time,
everybody!"

Don was excited and covered in sweat, feeling the oppressive August
heat. He removed his vest, saying, "We gotta get some wine into this
mix!" I rushed downstairs, found a liquor store, and brought back a bottle of good French wine. Don looked at the bottle and said, "That might

be good for a verse, but we got a whole song to write!" We hurried back down to the liquor store, and he picked out a big jug of generic red table wine. As we climbed back up the stairs, Don said, "Gotta bring this baby home before it just runs away!"

Don sat back on the couch and opened the jug, saying, "You know, Peter, almost everything I learnt was from Sam Cooke. What Elvis is to you rockers, Sam is to me, Pickett, Solomon, and Otis. We all started singing in church. Sam was one of the first gospel stars to write and record nonreligious songs, and he got a lot of flack for it, too, but he led the way for us younger cats."

Don put down the jug, picked up the guitar, and started singing Sam's "Having a Party." He reached the line "Dancing to the music / on the radio," and from there, we came up with the phrase "radio of love," which Don declared was "the real double-down insurance hook." He said, "DJs never feel they get the credit they deserve, so by adding 'radio of love,' we'll make 'em feel real important."

After a few more good swigs from the jug, Don jumped to his feet and declared, "We got it, man, we got it — the story, the hooks, lights out blast blast blast, radio of love, and then dancing in the dark. Man, it's a smash! Good God, have mercy!" He started jumping up and down like a prospector who realizes he's just discovered gold.

Don was on a roll, still elaborating on the importance of gospel music for any soul singer, and I was taking in every word. "The one gospel group that had the greatest impact on me was the Swan Silvertones. Just listen to their records, with Claude Jeter singing. Man, that cat inspired me to do all those high falsetto parts on my records." He took several more swigs from the jug. "Now, Peter, if you go to the Apollo Theater, I don't care what performer you see, if it's Pickett, Aretha, Jackie Wilson, or Joe Tex, man, they got to move that crowd. The audience at the Apollo is like a congregation in a church, and any performer that can't move them ain't doing their job!

"I was booked at the Apollo, top of the bill, with my hits 'Mercy Mercy' and 'See-Saw' riding high on the charts. My valet rushed into the dressing room telling me there's this young, big, pudgy guy out there onstage, hardly moving a muscle, singing one ballad after another, driving the ladies screamin' crazy. So I go to the side of the stage to check this dude out. Man, my valet was right. He had that crowd in the palm of his hand, and I thought, We gotta pink 'em!"

I was confused by this and asked, "What do you mean by 'pink 'em'?"

Don looked at me as if I were asking him the most rudimentary question, like how many cans of beer there are in a six-pack.

"Peter, how long have you been performing? Man! You never heard of pink 'em? Damn, every good performer knows about pink 'em. Little Richard taught it to me way back, and now I'm gonna teach it to you! Pink 'em is something ya just gotta use in special situations. You see, this young pudgy cat is killing them ladies with his ballads, right? I ain't gonna follow this cat, and I can't start my show off with any ballad, so I know I need to take action. I HAD TO PINK 'EM!!! I yelled to my valet, 'Start moving quick — we gotta pink 'em!' When this cat finishes his set and the curtain closes, all my staff, they start rolling out a big bright plush pink rug. I change into my finely tailored pink suit, my pink handkerchief, pink cufflinks, pink patent-leather shoes, a wide-brim pink hat with a pink feather to top it off, and a pink cane. This is a proven fact: women just love pink! Many of 'em don't even know they love it, but they do! When they see pink, it starts working up something deep inside 'em. Now just imagine this, all them ladies sitting at the Apollo. The curtain reopens, and when them women see my big plush pink rug spread out beautifully across the stage and I come walking out real slow in my full regal pink attire, let me tell you, the women, they just go wild — I mean wild! They can't control themselves!

"And that's how ya pink 'em!"

Don paused, smiling, as if he was reliving that very moment. "Hey, guess who that tall pudgy guy was? None other than the Big O himself — that's right, Otis Redding. Otis was it! Man, I loved the guy. We became real tight and wrote a bunch of songs together. I remember one of the last times I saw him, he was messin' around on a guitar. He'd been working on some verses that eventually became 'Dock of the Bay,' and he was searching for a line, so I threw him "loneliness won't leave me alone." Now, people always think I'm jiving and making that story up, but I don't care. If Otis was here, he'd tell ya. Like Sam's, Otis's death cost us all a lot. They both left big holes in our world that will never, ever be filled."

In the summer of 1984, Bruce Springsteen was about to release his album *Born in the USA*, and I heard through the grapevine that the title of his first single was "Dancing in the Dark." You can't copyright song titles. Back in the early 1930s, there had been a popular song also called "Dancing in the Dark." I immediately called Don with this news.

"We have a big problem. Bruce Springsteen is about to release his first new single, and it's called 'Dancing in the Dark.'"

"Well, Pete, there's a lot of songs with the same title," Don replied.

But I said, "Don, this is Bruce Springsteen, with the Columbia Records machine behind him. They're gonna make damn sure it gets played on every radio station in the country."

Don didn't say anything, and I could almost hear his brain thinking when he yelled, "Man, I got it! Bruce Springsteen might have done us a huge favor. 'Lights Out'! We gotta change it to 'Lights Out.' It's got energy; it's mysterious, man. Who knows what happens when the lights go out? 'Lights Out' along with the 'blast blast blast,' brother, you can't go wrong. Peter, it's a double-down guaranteed smash!"

Don proved to be right: it was the title of my first solo album, and the single "Lights Out" shot up to the top ten like a bullet.

In 1992, the Big M called to let me know that Don had had a serious stroke and it would be a good idea to call him. It was rough, hearing him try to speak. He kept repeating "Lights Out," which made it even sadder. He remained partially paralyzed and in a wheelchair for the rest of his life. In gratitude, the Rolling Stones, who were huge fans, bought him a special wheelchair van. I regularly stayed in touch. One of the last times we spoke, he mentioned he had one more hit for Aretha, and this time he was serious. As debilitated as his speech was, he still tried hard to sing it. When he finished, I told him, "Don, it's a double-down guaranteed smash, and with a song like that, you'll never need to pink 'em."

With the Soul Clan: L-R, Joe Tex, Ben E. King, Wilson Pickett, Solomon Burke, Don Covay

32

THE LAST TEMPTATION
Martin Scorsese

THE PHONE RANG, and I answered to a woman's voice on the other end.

"Mr. Peter Wolf?"

"Who's calling?"

"I'm from the production office for a new Martin Scorsese film being cast in New York."

A joke was certainly being played on me, so I answered, "Mr. Wolf is out at the moment. Could I have your number, and he'll be in touch?"

My assistant returned the call, and to my shock, it seemed legit. Scorsese was filming an adaptation of the Nikos Kazantzakis book *The Last Temptation of Christ*, and he actually wanted me to audition for the role of Pontius Pilate. I thought this was downright crazy. A beggar, perhaps one of the two thieves, or even Doubting Thomas — but me as Pontius Pilate?

In the 1960s, I had read most of this noted Greek author's books, including *The Last Temptation of Christ.* As a kid, I saw the Jules Dassin film *He Who Must Die*, based on Kazantzakis's *The Greek Passion.*

The script arrived later that week with a note requesting that I choose a date and time for my audition in New York.

I did not have a good track record with movies. Previously, I had turned down roles in the Alex Cox film *Sid and Nancy* and, more recently, in John Waters's *Hairspray.* But it turned out that the role of Pontius Pilate required only four or five lines. I resolved to give it a try.

Several weeks later, I drove to New York on the day of the audition. I checked into my hotel and, with my reading scheduled at 4:00 p.m., decided to distract myself from my nervousness with a visit to my adoptive "guru," Earl McGrath. He greeted me at the door with a big smile, wineglass in one hand, cigarette in the other. "Ah, our thespian arrives for some fortification before his grand debut!"

"No, Earl — I'm too nervous to even drink."

"Too nervous to drink? Are you mad? You know how many great actors pass through this very portal just to savor the fruits and encouragement of the gifts of Dionysus? Camilla will talk sense into you!"

Earl McGrath

Camilla, Earl's wife, was an elegant, wise, and refined woman descended from Italian royalty whose family relations included Pope Leo XIII. Camilla could immediately tell how nervous I was. She led me into the sitting room and gave Earl a disparaging look when he offered me a joint, admonishing him, "Earl, let him be, for God's sake!"

For Earl, that was just fuel for the fire. "Listen, if you have to read your lines in an hour, do them here, and let Camilla and I be your audience. You'll be more prepared and relaxed." Camilla was truly interested in hearing my reading, and Earl, with his caustic humor, added, "Who better than Camilla to hear your reading, with her close papal relations?"

I stood by the window, the flags of Carnegie Hall across the street waving in the wind, holding the script in my hand. I paused and began.

"Are you Jesus of Nazareth? They say you are the Messiah."

"Wait, hold on!" Earl interrupted. "What are you, a cab driver? You're Pontius Pilate, man! You have to speak with authority, nobility; you're ruling all of Jerusalem!"

I began again, this time with more emphasis on enunciation.

"Are you Jesus of Nazareth? They say you are the Messiah."

"Better!" Earl said. "But think of Olivier in *Henry V* — clearer and with more authority."

"Earl, let him be. He's doing fine. You're going to make him more of a nervous wreck than he already is. When did you become Cecil B. DeMille? Stop it!"

Earl sat back on the couch, chastised by Camilla, and poured himself another glass of wine.

I read my lines again and again, attempting to sound as eloquent as an Englishman can be — if he's from the Bronx. Earl and Camilla listened, argued, and listened some more.

Earl walked me out and bade me farewell with, "Well, here's to you, my young Barrymore. Go in there and break a leg!"

I arrived at the audition and took the elevator to the third floor. My stomach lurched as I approached room 302. A young woman sitting behind a long table piled high with scripts smiled. "Ah, yes, Mr. Wolf. Go through the door to the right and take a seat. Shirley will be calling you shortly."

The room had around twenty chairs against the wall, with twelve people seated, all holding or reading scripts. After ten minutes, a woman popped her head in, calling, "Mr. Wolf, follow me, please." She led me to Shirley, who would be conducting my audition.

"Good afternoon. May I call you Peter?"

"Yes, of course," I replied.

"I'm Shirley. You're here today to read for the part of Pontius Pilate. Tell me about yourself. Have you ever acted before?"

"Acted before? No, not really," I replied.

"Well, then, why don't you begin your reading?"

I cleared my throat and began. "Are you Jesus of Nazareth? They say you are the Messiah." I emphasized each word, speaking slowly and distinctly, enunciating with the clarity my guru, Earl, had instructed me to use.

"Excuse me, Peter. I don't mean to stop you, but are you from England?" she asked.

"No."

"Well, where are you from?"

"The Bronx."

"You see, what Marty is looking for is a natural approach to each character. So being from the Bronx, you should say the lines as if you were going into a local candy store and asking the owner something like, 'Can I get some candy and some comic books?' Just speak naturally. Now try it one more time, as if you're really in the candy store."

There was a puzzled look on my face, and she noticed.

"Peter, maybe you want to go in the other room and think about this approach, and I'll call you back in about fifteen minutes."

Glad for a reprieve, I was desperate to take a leak and walked to the men's room, where standing by the urinal was a notable screenwriter and director who years earlier went to Harvard, where our paths had crossed several times.

"What are you doing here? Reading for Scorsese, too?" I asked.

"Well, sort of. You wouldn't believe what happened to me the other day. I got to cast Bibi Andersson in a part! I've had the hots for her ever since I saw my first Bergman film. Every time I was with a woman, I'd fantasize it was Bibi. I met her three days ago, and I still can't get her off my mind. She's amazing!"

Then I noticed that he wasn't peeing but rubbing his penis up and down so hard I thought it would break right off into the urinal. "Damn, she was just amazing!" he yelled.

I forgot about my urge to pee, and I forgot about my Bronx interpretation of Pontius Pilate. I walked out to the front room and handed my script to the girl at the desk, asking her to tell Shirley, "I'll be back when I can deliver an authentic Bronx accent."

I had no intention of returning and, like Pilate, chose to wash my hands of the whole affair.

I walked across Columbus Circle, past Earl's apartment, past Carnegie Hall, then arrived at my hotel, checked out, and drove straight back to Boston.

The Last Temptation of Christ was released to mixed reviews and protests from Christian groups — even a ban from the Catholic Church.

On a rainy Tuesday afternoon I went to see the film when it opened in Boston at a nearly empty theater.

Judas, played by Harvey Keitel, betrays Jesus, played by Willem Dafoe. Suddenly on the screen appears David Bowie as Pilate, delivering his lines in pitch-perfect King's English.

"Are you Jesus of Nazareth? They say you are the Messiah."

In the words of George Burns, "Acting is all about honesty. If you can fake that, you've got it made!"

33

I NEVER LOVED A MAN (THE WAY
I LOVE YOU)
Aretha Franklin

With George Clinton, Aretha Franklin, and producer Michael Narada Walden

ONE DAY IN 1985, a message on my voicemail from the president of Arista Records took me by surprise. "Peter, Clive Davis. I'm having one of my A and R people call you tomorrow regarding a duet with Aretha Franklin." A duet with Aretha Franklin? That seemed as incongruous a combination as a nightingale harmonizing with an alley cat.

Sure enough, the following day an A and R person called to confirm Clive's request. I explained that I was honored, but it was a difficult concept to wrap my head around. Next, the producer of the project, Narada Michael Walden, called me, and I told him flat-out that I didn't think it would work. "Pete, it's Aretha. There are musicians who would give their right arm to record a duet with her. It doesn't get any better than Aretha."

"Michael, you hit the nail on the head. I'm honored that you're even thinking of me, but to save you, Aretha, and myself from unnecessary humiliation, I think it's best to pass."

"Pete, I'll send you the track. Just live with it and I'll get back to you."

He sent the track: a well-played basic dance groove. Michael persisted: "You'd better have changed your mind. We can cut it in any key, anything that will make you comfortable. Also, Carlos Santana is adding a guitar solo to the track, so just think about it some more."

His final call came two days later. His persistence paid off: I bit the bullet and flew out to Detroit before I could change my mind.

I loved the idea of recording in Detroit; it was a spiritual second home to me. When I arrived at the studio, Michael met me, all dressed in white; there was a peaceful calm about him. The studio was lit with candles and incense sticks, and NO SMOKING signs hung everywhere. As we listened to the track, entitled "Push," he explained the approach he envisioned. "Pete, when Aretha gets here tomorrow, this place will be on fire."

As we were leaving the studio, I ran into funk master George Clinton, who was there working on a new album with the Red Hot Chili Peppers. "Pete, you're gonna do a song with Aretha? Damn, it doesn't get better than that. But look out — she can be a tough one." Hearing this certainly didn't calm my nerves.

The next afternoon, Michael and I waited in the overly warm control room. Aretha didn't like air-conditioning. It was already a half hour past the time she was scheduled to show up. An hour passed, then another, and I sensed Michael, too, was getting a bit nervous. Finally, from the window of the studio lounge, I saw a long black Cadillac making its way to the entrance. The car's back door opened, and two mustachioed men dressed in dark suits, fedoras, and sunglasses got out; you surely didn't want to mess with either of them. After five minutes, the taller of the two opened the door. Out stepped the Queen of Soul in a full-length mink coat.

I ran to tell Michael that Aretha had arrived. I nervously sat behind the glass wall of the control room as he went outside to meet her, then I watched as Aretha, her bodyguards, and Michael entered the studio.

Michael waved me over for a formal introduction. Aretha just nodded as she took off her mink and placed it on top of the baby grand piano.

I knew she was accustomed to hearing praise, but we were both there to work, so I stopped myself from being too effusive in my admiration. She asked me where I lived and when I had arrived in Detroit. What took me by surprise was her heavy British accent. I answered her questions, trying hard not to show my bewilderment.

Aretha started singing some deep gospel licks that — especially when heard up close — were powerful and dramatic. She glided through the first verse of the song with ease, adding impromptu touches that few singers are capable of mastering. We both sang the chorus, and I joined in on the second verse. After a long instrumental section, Aretha started ad-libbing in her British accent.

"Darling, you are looking so well tonight."

"The gown you're wearing makes you the belle of the ball," I replied.

Aretha started laughing so hard that she asked Michael to stop the tape and get her some water. I went to the control room to grab her a bottle and asked Michael, "What's with the British accent?"

Michael laughed. "She's imitating Joan Collins. Aretha is a huge *Dynasty* fan and watches it every week without fail. She obviously feels comfortable to be joking with you. If something is bugging Aretha, she's not shy letting you know, that's for sure."

When I gave her the water, still in her British accent, she said, "I'd just love a spot of tea. No milk and a dash of sugar." I gladly offered to get it for her.

While I was in the lounge preparing the tea, the bodyguards were watching me. The taller one asked, "You look familiar. Are you in a famous rock band or something?"

I told him I used to be on Atlantic Records, and thanks to the Big M and King Curtis, I once saw Aretha recording in the Atlantic studios. In a surprisingly high-pitched voice, like one you'd expect from Minnie Mouse, the heavier guard shouted, "You knew King Curtis? Wait till I tell Aretha!"

King Curtis was a highly talented and beloved musician who had led Sam Cooke's band. He was fatally stabbed in 1971 in front of his own brownstone in New York City after asking a group of men, high on drugs, to quiet down and get off the front steps of his house. It was a tragedy that shook up the music industry and the soul world in particular.

When I returned with Aretha's tea, she sat down on the piano bench. Dropping the British accent, she asked, "You knew Curtis?"

I told her, "When Jerry Wexler was thinking of dropping the Geils band before we recorded our first album, it was King Curtis who convinced him to keep us on the label." We reminisced about all the great characters and artists who hung around the studio and offices of Atlantic. When I mentioned that I wrote my first solo single with Don Covay, she really came to life.

"Oh, mercy! What a character that man is. He wrote me a number one song, 'Chain of Fools,' and I can remember the day he and Jerry Wexler first pitched it to me. We cut it so fast, and when we were done, we all felt it was going to be a huge hit. I can sure use several more songs like that. Next time you speak to that crazy man, tell him Re sends her love, and tell him to write me a couple more hits."

She reached into her handbag for cigarettes. Seated right underneath a large NO SMOKING sign, she lit up a Kool. She became quiet. With a far-off look she said, "King Curtis — what a loss."

She turned around to the piano and opened the lid. She started playing chords in a slow tempo, then began singing Little Willie John's "Talk to Me." Her version was breathtaking. If the mike had been on to record it, she would have had the number one hit she was looking for.

"Peter, I do miss them, but most of all Sam. Oh, Sam — he was my first love and will always be my first love." She played a little while longer, caught up in the reverie. It was powerful to hear her speak so intimately about Sam Cooke.

Michael came into the studio, breaking her trance, to tell her we still needed to jam out on the vamp part of the song.

We returned to the microphones, and Aretha wailed. Michael said, "Try it once more, Re. I think you got a better one in you."

She stopped cold. "You think I got a better one in me. So you mean I don't know if I got a better one in me? I've got to be told?" I thought she was fooling with him until she said, "Listen, if I thought I had a better one in me, I'd just do it again. I don't need anyone telling me what I got in me. You think you can tell me what my own mind and ears can't?"

She walked over to the piano, grabbed her mink, and strode to her Cadillac, bodyguards trailing behind.

Years later, in 2005, the Rock & Roll Hall of Fame held a tribute to Sam Cooke. It was an all-star event with a roster including Solomon Burke, Cissy Houston, Elvis Costello, the Manhattans, the Dixie Hummingbirds, and the Blind Boys of Alabama. In the audience was Sam's family, seated with writer Peter Guralnick, author of *Dream Boogie*, the definitive biography of Sam Cooke.

Because Aretha didn't want air-conditioning backstage, it was like a hothouse. Everyone performed a rendition of Sam's songs. I sang "Everybody Loves to Cha Cha Cha." Costello did a duet with William Bell. When it was time for Aretha to go on, however, there was a long delay. No one was allowed in her dressing room, and everyone was getting nervous, wondering if she would even come out to perform. The question of the night was, Who would sing Sam's iconic "A Change Is Gonna Come"? It was assumed that it would be Aretha, but for some reason, she didn't want to perform it.

As I walked past her dressing-room door, one of her bodyguards recognized me. I asked him if I could say a quick hello to Aretha. To my surprise, he opened the door and let me in.

Aretha performed her set backed by her own band rather than the house band. Next up, seated on a large red-satin-draped throne, wearing a glittering purple sequined suit, was a larger-than-life Solomon Burke. When he started to sing the final song of the night, "A Change Is Gonna Come," the audience went wild. He was channeling Sam that evening like no one else could. I stood next to Aretha, who was watching from the side of the stage, and her eyes moistened. Slowly, she started singing along. She kicked off her heels, took a spare microphone from its stand, turned to me, and said, "Peter, grab the train of my gown."

I held it as I followed her slow progress toward center stage, where she joined Solomon. The entire hall came to its feet. Soon after, all the performers joined in. When the song ended, as she was leaving the stage, I rushed toward her and grabbed the train of her gown. I walked behind the Queen as she made her way to the dressing room, and she said, "After a first love like Sam, there's no encore."

34

PARTNERS IN RHYME
Tim Mayer and Will Jennings

Tim Mayer

S OME OF THE most intense relationships in a songwriter's life come from collaborations — they can be incredibly fruitful; they can also be fraught. I am at my best when working in a collaborative partnership. Alone, I can too easily fall prey to my own lack of discipline and to self-doubt. The creative process is a challenge that can at times be overwhelming. When you can't find the words to express something, a collaborator is that rare individual who sparks ideas and helps lead you to what you're trying to accomplish. I've been fortunate to have several important partners since the breakup of the Geils band.

It was 1988 when I stood alongside others in a small anteroom just off a main hall, trying to think of anything except the one reason why I was there. Staring down at the cigarette butts littering the floor, I noticed the black sheen of Donald Fagen's shoes and the well-worn suede of Bill

Murray's loafers and how they contrasted with the stiffened leather of my wing tips. We could easily have been mistaken for a group of overgrown prep-school scruffs loitering aimlessly outside the headmaster's office.

Our soft-spoken conversations were interrupted when we were summoned to take up positions beside the coffin of our beloved and gifted friend Tim Mayer. Together, James Taylor, Bill and his brother Brian Doyle-Murray, Donald Fagen of Steely Dan, and I shouldered the weight of this enigmatic and boundlessly gifted playwright, stage director, poet, and lyricist on the final leg of his journey.

Tim was a wordsmith with a Harvard pedigree, equally adept at translating the *Iliad* and composing song lyrics. He was there at the beginning of *National Lampoon* and *Saturday Night Live*, using his razor-sharp intelligence to bring cutting-edge comedy to the masses. He was, to quote the poet Paul Schmidt, a "firework of wit."

I had met Tim in my early years in Boston, but it was not until much later that our fruitful collaboration began. I was in the midst of putting together a new solo album, and Tim happened to read one of my lyrics. He thought he could improve upon what I had written, and he was right. Thus began many sessions of writing together. Conveniently, we lived in the same building. It was not uncommon for me to answer the phone and hear his raspy voice on the other end.

"Commander, you wouldn't happen to have two Valium at hand? I'll be right over with my strawberry milkshake." These ingredients comprised Tim's magical hangover cure.

If Tim was feeling especially highbrow, bringing his "ascot and cuff-links" attitude to my lowbrow Bronx tough guy, we would argue endlessly over the finer points of a word or phrase. Eventually we would meet somewhere in the middle. We exchanged lyrics back and forth until we felt we had something satisfying and worthy. Tim valued the challenge of finding a street vernacular that would be true to my own experience and style. To say he had a way with words would be putting it mildly. When he died of cancer at a young age (forty-four), I lost not only a writing partner but also a close friend.

I knew well the lyrics of the next collaborator I sought to work with. His words conveyed warmth and wit, with a depth of honesty that few could match. He was most definitely not a gun for hire. It was not a question of whether I could hire him but rather a case of whether he might consider working with me.

I spent months making phone calls and sending letters and faxes before I at last had the chance to meet the reclusive and enigmatic Will Jennings. Like a 1930s gumshoe, following one lead after another, I tracked him down, and he agreed to meet me in Nashville. Finally I stood in a hotel corridor and knocked tentatively on his door. A long silence followed. I didn't know it at the time, but I was about to meet a

Will Jennings

person who would become one of my most important collaborators and a treasured friend.

Will greeted me with a firm Texas handshake. There was a regal air about him; he was dressed like an English country gentleman out for an autumn stroll in an Irish tweed walking cap, cashmere scarf, and jeans. With a kindly face, mustachioed smile, and eyes that gave the impression that there wasn't much they missed, Will brought to mind a favorite of mine: the distinctive British actor Sir Ralph Richardson.

I followed him to the far corner of a dimly lit room where snug armchairs awaited us beside a coffee table set with an ice bucket and two wine bottles — one empty, the other on its way.

"Didn't mean to be rude and start without you," Will said, breaking the silence. "I just received the sad news that Chet Baker committed suicide in Amsterdam. He was one of my favorite jazz musicians. Besides his trumpet playing, I loved the way he sang. Feel like joining me in a toast to the man?"

We finished the bottle, then adjourned to a seafood joint on the main drag in downtown Nashville. After several more bottles of wine and a dinner's worth of conversation, we ended up in a bar on the top floor of a new luxury hotel where a view of the entire city of Nashville lay spread below. We barely noticed. Over vodka cocktails, we discussed literature, classical music, bebop, jazz, old honky-tonk classics, and western swing. After several rounds, and more toasts to Chet, we turned to poetry as Will announced, "Yeats! Now, that's my man!" He raised his glass high and proceeded to recite several of the bard's poems, ending with a verse of "Mad as the Mist and Snow."

> Bolt and bar the shutter,
> For the foul winds blow:
> Our minds are at their best this night,
> And I seem to know
> That everything outside us is
> Mad as the mist and snow.

He abruptly took my hand with a firm grip and said, "Buddy, call me in a week, and we can set up a get-together out on the West Coast. I can't stay in this town too long — it just gives me the heebie-jeebies."

I left him chatting with the bartender. In the elevator, I realized we had talked about many things except the one that brought me there: songwriting.

Will was from East Texas. He studied trombone and trumpet, married his high school sweetheart, and became an English teacher at the University of Wisconsin–Eau Claire.

In 1971, on a whim, he and his wife, Carole, packed up their worldly belongings and drove to Nashville so Will could try his hand at a career in songwriting. By chance, early on, he met songwriters Kris Kristofferson and Mickey Newbury. They introduced him to some of the city's key publishers, and he never looked back, going on to win several awards, including Oscars, Grammys, and Golden Globes. He never mentioned those accolades, nor were they noticeably displayed in his home.

Will had no set approach to working. We'd begin in the afternoon, each with a clipboard in hand, and I'd start my usual pacing around the room. If I made a suggestion that Will didn't seem to like, he would quietly stare into space as if nothing had been said, which, I soon came to learn, meant it was not an idea worth pursuing. There were a lot of quiet stares from Will.

When we did finish a song, we'd make a rough recording with me singing and Will playing the keyboards or guitar. I always asked Will to record a version with just him singing. I loved the emotional feel his voice gave to each song and his unique way of phrasing and staying just a bit behind the beat, making each word count. For him, each word always did.

From my first meeting with Will, I felt immediately at ease. I recognized in him the humble gentility of my recently deceased father. His humor and positivity made anything seem possible. And he could be hilarious — nobody could outdo his James Mason or Eugene Pallette impressions.

We would work until about eight, have a light dinner, and then raid his wine cellar before ending the night upstairs in a place Will called the hut. It was a narrow V-shaped room over his garage stacked with mountains of books (including some very rare first editions) and his vast collection of more than twenty thousand CDs, organized from Bach, Basie, and Beethoven to zydeco. It was on these nights, with him as the teacher and me as the eager student, that our long friendship began. Many an evening would end with one of us reciting a poem or work of prose. Will might pick up his mandolin or guitar and play one of his favorite Jimmie Rodgers songs, most often "Peach Pickin' Time Down in Georgia."

On one occasion, Will interrupted our writing session, mentioning that he had to meet up with a friend in the valley to discuss some personal matters. I later found out that every Wednesday, Will would meet with Roy Orbison. They would drive their Cadillacs to a local car wash and have what they called a chatting session. I was privileged to hear some of the songs he and Roy wrote and recorded together. Will was amazed at how softly Roy sang into the microphone and how completely the recording of Roy's enormously full, operatic voice filled the room when it was played back. The two men remained so close that Will was asked by Roy's wife to give the eulogy at Roy's funeral.

For lunch, Will sometimes liked to eat at a casual restaurant that looked like a refurbished Denny's but served much tastier food. On one particular afternoon there, I noticed the actor Rod Steiger sitting with a woman several booths away. I wanted to say hello, but Will was far too polite and reserved to ever intrude on another's privacy. I waited until I saw the waitress hand Steiger the check. With what Will would call my New York assertiveness, I walked over to Mr. Steiger's booth. Thinking I might be a bit more creative than the average fan, I wasn't going to ask about or mention his classic role as Marlon Brando's brother in *On the Waterfront*. Instead I uttered the dreaded cliché that every celebrity puts up with: "Sorry to bother you." I quickly added, "Mr. Steiger, I must say you were really magnificent in the role of Mussolini."

"Mussolini?" He looked up in surprise. "Mussolini—well, that's real nice to hear. I put a lot of work and research into that part, and it all pretty much went unnoticed. It's nice to know someone liked it." He was dressed all in black, had a large Navy Cross dangling from his thick neck, and wore tinted glasses that looked huge on his massive bald head.

He introduced his wife, and I called over to Will, who very reluctantly approached. I introduced Will as Steiger continued, uninterrupted.

"Nobody gives me credit for the research and detail I gave to every role. Do you know I played more historic figures than probably any other Hollywood actor? I was Ulysses S. Grant, Napoleon, W. C. Fields, Pontius Pilate, Rasputin, Dutch Schultz, Al Capone, and I even played Rudolf Hess. All overlooked! I turned down lots of parts, some really big—*Patton, The Godfather*! I could have made lots and lots of money, retired from all this bullshit if I wanted! Why? Why did I turn down those roles, you might ask? Depression. I've been battling clinical depression for years, maybe even all my damn life when I think about it. I've tried psychiatrists, meds, and even electric shock, the whole works. I'm dealing with it all the time. Why? Who the hell knows why? When I think about my life and all the things I could have done, well, maybe, maybe, it's just too late for me."

Will and I looked at each other, hearing a new song title ring in our ears like church bells. The song, "It's Too Late for Me," became one of my favorite recordings.

In 2006 Will was inducted into the prestigious Songwriters Hall of Fame. I attended the ceremony, noting that Will was seated at the front table alongside Kris Kristofferson, who championed him early in his career and was there to receive the Johnny Mercer Award. Kris dedicated his award that night to Mickey Newbury, who helped both him and Will at the start of their careers. After the ceremony, there was a large reception attended by many notable award-winning songwriters, publishers, and major media outlets. I watched Will, who was uncomfortable in such a large gathering, do the polite meet and greets. Later that evening I assumed I'd find him in the bar of his hotel, but there was no sign of him.

I was about to leave when I noticed him sitting by himself outside, at a small café table. He seemed deep in thought, and I wasn't sure if he even wanted company, but he beckoned me over. "What a nice surprise. Glad you're here — now we can properly celebrate this grand occasion." He ordered a bottle of champagne and a friendly backup bottle if needed. It wasn't long before we were emptying the second bottle.

We sat quietly, two friends enjoying the deserted street scene, until the arrival of garbage trucks, sidewalk cleaners, and the early morning delivery vans interrupted the tranquility of the moment. With the sunrise reflected in his glasses, Will smiled warmly. In his typically modest way, he said, "Well, pal, thanks for coming. I guess it's time for me to turn in. It's been a long day, and there are still many more songs to write."

35

EVERY FOOL HAS A RAINBOW
Merle Haggard

F RANK MULL LIMPED his way to the tour bus as I followed behind, noting that he greeted everyone in passing with a raised tip of his hand-carved walking stick. Frank, a well-respected tour coordinator, was in his late sixties, balding, with a trimmed gray beard that accentuated his smiling round face. He wore a straw fedora, wide tinted glasses, and a loose-fitting seersucker suit that gave him the air of a traveling carny. The tour bus to which we were headed was owned by his closest friend, the reclusive, moody, unpredictable, and legendary singer-songwriter Merle Haggard. My mission: Would Merle agree to record a duet for a song I had written with Will Jennings, "It's Too Late for Me"?

Merle had a mythical quality and an outlaw spirit. As a young man, incarcerated in San Quentin, he experienced a life-changing event — Johnny Cash's famous San Quentin prison concert. In his own words, "It set a fire under me that hadn't been there before."

When Merle first burst onto the country charts, in the mid-1960s, he was movie-star handsome. With age, his classic features transformed into an even more riveting combination of character and distinction.

I nervously stood behind Frank as he typed out the code on the keypad and unlocked the door to the bus. There, seated in the back, was Merle, listening to several versions of a new song he had just recorded.

Merle greeted me with a nod as he played the different mixes. I was caught off guard when he turned and asked me, "Which one do you like?"

I thought carefully before answering. "Well, if I had to choose, I think I'd go for the first mix. It doesn't have as much reverb, so it sounds more intimate. It loses something if there's too much effect on the voice, especially one as good as yours."

Merle didn't respond, leading me to think that perhaps I had said too much. He played the mixes back and, after a long pause, which to me felt like an eternity, replied, "Engineers always seem to want to add effects. You're right: the first mix is the better one."

That seemed to break the ice and put me somewhat at ease. Out of the blue, Merle turned and asked me, "Frank played me your track. That isn't an old Lefty Frizzell song, is it? Because I know almost everything Lefty ever recorded."

Merle could not have given me a better compliment. Lefty Frizzell was a popular country star in the early 1950s and one of Merle's biggest influences. When I first saw Merle perform, in the mid-1960s, his vocal style was so closely modeled on Lefty's that if you closed your eyes during his performance, you could almost hear a young Lefty out there on the stage.

It was a thrill and an honor just being allowed on Merle's bus. For the benefit of the uninitiated, a bus is not simply a traveling home for many country musicians but also a prominent status symbol, even more significant if it's customized. They aren't cheap and can run more than

$1 million, but if you want to be thought of as a success in country music, having your own bus is usually one of the requirements.

I came to realize the importance that buses bestowed upon country stars in Nashville during the mid-1980s, when I was invited to a recording session for the making of the famed *Highwayman* album, a collaboration featuring Johnny Cash, Willie Nelson, Waylon Jennings, and Kris Kristofferson. I walked into the control room with record producer Tony Brown to find Waylon Jennings loudly venting his disapproval of the vocal blend on a rough mix and making sure that everyone there knew it. Willie was calmly sitting in a chair listening to Waylon's rant, while Kris tried unsuccessfully to quiet him down. Finally, Willie told Kris, "Better get Johnny from his bus."

Moments later, in walked Johnny Cash, with Kris right behind. Johnny asked, "Waylon, what the hell is all this commotion about? It's just a rough of the song; it's not the final mix."

"Hoss," Waylon shouted to him over the mixing console, "listen, I know how this shit works. They blend the voices in this so-called rough mix, and that's the way it'll end up on the record."

"Waylon, this is going to change at least twenty times before we're through," said Johnny, trying to reason with him.

"Bullshit! I've dealt with this shit before," Waylon exploded, waving his hands in the air as if he were swatting away a swarm of bees. Johnny noticed that Tony Brown, several other guests, and I were silently observing this tirade and said, "Waylon, why don't we move all this bantering to my bus?"

"Banter nothing, Hoss. If we're all going anywhere, it's going to be on my bus."

"What the hell is wrong with my bus?" Johnny shouted back.

Tony, standing next to me, whispered, "This studio has the most comfortable private lounge in all of Nashville, but these guys never set foot in it. They're just all about their buses."

* * *

As Merle's stardom rose, he remained a historian of the roots of the music he loved. He recorded tributes to the Singing Brakeman, Jimmie Rodgers (considered the father of country music), Elvis Presley, and Bob Wills, the King of Western Swing.

Merle asked if I had ever heard the transcription recordings of Bob Wills. When I mentioned I hadn't, he replied enthusiastically, "You'll be in for a big surprise when you hear them."

Frank returned to the back of the bus, saying it was time for Merle to join the fellas and hit the stage. As we were all leaving, Merle said, "Next time we get together, I'll get you a box of those transcriptions."

Next time — now, that sounded like another promising opportunity to pitch our duet.

Merle was playing in Tarrytown, New York, and I drove out to see him, hoping that I might persuade him to do the duet. I was warmly greeted by Frank Mull and entered Merle's bus, shocked to find seated in the front lounge a gentleman I immediately recognized. He was a lawyer who was once a top dealmaker in the music industry. He had represented clients such as Paul Simon and Bruce Springsteen. Long retired, he was pretty much forgotten, but I remembered him and the ridiculously overinflated figure he quoted for his services when I was searching for a lawyer to help get a record deal for the Geils band. Needless to say, his fee was well beyond our meager reach.

He was a coldhearted businessman, and I wondered what he was doing on Merle's bus. Years before, he had been hired by one of Merle's people at a time when Merle was in deep trouble with the IRS. This lawyer proposed a yearlong tour to pay the IRS debt, the hitch being that Merle had to use a backup band of younger musicians who would be far cheaper than his own. When Merle heard about the situation, he nixed the whole scheme. Instead, he liquidated some of his publishing rights. As Frank was telling me this, the lawyer chimed in, "I got to hand it to Merle. Time proved he was right. He chose to keep his band, and after forty years, he's still playing with most of the same musicians from back then, and the IRS debt has been long paid in full. So my hat's off to him."

Later, I asked Frank why this lawyer was even on the bus. "Oh, he calls me or Merle out of the blue from time to time, and I think when Merle sees him, it still makes him feel real good to rub it in his face that he didn't take his advice and instead rightly stood his ground."

I admired him for this loyalty and for touring with the same musicians, one of whom was his ex-wife, singer Bonnie Owens. Bonnie was the second of Merle's five wives. She not only sang backup but also played an important part in Merle's prolific songwriting, transcribing his words and offering her wise opinion. The strength of their post-divorce relationship was so powerful that she even attended the celebrations of his subsequent marriages. In later years, when Bonnie developed Alzheimer's and needed full-time care, Merle would visit her facility and perform for Bonnie and the other residents.

Merle summoned me to the back of the bus and presented me with the Bob Wills transcription box, as promised. I was relieved when he at last discussed recording the duet acoustically on his bus next time he rolled through New England.

I had become friendly with Merle's keyboard player, who one day surprised me with a phone call, letting me know that "Merle keeps

With Merle on his bus

playing that song you gave him, and he's planning to record it for an album." Hearing this, I immediately called Frank to ask if he could tactfully remind Merle that I wanted to record it as a duet. Every time I thought I was getting closer to his agreeing to the duet, he seemed to avoid making a commitment one way or the other.

Merle played Connecticut; I was there. Vermont; I was there, and yet again, the duet wasn't mentioned. Then came the news that he'd be touring with Ray Price and Willie Nelson and they'd be coming to Harbor Lights, an outdoor pavilion in Boston. I knew this would be my best shot if the duet was ever going to happen. I called Frank to let him know I'd try to set up a situation so Merle and I could record the track at the venue. Frank said he'd run it by Merle but couldn't promise anything. I called my old friend Don Law, the promoter of the venue, to ask if I could use an extra dressing room to set up some recording equipment. By coincidence, Don's father, Don Law Sr., was a respected country music producer, responsible for most of Ray Price's recordings. He had also produced music by Lefty Frizzell, as well as some of Johnny Cash's biggest hits and the entire known recordings of the legendary bluesman Robert Johnson.

In setting up this mobile recording session, I could not have prepared a bank heist with greater attention to detail. Once the date was set, I hired one of the best engineers in town and brought in lead guitarist Duke Levine, who also played on the track. By late morning, we had created a damn good mobile studio in a vacant dressing room, right on the concert site. I brought in lamps to give the room some mood, even hanging vintage photos of Lefty Frizzell and a young Ray Price standing alongside Don Law Sr. Now all we needed was Merle.

At around noon, Willie's buses pulled into the venue, and about a half hour later, Ray Price's bus arrived.

I anxiously awaited Merle, not sure if he'd even be willing to sing on the track. Several hours passed, and still no Merle. I was sitting in catering with my old friend and harp player from Willie's band, Mickey Raphael, when I heard the sound of a bus arriving. I rushed out to discover it was Merle's band, but no sign of Merle. I asked Merle's piano player how far behind he thought the bus might be.

"Well, Pete, his bus turned off several exits back. Merle can be kind of funny. When he gets in a mood, he could just pick up and head right back to California. He's pretty unpredictable that way."

That was not what I wanted or needed to hear. I tried calling Frank, but there was no answer. Another hour had passed while I nervously paced back and forth, testing and retesting all the equipment, when Merle's piano player came rushing in to the little makeshift studio to let me know that Merle's bus was just now pulling in.

I quickly went outside and stood by the dressing-room complex, where I knew Merle would definitely see me. Finally, after twenty minutes, the door of his bus opened, and out stepped Frank, followed by Merle's longtime manager and producer, Fuzzy Owen, and then, at last, Merle himself. Fuzzy and Frank headed for the catering tent as Merle came walking toward me, but other than giving me a simple nod, he didn't greet me—he just walked right past and headed to his dressing room.

At that moment, I was pretty sure there wasn't going to be any recording session.

Feeling disappointed and depressed, to say the least, I wandered back to the catering tent. Then, surprisingly, I saw Merle walking toward me again. "Pete, you think you and I could run over the song?" I was trying hard to hide my excitement as Merle followed me into the makeshift studio, where I had an acoustic guitar, a music stand, a lyric sheet, headphones, and a chair ready for him.

After checking microphone levels, we did a quick acoustic run-through, then we all put on headphones and played the track. Once the music started, Merle's eyes closed—he didn't even need a lyric sheet. No one in the room could miss the intense emotion Merle gave to every word and line he sang. Instantly, the song took on a deeper meaning, credibility, and a more profound sadness than it ever had before. The power and depth of his interpretation stunned everyone in the room. When the music stopped, nobody moved or made a sound until Merle opened his eyes, looking as if he was returning from a place where only a special few have ever traveled.

Taking his headphones off, Merle said, "Well, Pete, that's one song you got to get deep inside of to make it work." I handed him my guitar and asked if he wouldn't mind signing it.

"Is it yours?" he asked.

"Sure is," I answered.

He played it a bit, signed it, and passed it back. "Well, she's a sweet one. Now, let's get us some Dickel's," he said. I wasn't sure what he meant. I followed him to his bus, where he grabbed a bottle of George Dickel Tennessee Whisky. He handed it to me. "Help yourself, Pete." I took a slug that felt so good and warm going down even as it went straight to my head.

"Merle, I can't thank you enough for what you did today." Then I added, "For a while, I didn't think you were even going to show up."

"Well, there's a story there," he replied. "As we were heading up into Massachusetts on 84, I saw a sign through some trees that read CRACKER BARREL 2 MILES NEXT EXIT. So I told our bus driver to turn off. We stopped and had a nice relaxing lunch. I had some hot biscuits and gravy, and look here." He pulled a card from his wallet — his very own Cracker Barrel VIP card.

"When a place offers you one of these, Pete, it's sort of insulting if you pass 'em by and don't use it. I love Cracker Barrel. Come on, let's check out Willie's bus and see what trouble that boy's up to." I followed Merle, his bottle in hand, as we climbed the steps to Willie Nelson's bus.

Willie and his mentor, the eighty-one-year-old honky-tonk pioneer Ray Price, were in the front lounge passing each other a large vape pipe attached to a hookah sitting on a table in front of Willie. Ray, once roommates with Hank Williams, was an important originator of the real whiskey-soaked honky-tonk sound, with a young Willie Nelson on bass in his band.

"Hey, Merle, what's in that bottle you're holding?" Ray asked. "How about giving my coffee a bit of a booster shot?"

"Same for me," said Willie. I thought Willie had stopped drinking, but maybe this was a special occasion. Merle obliged and said, "Pete, grab yourself one of those coffee cups and let me give you a refill." They passed the pipe to Merle, who held on to it, taking several long, deep inhales.

"We just did some recording, and Pete here set up a whole studio in the dressing room."

"Hope it's a hit," Willie said.

Merle continued chatting as he reluctantly handed back Willie's pipe after I passed on having some. Merle began telling a story about the time I first met his longtime right-hand man, Fuzzy Owen, one of the architects of what became known as the Bakersfield Sound in country music. Merle said, "One night Pete came to my show and joined me and the band in catering. Pete sat right across the table from Fuzzy, and I introduced him. He seemed really excited about meeting Fuzzy, so he starts asking Fuzzy all sorts of questions about how he produced his records back in the day, how big the studios were, what kind of microphones he used, what amplifiers did the players have, all sorts of questions. Fuzzy just kept nodding his head and sometimes just saying, 'Yes, sir, them sure were the good old days.' Pete keeps asking Fuzzy questions, and Fuzzy just keeps nodding his head, until I finally had to break in and say, 'Pete, you're just wasting your breath. He ain't got on his hearing aids. Fuzzy's stone deaf. He can't hear one damn word you're saying!'"

Both Willie and Ray started laughing as if it was the funniest thing either of them had ever heard.

The topic turned to women, the marriages and the divorces, and Merle asked me, "Peter, are you still in touch with Faye?"

"We talk every now and then," I replied.

"Well, fellas, here's one I think that of all the people who will understand the embarrassment and humor of this story, Peter will. After I saw *Bonnie and Clyde*, I fell head over heels for Faye Dunaway."

"Who wouldn't?" said Ray.

Merle continued. "Damn, almost every country guitar picker I knew felt the same way. I even wrote a song and an album called *The Legend of Bonnie & Clyde*. It so happened that one of these awards shows asked if I'd be willing to appear on their television ceremony, and if I agreed, they would not only pay me a lot of money but also present me with some fancy award. Sounded like a pretty good deal, so I told them the only way I'd do it was if they got Faye Dunaway to present it to me. The producers got in touch with her people, but she said she wanted to speak with me first.

"Well, I couldn't believe it. I told them to definitely make sure she gets my number. Months passed, and I never heard from her. I was playing out in Vegas, and I always enjoy a good poker game. After our show, I got into a nightly routine of visiting a nearby casino where there was this gorgeous waitress, and I made sure to always sit at her station. We got to know each other, chatting every night, and damn, there were sparks between us. We planned a rendezvous for the next day at my hotel suite, so I warned Fuzzy to guard the elevator and make sure my wife wasn't heading back up. Well, me and this lady were hot and heavy in the midst when suddenly the phone rings. I knew it must be Fuzzy, so I picked it up and yelled, 'What the hell! You got me damn in the middle!' I near went into shock when I heard that unmistakable voice asking, 'Is this Merle Haggard? It's Faye Dunaway calling.' Goddamn, I couldn't believe it, and I couldn't catch my breath, laying there with this beautiful lady, but I still tried muttering a couple of words and then got so flustered I just hung up. Peter, when you speak to her again, please don't mention the details, but just let her know I'm not as crazy as she probably thinks."

Again, both Ray and Willie broke out in uncontrollable laughter. Ray just about spilled his coffee cup onto his fine silk suit and almost fell to the floor he was laughing so hard. It was then I realized just how stoned the three of them were. It's well known in the country music world that Willie carries the strongest weed you can find on either side of the Mississippi, and there are numerous stories of musicians who make the pilgrimage to Willie's bus only to make the mistake of trying to keep up with the man. The three of these musical giants just kept on smoking, drinking, and laughing right up until showtime, when they hit the notes pitch-perfect, exactly where they should be. Their tour was rightfully called the Last of the Breed.

I couldn't wait to send Merle and Will Jennings a copy of the finished mix. One afternoon my phone rang, and it was Merle, letting me know he was really pleased with how it turned out. This was the first of many calls I received from him, and I was always pleasantly surprised to hear his voice on the other end of the line. He'd talk about simple things — the weather, fishing — and invite me to his farm, in Redding, California.

Once I asked him about songwriting.

"I'm blessed, I guess, that songwriting seems to come quickly. If I'm struggling after fifteen minutes, I just move on to something else. I love noodling around on the guitar; I get great pleasure in that. What I have to work on the hardest is singing." That certainly took me by surprise, for his beautiful baritone always sounded so effortless.

Merle continued touring, playing rodeos, casinos, performance centers, and out-of-the-way clubs and honky-tonks. Even while his health was failing, he toured with Bob Dylan and played with the Rolling Stones; it was hard keeping him off the road. As he grew weaker and was hospitalized, it was apparent to those around him, as well as to Merle himself, that he was near the end of the run. He insisted on spending his final days on his bus. He died on the day he predicted, during the early morning of his seventy-ninth birthday.

When I hear his singing on our duet, "It's Too Late for Me," it takes me back to experiencing the greatness of Merle. In seeking him out, I fulfilled a dream. His voice connects me to a "long line" that winds its way through music history, like a river running through time.

Acknowledgments

First and foremost, my deepest gratitude and thanks go to Grace O'Connor, who was with me every step of the way as I wrote this book. Her persistence, wisdom, and encouragement kept me going, and her perspectives were invaluable in the shaping of everything from the first draft to the finish.

To Nora, thank you for the love and support, and for encouraging me during my early drafts.

I owe an enormous debt to the acclaimed writer Peter Guralnick, whose books I hold in high esteem. He and his wife, Alexandra, not only helped me jump-start this book, they also read many of the early drafts and offered helpful insights, suggestions, and support along the way.

I would also like to thank Andrew Wylie, agent extraordinaire — il capitano — whose belief in my first drafts remained a life raft throughout the writing process. I relied heavily on his advice and counsel. His able colleague Katie Cacouris was always at hand when needed.

Thanks also to the staff at Little, Brown, including Joshua Kendall and Betsy Uhrig, as well as Bruce Nichols, Craig Young, and Michael Pietsch.

Barbara Clark is an editor scrupulous about details and research. I value her opinion as well as her patience as we worked our way through my many changes.

My gratitude goes to Bill Flanagan for his wise counsel and feedback.

Thanks are due to David Bieber, whose ear was always available in the wee hours of the morning.

A big thank-you to Paul Sternburg, a brother and friend who always has my back, and my consiglieri, Steven Van Zandt, who was there to listen whenever I called. For their guidance and friendship, thanks to Jeff Rosen, Mario "the Big M" Medious, John Doumanian, Dr. Henry Friedman, John Solon, and Holly Walton.

Thank you to Grace O'Connor for her jacket photograph; to my sister, Nancy, who reviewed some of the early drafts, helped search for family photographs, and introduced me to the music of doo-wop, which, like jazz, is a true American art form; and to Joe Greene and Alan Shapiro for their assistance in digitizing my photo collection.

With his wisdom and insight, Frank Riley — my booking agent, the last of the independents — helped my music train continue on down that "long line."

I am indebted to the multitalented Kenny White — songwriter, performer, and producer of many of my favorite solo recordings (we first made a musical connection when we recorded the song "Waiting on the Moon"). My band of brothers, the Midnight Travelers, have stood shoulder to shoulder with me and always kept the music bar high.

I'd also like to thank Barry Tashian, who guided me as I was forming my first band.

I will always appreciate Shirley Shore, my high school English teacher, who understood my disabling dyslexia and helped me feel comfortable with reading and writing.

I'm grateful to the talented, generous, and patient songwriting collaborators Will Jennings, Tim Mayer, and Angelo Petraglia and to all the other extraordinary musical collaborators and players who joined me in burning the midnight oil throughout the years. I took this book's part titles and subtitles — as well as the title of the book itself — from some of the songs we wrote together:

"Growin' Pains" — Wolf/Petraglia
"Rolling On" — Wolf/Jennings
"I Rode This Dream" — Wolf
"Long Way Back Again" — Wolf/Jennings
"Long Line" — Wolf/Petraglia/Kimball
"Waiting on the Moon" — Wolf/Jennings

Thank you to my father, who allowed ten-year-old me to interrupt my sister's date and attend Alan Freed's Cavalcade of Stars show, where I witnessed performances by many of rock's originators: Little Richard, Chuck Berry, Jerry Lee Lewis, Buddy Holly, the Everly Brothers, the Shirelles, Frankie Lymon and the Teenagers, Fats Domino, the Chantels, Screamin' Jay Hawkins, the Platters, the Moonglows, Dion and the Belmonts, and the Flamingos.

My gratitude to the charismatic disc jockeys Alan Freed, Jocko Henderson, the Magnificent Montague, and Symphony Sid, who introduced me to a world of music that still inspires me to this day...and to all the legendary artists I experienced as a loyal audience member at the historic Apollo Theater and Birdland ("the Jazz Corner of the World"). These performances transformed my life.

And, of course, my thanks go to the loyal fans, whose support has kept me rollin' on.

Photo Credits and
Permissions

About the Author

Peter Wolf was born in the Bronx, moved to Boston to study painting at the School of the Museum of Fine Arts, then left to pursue a life in music with the J. Geils Band. In 1984, he began his career as a solo artist. Wolf continues to paint, record, and tour from his home base in Boston, Massachusetts.